NEXT GENERATION GRAMMAR

4

Sigrun Biesenbach-Lucas

Donette Brantner-Artenie

Series Editor
David Bohlke

Next Generation Grammar 4

Pearson Education, 10 Bank Street, White Plains, NY 10606

Staff credits: The people who made up the *Next Generation Grammar 4* team, representing editorial, production, design, and manufacturing—are Andrea Bryant, Aerin Csigay, Dave Dickey, Nancy Flaggman, Gosia Jaros-White, Mike Kemper, Maria Pia Marrella, Amy McCormick, Liza Pleva, Massimo Rubino, Ruth Voetmann, and Adina Zoltan.

Cover art: Diane Fenster
Text composition: ElectraGraphics, Inc.
Text font: Minion Pro

Library of Congress Cataloging-in-Publication Data
Cavage, Christina.
  Next generation grammar 1 / Christina Cavage, Stephen T. Jones.
    p. cm.
  ISBN 978-0-13-256063-4 — ISBN 978-0-13-276054-6 — ISBN 978-0-13-276055-3 — ISBN 978-0-13-276057-7
1. English language—Grammar—Study and teaching. 2. English language—Study and teaching—Foreign speakers.
I. Jones, Stephen T. II. Title. III. Title: Next generation grammar one.
  PE1065.C528 2013
  428.2'4—dc23

                                                                                2012024734

For text, photo, and illustration credits please turn to the pages following the index at the back of the book.

PEARSON ELT ON THE **WEB**

PearsonELT.com offers a wide range of classroom resources and professional development materials. Access our course-specific websites, product information, and Pearson offices around the world.

Visit us at **pearsonELT.com**

Printed in the United States of America

ISBN 10: 0-13-276057-6 (with MyEnglishLab)
ISBN 13: 978-0-13-276057-7 (with MyEnglishLab)

1 2 3 4 5 6 7 8 9 10—V082—18 17 16 15 14 13

Welcome to *Next Generation Grammar*

When do we use one of the present forms for future, as opposed to using *will* or *be going to*? Which modal verbs do we tend to use to make requests, from least formal to most formal? In what types of writing might we find more instances of passive forms than active forms? And how and why do we reduce certain adverbial clauses? These and many other questions are all answered in *Next Generation Grammar,* a groundbreaking new series designed to truly meet the needs of today's students. In addition to learning through the textbook, learners engage with innovative digital content, including interactive learning software, video, and continuous online assessment.

At its heart, *Next Generation Grammar* is a comprehensive grammar course that prepares students to communicate accurately in both writing and speaking. The grammar points are presented naturally, through a variety of high-interest reading texts followed by extensive practice and application. Each new grammar point is practiced using all four skills, with extra emphasis on grammar for writing. This task-centered approach allows immediate feedback on learning outcomes so students can track their own progress.

The series is truly for a new generation—one that is busy, mobile, and demanding. It respects that learners are comfortable with technology and use it as part of their daily lives. The series provides a traditional textbook (in either print or eText format) along with dynamic online material that is an integral, not a supplementary, part of the series. This seamless integration of text and digital offers a streamlined, 21st century learning experience that will engage and captivate learners.

Next Generation Grammar boasts a highly impressive author team. I would like to thank Sigrun Biesenbach-Lucas, Donette Brantner-Artenie, Christina Cavage, Arlen Gargagliano, Steve Jones, Jennifer Recio Lebedev, and Pamela Vittorio for their tireless dedication to this project. I would also like to thank Pietro Alongi, Andrea Bryant, Gosia Jaros-White, Amy McCormick, Massimo Rubini, and the entire Pearson editorial, production, and marketing team for their vision and guidance through the development of this series.

David Bohlke
Series Editior

What's **next** in grammar?

Imagine a grammar course that gives you the freedom to devote class time to what you think is most important; a grammar course that keeps students engaged and on-track; a grammar course that extends learning beyond the classroom through compelling digital content.

Introducing *Next Generation Grammar*

Print or eText?

You make the choice. The course book content is presented in two formats, print or eText, offering maximum flexibility for different learning styles and needs.

Blended instruction

Optimize instruction through a blend of course book (in either print or eText format) and online content. This seamless integration will allow for spending more class time on meaningful, communicative work. Learners will practice and apply new language online and can also access our engaging video reviews if they have missed a lesson, or simply need additional help with a grammar point.

Rich online content

Explore the online component. It offers a wealth of interactive activities, grammar reference material, audio files, test material, and video reviews with our Grammar Coach, Jennifer Lebedev, YouTube's *JenniferESL.* The dynamic multimedia content will keep learners focused and engaged. You can also track class progress through an intuitive and comprehensive learner management system.

Ongoing assessment

Use the extensive assessment suite for targeted instruction. The interactive nature of the assessments (including timely feedback, goal tracking, and progress reports) allows you to track progress, and also allows learners to see for themselves which areas have been mastered and which require more effort. In the course book, assessment occurs at the end of each unit. The online component offers pre- and post-unit tests, as well as end-of-chapter tests.

The **next generation of grammar** courses is here. **Anytime, anywhere, anyplace.**

Teacher-directed

Student-centered

Print or eText

Practical tasks

Seamless integration of course book and digital

Grammar coach

Ongoing assessment

Anytime, anywhere, anyplace

CONTENTS

UNIT 1 BUSINESS AND THE ECONOMY	Student Book Outcomes	MyEnglishLab
Chapter 1 page 2 **Business in Economic Hard Times** Simple past and past progressive Modals of advisability and suggestion	Getting Started Reading: *Increasing Sales in a Recession* Grammar Focus 1 and 2 Listening, Speaking, and Writing	Vocabulary Check + Reading Comprehension Grammar Plus 1 and 2 Listen for it, Sounding Natural Linking Grammar to Writing Diagnostic Test
Chapter 2 page 10 **Marketing Company Logos** Simple past and present perfect Noun clauses with the subjunctive	Getting Started Reading: *Warmer, Fuzzier: The Refreshed Logo* Grammar Focus 1 and 2 Listening, Speaking, and Writing	Vocabulary Check + Reading Comprehension Grammar Plus 1 and 2 Listen for it, Sounding Natural Linking Grammar to Writing Diagnostic Test
Unit Assessments page 20	Grammar Summary Self-Assessment Unit Project	Grammar Summary Unit Test Search it!
UNIT 2 PSYCHOLOGY AND PERSONALITY	**Student Book** Outcomes	MyEnglishLab
Chapter 3 page 24 **Winning and Losing** Adjectives and adverbs Adjectives clauses with subject relative pronouns	Getting Started Reading: *Winners and Losers* Grammar Focus 1 and 2 Listening, Speaking, and Writing	Vocabulary Check + Reading Comprehension Grammar Plus 1 and 2 Listen for it, Sounding Natural Linking Grammar to Writing Diagnostic Test
Chapter 4 page 32 **Traits of Successful People** Adjective clauses with object relative pronouns Reducing adjective clauses to adjective phrases	Getting Started Reading: *The Qualities of Successful People* Grammar Focus 1 and 2 Listening, Speaking, and Writing	Vocabulary Check + Reading Comprehension Grammar Plus 1 and 2 Listen for it, Sounding Natural Linking Grammar to Writing Diagnostic Test
Unit Assessments page 40	Grammar Summary Self-Assessment Unit Project	Grammar Summary Unit Test Search it!
UNIT 3 SOCIETY, CONFLICT, AND JUSTICE	**Student Book** Outcomes	MyEnglishLab
Chapter 5 page 44 **Conflict Resolution** Noun clauses as subjects, objects, and complements Gerunds and infinitives as objects	Getting Started Reading: *Lessons from the Playground* Grammar Focus 1 and 2 Listening, Speaking, and Writing	Vocabulary Check + Reading Comprehension Grammar Plus 1 and 2 Listen for it, Sounding Natural Linking Grammar to Writing Diagnostic Test
Chapter 6 page 54 **Alternative Forms of Justice** Quantifiers Connecting structures for comparison and contrast	Getting Started Reading: *A Jury of Their Peers: Teen Courts Help Communities Get Smart about Being Tough* Grammar Focus 1 and 2 Listening, Speaking, and Writing	Vocabulary Check + Reading Comprehension Grammar Plus 1 and 2 Listen for it, Sounding Natural Linking Grammar to Writing Diagnostic Test
Unit Assessments page 64	Grammar Summary Self-Assessment Unit Project	Grammar Summary Unit Test Search it!

UNIT 4 THE IMPACT OF SOCIAL MEDIA	Student Book Outcomes	MyEnglishLab

Chapter 7   page 68
 	
The Digital Gap
 	
Equatives
Comparatives and comparative
   clauses
Degree complements
	Getting Started
	Reading: *Old and Young Use Internet*
	   Differently
	Grammar Focus 1, 2, and 3
	Listening, Speaking, and Writing
		Vocabulary Check + Reading Comprehension
		Grammar Plus 1, 2, and 3
		Listen for it, Sounding Natural
		Linking Grammar to Writing
		Diagnostic Test

Chapter 8 page 78 **Digital Footprints** Present and future unreal conditionals Reported Speech	Getting Started Reading: *Trends in Online Reputation* *Management* Grammar Focus 1 and 2 Listening, Speaking, and Writing	Vocabulary Check + Reading Comprehension Grammar Plus 1 and 2 Listen for it, Sounding Natural Linking Grammar to Writing Diagnostic Test
Unit Assessments page 86	Grammar Summary Self-Assessment Unit Project	Grammar Summary Unit Test Search it!
UNIT 5 PLANNING PUBLIC SPACES	Student Book Outcomes	MyEnglishLab
Chapter 9 page 90 **The Role of Public Spaces in Communities** Stative passives Adjective clauses with *where, when,* and *why* Adjective clauses with quantifiers	Getting Started Reading: *Great Public Spaces* Grammar Focus 1, 2, and 3 Listening, Speaking, and Writin	Vocabulary Check + Reading Comprehension Grammar Plus 1, 2, and 3 Listen for it, Sounding Natural Linking Grammar to Writing Diagnostic Test
Chapter 10 page 102 **The Role Public Spaces on Campuses** Subject-verb agreement Dynamic passives	Getting Started Reading: *Library Examines Space,* *Socialization* Grammar Focus 1 and 2 Listening, Speaking, and Writing	Vocabulary Check + Reading Comprehension Grammar Plus 1 and 2 Listen for it, Sounding Natural Linking Grammar to Writing Diagnostic Test
Unit Assessments page 112	Grammar Summary Self-Assessment Unit Project	Grammar Summary Unit Test Search it!
UNIT 6 PUBLIC HEALTH: PANDEMICS	Student Book Outcomes	MyEnglishLab

Chapter 11   page 116
 	
Current Virus Threats
 	
Coordinating conjunctions
Adverbial time clauses and time
   phrases
	Getting Started
	Reading: *Pandemic Challenges*
	   of Today
	Grammar Focus 1 and 2
	Listening, Speaking, and Writing
		Vocabulary Check + Reading Comprehension
		Grammar Plus 1 and 2
		Listen for it, Sounding Natural
		Linking Grammar to Writing
		Diagnostic Test

Chapter 12 page 124 **The Flu Pandemic of 1918** Past perfect and past perfect progressive Past unreal conditionals	Getting Started Reading: *The Great Pandemic* Grammar Focus 1 and 2 Listening, Speaking, and Writing	Vocabulary Check + Reading Comprehension Grammar Plus 1 and 2 Listen for it, Sounding Natural Linking Grammar to Writing Diagnostic Test
Unit Assessments page 132	Grammar Summary Self-Assessment Unit Project	Grammar Summary Unit Test Search it!

UNIT 7 ERADICATING POVERTY	Student Book Outcomes	MyEnglishLab
Chapter 13 page **136** **Empowering Women** Connecting structures of cause / reason Conjunctive adverbs of effect	Getting Started Reading: *Empowering Women to Eradicate Poverty* Grammar Focus 1 and 2 Listening, Speaking, and Writing	Vocabulary Check + Reading Comprehension Grammar Plus 1 and 2 Listen for it, Sounding Natural Linking Grammar to Writing Diagnostic Test
Chapter 14 page **144** **Fair Trade** Articles Parallel structures	Getting Started Reading: *Fair-Trade Chocolate* Grammar Focus 1 and 2 Listening, Speaking, and Writing	Vocabulary Check + Reading Comprehension Grammar Plus 1 and 2 Listen for it, Sounding Natural Linking Grammar to Writing Diagnostic Test
Unit Assessments Page **152**	Grammar Summary Self-Assessment Unit Project	Grammar Summary Unit Test Search it!
UNIT 8 ANTHROPOLOGY—BODY ART	Student Book Outcomes	MyEnglishLab
Chapter 15 page **156** **Body Art in the Workplace** Modals and phrasal expressions: Degrees of necessity Causatives	Getting Started Reading: *Young Workers Have Something Up Their Sleeve* Grammar Focus 1 and 2 Listening, Speaking, and Writing	Vocabulary Check + Reading Comprehension Grammar Plus 1 and 2 Listen for it, Sounding Natural Linking Grammar to Writing Diagnostic Test
Chapter 16 page **164** **Cultural Identity through Body Art** Expressing purpose with infinitives: Using *for* and *so that* Conjunctive adverbs of exemplification, emphasis, and clarification	Getting Started Reading: *Cultural Expression through Body Art* Grammar Focus 1 and 2 Listening, Speaking, and Writing	Vocabulary Check + Reading Comprehension Grammar Plus 1 and 2 Listen for it, Sounding Natural Linking Grammar to Writing Diagnostic Test
Unit Assessments page **172**	Grammar Summary Self-Assessment Unit Project	Grammar Summary Unit Test Search it!

UNIT 9 COMMUNITY SERVICE		Student Book Outcomes	MyEnglishLab
Chapter 17 **Professionals Making a Difference** Gerunds as objects of prepositions Reducing adverbial phrases of cause / reason	page **176**	Getting Started Reading: *Engineering without Borders* Grammar Focus 1 and 2 Listening, Speaking, and Writing	Vocabulary Check + Reading Comprehension Grammar Plus 1 and 2 Listen for it, Sounding Natural Linking Grammar to Writing Diagnostic Test
Chapter 18 **Youth Making a Difference** Gerunds and infinitives as subjects and subject complements Interaction of verb tenses: Time frame shifts	page **184**	Getting Started Reading: *Mixing Sweat with Earth* Grammar Focus 1 and 2 Listening, Speaking, and Writing	Vocabulary Check + Reading Comprehension Grammar Plus 1 and 2 Listen for it, Sounding Natural Linking Grammar to Writing Diagnostic Test
Unit Assessments	page **192**	Grammar Summary Self-Assessment Unit Project	Grammar Summary Unit Test Search it!

UNIT 10 THE ENVIRONMENT		Student Book Outcomes	MyEnglishLab
Chapter 19 **When Predators Disappear** Infinitives as noun and adjective complements Pronoun agreement and reference	page **196**	Getting Started Reading: *Nature Out of Balance* Grammar Focus 1 and 2 Listening, Speaking, and Writing	Vocabulary Check + Reading Comprehension Grammar Plus 1 and 2 Listen for it, Sounding Natural Linking Grammar to Writing Diagnostic Test
Chapter 20 **Vanishing Islands** Future time Modals of prediction and certainty	page **204**	Getting Started Reading: *The Uncertain Future of Island Nations* Grammar Focus 1 and 2 Listening, Speaking, and Writing	Vocabulary Check + Reading Comprehension Grammar Plus 1 and 2 Listen for it, Sounding Natural Linking Grammar to Writing Diagnostic Test
Unit Assessments	page **212**	Grammar Summary Self-Assessment Unit Project	Grammar Summary Unit Test Search it!

Appendices
A   Irregular verbs .... page A-1
B   Verbs and adjectives followed by the subjunctive .... page A-6
C   Verbs followed by gerunds and infinitives... page A-6
D   Common noncount nouns.. page A-7
E   Tense and place / time shifts .... page A-8
F   Common stative passive + preposition combinations............................... page A-9
G   Common intransitive verbs .... page A-9
H   Common noun + preposition + gerund, and adjective +
     preposition + gerund combinations... page A-10
I   Abstract nouns.. page A-10
J   Adjectives commonly followed by infinitives... page A-10
Index .... page I-1

Tour of a Unit

Each unit in **Next Generation Grammar** begins with an engaging opener that provides a quick overview of the unit. A list of learning outcomes establishes each chapter's focus and helps students preview the grammar content. The outcomes can also be used as a way to review and assess progress as students master chapter content.

MyEnglishLab

Before they begin the unit, students go online and complete the **What do you know?** section to assess what they already know about the grammar featured in the unit. This directs students' focus to the grammar and also helps teachers target instruction to their learners' specific needs.

UNIT 7

Relationships

Outcomes

After completing this unit, I will be able to use these grammar points.

Chapter 13

Grammar Focus 1
Enough and too

Grammar Focus 2
Permission: Modals and expressions

Grammar Focus 3
Requests: Modals and expressions

Chapter 14

Grammar Focus 1
Reflexive and reciprocal pronouns

Grammar Focus 2
Unreal conditional

MyEnglishLab

▶ What do you know?

The ***Getting Started*** section begins with the introduction of the chapter's themes. Students engage in lighthearted, motivating, and personal tasks that introduce and preview the chapter's grammar points.

In the ***Reading*** section students are further exposed to the chapter's grammar through high-interest, real-world texts that reflect the unit's theme. Beginning with a pre-reading warm-up, tasks progress from schema building to a detailed comprehension check.

The ***Vocabulary Check*** activities on *MyEnglishLab* allow students to review and practice the vocabulary necessary for reading comprehension. Students are encouraged to complete these activities before they begin the ***Reading*** section.

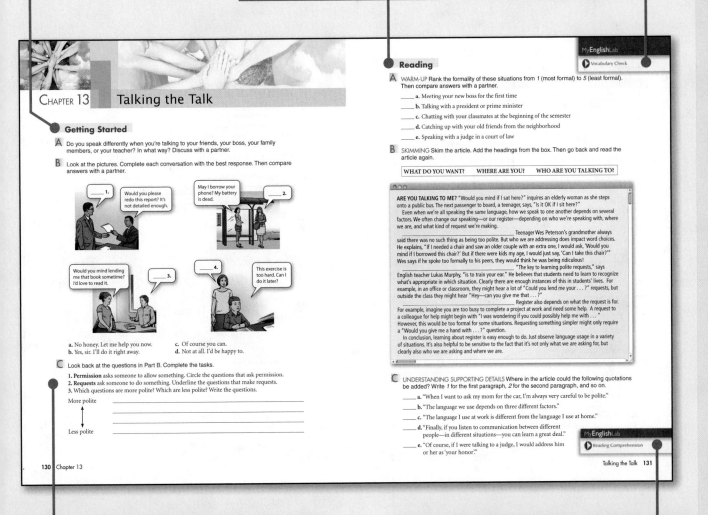

CHAPTER 13   Talking the Talk

Getting Started

A Do you speak differently when you're talking to your friends, your boss, your family members, or your teacher? In what way? Discuss with a partner.

B Look at the pictures. Complete each conversation with the best response. Then compare answers with a partner.

1. Would you please redo this report? It's not detailed enough.

2. May I borrow your phone? My battery is dead.

3. Would you mind lending me that book sometime? I'd love to read it.

4. This exercise is too hard. Can I do it later?

a. No honey. Let me help you now.
b. Yes, sir. I'll do it right away.
c. Of course you can.
d. Not at all. I'd be happy to.

C Look back at the questions in Part B. Complete the tasks.

1. **Permission** asks someone to allow something. Circle the questions that ask permission.
2. **Requests** ask someone to do something. Underline the questions that make requests.
3. Which questions are more polite? Which are less polite? Write the questions.

More polite _____

Less polite _____

Reading

MyEnglishLab ▶ Vocabulary Check

A WARM-UP Rank the formality of these situations from *1* (most formal) to *5* (least formal). Then compare answers with a partner.

_____ a. Meeting your new boss for the first time
_____ b. Talking with a president or prime minister
_____ c. Chatting with your classmates at the beginning of the semester
_____ d. Catching up with your old friends from the neighborhood
_____ e. Speaking with a judge in a court of law

B SKIMMING Skim the article. Add the headings from the box. Then go back and read the article again.

| WHAT DO YOU WANT? | WHERE ARE YOU? | WHO ARE YOU TALKING TO? |

ARE YOU TALKING TO ME? "Would you mind if I sat here?" inquires an elderly woman as she steps onto a public bus. The next passenger to board, a teenager, says, "Is it OK if I sit here?"
  Even when we're all speaking the same language, how we speak to one another depends on several factors. We often change our speaking—or our register—depending on who we're speaking with, where we are, and what kind of request we're making.
  _____ Teenager Wes Peterson's grandmother always said there was no such thing as being too polite. But who we are addressing does impact word choices. He explains, "If I needed a chair and saw an older couple with an extra one, I would ask, 'Would you mind if I borrowed this chair?' But if there were kids my age, I would just say, 'Can I take this chair?'" Wes says if he spoke too formally to his peers, they would think he was being ridiculous!
  _____ "The key to learning polite requests," says English teacher Lukas Murphy, "is to train your ear." He believes that students need to learn to recognize what's appropriate in which situation. Clearly there are enough instances of this in students' lives. For example, in an office or classroom, they might hear a lot of "Could you lend me your . . . ?" requests, but outside the class they might hear "Hey—can you give me that . . . ?"
  _____ Register also depends on what the request is for. For example, imagine you are too busy to complete a project at work and need some help. A request to a colleague for help might begin with "I was wondering if you could possibly help me with . . . " However, this would be too formal for some situations. Requesting something simpler might only require a "Would you give me a hand with . . . ?" question.
  In conclusion, learning about register is easy enough to do. Just observe language usage in a variety of situations. It's also helpful to be sensitive to the fact that it's not only what we are asking for, but clearly also who we are asking and where we are.

C UNDERSTANDING SUPPORTING DETAILS Where in the article could the following quotations be added? Write *1* for the first paragraph, *2* for the second paragraph, and so on.

_____ a. "When I want to ask my mom for the car, I'm always very careful to be polite."
_____ b. "The language we use depends on three different factors."
_____ c. "The language I use at work is different from the language I use at home."
_____ d. "Finally, if you listen to communication between different people—in different situations—you can learn a great deal."
_____ e. "Of course, if I were talking to a judge, I would address him or her as 'your honor.'"

MyEnglishLab ▶ Reading Comprehension

This section culminates with an important inductive step that asks students to look back at the previous tasks and focus on form or function. By circling, underlining, charting, or answering questions, students focus on differences in meaning.

Upon completion of the ***Reading*** section, students can further engage with the chapter's reading selection on *MyEnglishLab*. The ***Reading Comprehension*** activities provide students with an additional check of understanding.

The **Grammar Focus** sections present the chapter's target structures in clear, easy-to-read charts. Each chart presents example sentences taken from the chapter reading that illustrate the structure in context.

The language notes give short and clear explanations of the form, meaning, and use of the target structure.

Grammar Focus 1 *Enough and too*

Examples	Language notes
(1) She was **smart enough**, but she didn't try. Did he finish **quickly enough?** I **didn't study enough**. I failed the test.	As we saw in Chapter 11, the word **enough** means "sufficient" or "the right amount." It has a positive meaning. In addition to modifying nouns, **enough** can also modify **adjectives, adverbs,** and **verbs.** Use: **adjective / adverb / verb + enough**
(2) This report is **not detailed enough.** He didn't work **fast enough.** You **aren't eating enough.**	**Not enough** means that something is insufficient or less than the right amount. Use: **not + adjective + enough** **not + verb + adverb + enough** helping verb + **not + verb + enough**
(3) He didn't move **fast enough to get** a seat. Do you think she has **enough to do?**	We often add an **infinitive:** **enough + infinitive**
(4) Don't be **too friendly** with strangers. Does he speak **too formally** to his peers?	As we saw in Chapter 11, the word **too** means "more than is needed." The meaning is usually negative. In addition to modifying quantifiers, **too** can also modify **adjectives** and **adverbs.**
(5) My kids aren't **too interested** in history. Don't work **too hard!**	We use **not too** to say that something is **lacking.** Use: **not + too + adjective / adverb**
(6) You are **too busy to complete** a project. Did he arrive **too late to get** into the movie?	We often add an **infinitive:** **too + adjective / adverb + infinitive**
(7) There are **too many people** on the bus. There are **too few seats** on the bus. **Q:** Did the teacher present **too much information?** **A:** No, she presented **too little. /** She didn't present **enough.**	As we saw in Chapter 11, we can also use **(not) enough** and **too** with count and noncount nouns. • The opposite of **too many** is **too few** (for count nouns). • The opposite of **too much** is **too little** (for noncount nouns). We more commonly say "not enough."

Grammar Practice

A Complete the sentences. Use *enough* or *too.*

> MyEnglishLab
> Grammar Plus 1
> Activities 1 and 2

1. I don't have _____ money to pay my taxi fare.
   Could you lend me some?
2. You are speaking _____ quickly. Would you mind slowing down?
3. Kevin hates to wait. He has _____ little patience.
4. I had no trouble finding your house. Your directions were easy _____.
5. Your instructions aren't clear _____. Can you say it in a different way?
6. Hal is _____ short to get the book off the shelf. He needs a ladder.
7. Nancy doesn't have a driver's license. She's not old _____.

132   Chapter 13

8. The movie is sold out. We arrived _____ late.
9. My grandma says I'm too thin. She always says, "You don't eat _____."

B Rewrite these sentences to say the opposite. Use *enough* or *too.* More than one correct answer may be possible.

1. She is walking too quickly. *She is not walking fast enough.*
2. He is old enough to enter the contest. _____
3. We were too slow to get seats on the subway. _____
4. There are too many people in our discussion group. _____
5. She was strong enough to lift the box. _____
6. There are too few grammar exercises in this book. _____

C Look at the picture. Write sentences with *enough* or *too.*

1. _____
2. _____
3. _____
4. _____
5. _____
6. _____

Talking the Talk   133

In the **Grammar Practice** sections, students are given the opportunity to apply the grammar structures in a variety of contextualized, controlled exercises that allow them to practice both the forms and the uses of the new structures.

MyEnglishLab

Grammar practice continues online in the **Grammar Plus** activities. Each **Grammar Plus** includes two additional practice activities to further reinforce new structures. Instant scoring and meaningful feedback show students their progress and highlight areas that may require more effort. Students also have the opportunity to see a video review featuring our expert grammar coach. The videos provide a quick, engaging review—perfect for allowing students to check their understanding before proceeding to further assessment.

In the **Listening** sections students have the opportunity to hear the target grammar in context and to practice their listening skills. Activities are developed to practice both top-down and bottom-up listening skills.

MyEnglishLab

Listening activities continue online with **Listen for it**. These activities assess both grammar in context and listening comprehension, and include instant scoring and feedback.

MyEnglishLab

Before students do the **Writing**, they go online to complete **Linking Grammar to Writing**. Several guided writing tasks link the grammar to the skill of writing, enabling students to then move back to the textbook and complete the **Writing** section with full confidence.

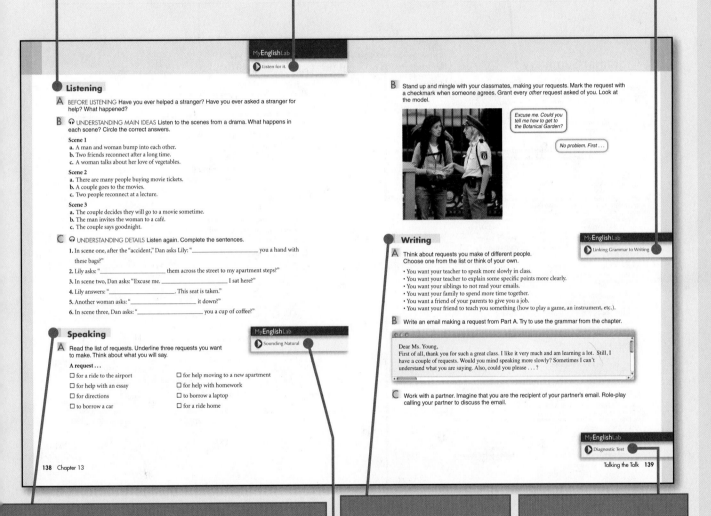

The **Speaking** section provides students with the opportunity to use the chapter's grammar naturally and appropriately in a variety of engaging interactive speaking activities.

MyEnglishLab

The **Sounding Natural** activities are pronunciation activities relating to the chapter's grammar and alternating between productive and receptive tasks. In the receptive tasks, students listen to prompts and select correct answers. In the productive tasks, students listen to prompts, record themselves, and compare their submissions with a model.

The **Writing** section provides students with the opportunity to use the chapter's grammar naturally and appropriately in a variety of activities. Students are provided with a whole or partial model and a more open-ended writing task.

Each chapter culminates with an online **Diagnostic Test** that assesses students' comprehension and mastery of the chapter's grammar structures. The test tracks students' progress and allows teachers to focus on the specific student needs.

The **Grammar Summary** chart provides a concise, easy-to-read overview of all the grammar structures presented in the unit. It also serves as an excellent reference for review and study.

A quick 20- or 25-point **Self-Assessment** gives students an additional opportunity to check their understanding of the unit's target structures. This gives students one more chance to assess what they may still need to master before taking the online **Unit Test**.

Grammar Summary

MyEnglishLab
▶ Grammar Summary

Enough means "sufficient" or "the right amount." Place it after adjectives, adverbs, and verbs. To say something is insufficient, use *not + adjective / adverb / verb + enough*. The meaning is usually negative. We can add an infinitive after *enough*.

Enough	Not enough
He's **tall enough to reach** the shelf.	He's **not tall enough to reach** the shelf.
She ran **fast enough to catch** the bus.	She didn't run **fast enough to catch** the bus.
I **studied enough**.	I didn't **study enough**.

The word *too* means "more than needed." Place it before adjectives and adverbs. The meaning is usually negative. We can add an infinitive after the phrase.

Too	
I'm **too tired**.	I'm **too tired to stay** awake.
He walks **too slowly**.	He walks **too slowly to keep** up with me.

We use *can, could,* and *may,* and other expressions to **ask permission**. We use *can, could,* and *would* and other expressions to **make requests**. By using expressions such as *Would you mind . . . ?* we imply that the action may be annoying or imposing. We can grant and refuse permission with *can* and *may* (not): *Yes, you can. / No you may not.* We can grant and refuse requests with a variety of responses (*Sure. / Not at all. / Sorry.*)

Asking permission	Making requests
Can / Could / May I see your homework?	**Can you** open the door?
Is it OK if I sit here?	**Would you** say your name again?
Do you mind if I sit here?	**Could you not** make that noise, please?
Would it be OK if I sat here?	**Would you mind** turning down the TV?
Would you mind if I sat here?	**Do you mind** waiting?
I was wondering if I could sit here.	**I was wondering if** you'd mind helping.

Reflexive pronouns are used when the subject and object of a sentence refer to the same person or thing. We also use them for emphasis. *By* + a reflexive pronoun means "alone."

Singular	Plural
I forced **myself** out of bed.	We are pushing **ourselves** today.
Admit the truth to **yourself**!	You and Mika express **yourselves** well.
The cat gave **itself** a bath.	The children fixed breakfast **by themselves**.
He wanted to go hiking **by himself**.	

Use the **reciprocal pronouns** *each other* (for two people) and *one another* (for more than two people) when the subject and object refer to the same people or things.

Reciprocal pronouns
Bill and Carrie are looking at **each other**.
The group of students were helping **one another** finish the project.

We use the **unreal conditional** to talk about unreal or imaginary conditions. Use an *if*-clause (simple past or past continuous) + a main clause (*would / might / could* + base verb). Although the *if*-clause is in the simple past, it refers to the present or future.

If-clause	Main clause
If I **had** the time,	I would **travel** more.
If I **were** a pilot,	I could **see** the world.
If I **were earning** more money,	I might **travel** for six months.

Self-Assessment

A *(5 points)* Rewrite the sentences. Add *too* or *enough*.
1. Lara didn't eat. (enough) _____
2. I have little time to finish my report. (too) _____
3. Damien gave up the race easily. (too) _____
4. The presentation was not detailed. (enough) _____
5. They didn't read the map closely. (enough) _____

B *(8 points)* Circle the correct words.
1. **Can / May** you please speak more slowly?
2. Would you mind **close / closing** that window?
3. **May / Would** I please see your I.D. card?
4. I was wondering if you'd mind **help / helping** me.
5. Do you mind if I **borrow / borrowed** your notes?
6. Is it OK if I **move / moved** your bag over there?
7. **Do / Would** you mind if I sat here?
8. I was wondering if I **can / could** use your laptop.

C *(6 points)* Complete the sentences. Use reflexive or reciprocal pronouns.
1. Look at _____! You are wearing two different shoes!
2. After Pedro scored the winning goal, he and his coach looked at _____ in disbelief.
3. My coworkers always try to solve their problems _____.
4. No one knows why Mr. Parker decided to give _____ a haircut.
5. For their birthdays, the three best friends bought _____ dinner.
6. Some people prefer to travel with a group, but I like traveling by _____.

D *(6 points)* Complete the sentences. Use the unreal conditional.
1. If my friends _____ (go) out without me, I _____ (be) upset.
2. If I _____ (not / live) so far away from campus, I _____ (walk) to school.
3. Tom _____ (not / be) in this advanced class if he _____ (not / study) so hard.
4. Kara _____ (quit) her job today if she _____ (have) any savings.
5. If I _____ (be) a veterinarian, I _____ (specialize) in cats.
6. If I _____ (see) a crime, I _____ (call) the police immediately.

MyEnglishLab

Students can go to *MyEnglishLab* for a **Grammar Summary** review, which includes activities and a video to help students prepare for the **Self-Assessment** and **Unit Test**.

Each unit ends with an interesting and engaging group **Unit Project** that encourages students to synthesize the new grammar structures and to integrate the unit's theme and skills. The project promotes collaboration, creativity, and fluency and exposes students to a variety of real-world situations.

Unit Project: Sphere of influence

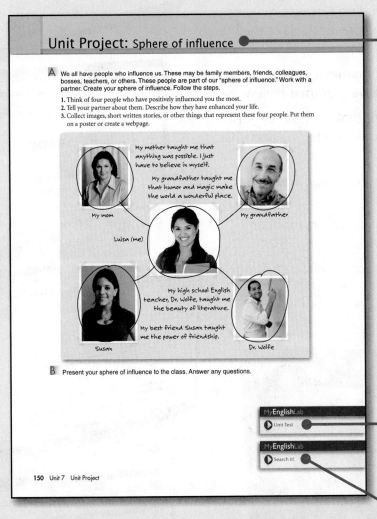

A We all have people who influence us. These may be family members, friends, colleagues, bosses, teachers, or others. These people are part of our "sphere of influence." Work with a partner. Create your sphere of influence. Follow the steps.

1. Think of four people who have positively influenced you the most.
2. Tell your partner about them. Describe how they have enhanced your life.
3. Collect images, short written stories, or other things that represent these four people. Put them on a poster or create a webpage.

My mother taught me that anything was possible. I just have to believe in myself.

My grandfather taught me that humor and magic make the world a wonderful place.

My mom

My grandfather

Luisa (me)

My high school English teacher, Dr. Wolfe, taught me the beauty of literature.

My best friend Susan taught me the power of friendship.

Susan

Dr. Wolfe

B Present your sphere of influence to the class. Answer any questions.

MyEnglishLab
▶ Unit Test

MyEnglishLab
▶ Search it!

MyEnglishLab

The unit's final, cumulative assessment is a comprehensive online **Unit Test**. This test allows students to check their mastery of the unit's grammar structures, see their progress, and identify areas that may need improvement. The test allows teachers to track students' progress and to focus on areas that might benefit from more attention.

MyEnglishLab

The **Search it!** activity allows students to do a fun online search for content that relates to the chapter's theme. Teachers may choose to have students complete these real-world tasks individually, in pairs, or in small groups.

Next Generation Grammar Digital

MyEnglishLab

A dynamic, easy-to-use online learning and assessment program, integral to the *Next Generation Grammar* program

▶ **Original activities** focusing on grammar, vocabulary, and skills that extend the *Next Generation Grammar* program

▶ **Multiple** reading, writing, listening, and speaking activities that practice grammar in context, including *Linking Grammar to Writing*, which guides students in the practical use of the chapter's grammar

▶ **Video** instruction from a dynamic grammar coach that provides an engaging and comprehensive grammar review

▶ **Extensive** and ongoing assessment that provides evidence of student learning and progress on both the chapter and unit level

▶ **Individualized** instruction, instant feedback, and study plans that provide personalized learning

▶ A **flexible gradebook** that helps instructors monitor student progress

And remember, *Next Generation Grammar* is available both in print and as an eText.

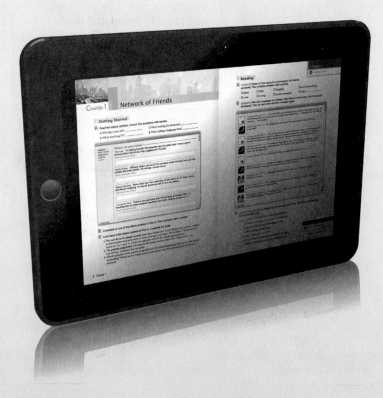

ActiveTeach

A powerful digital resource that provides the perfect solution for seamless lesson planning and exciting whole-class teaching

▶ A **Digital Student Book** with interactive whiteboard (IWB) software

▶ **Useful notes** that present teaching suggestions, corpus-informed grammar tips, troublesome grammar points, and culture notes

▶ Instant one-stop **audio** and **video grammar coach**

▶ **Printable** audio scripts, video scripts, and answer keys

▶ **Capability** for teachers to:
  • Write, highlight, erase, and create notes
  • Add and save newly-created classroom work
  • Enlarge any section of a page

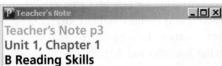

P Teacher's Note   _ □ ✕

Teacher's Note p3
Unit 1, Chapter 1
B Reading Skills
When you **skim** a text, you look it over quickly to get a general idea of what it is about. Do not read every word and do not use a dictionary. Instead, look at the title, pictures, bold, or italicized words, and the first line of each paragraph to get a sense of the general idea.

About the Authors

Dr. Sigrun Biesenbach-Lucas received her M.A.T. in TESOL and Ph.D. in Applied Linguistics from Georgetown University. Within the past twenty-five-plus years, she has taught English as a Second Language (ESL) as well as Linguistics at Georgetown University and at George Washington University. Before joining the CLED-EFL faculty at Georgetown in 2006, she taught in the TESOL Teacher Training Program at American University for eight years. In the Georgetown University intensive English program, she teaches advanced level academic preparation courses, and she also serves as the program's college applications advisor. In 2006, she was recognized as a World Teacher Honoree for outstanding teaching by TESOL. Dr. Biesenbach-Lucas is a member of several professional/academic organizations. She has presented at numerous international, national, and local conferences, has been invited to lead workshops, and has published in several scholarly journals and other venues. She is also a Member of the Editorial Board at *Language Learning & Technology,* a peer-reviewed academic journal. Additionally, she is a site reviewer for the Commission for English Language Program Accreditation (CEA). Her professional interests include English for Academic and Professional Purposes, instructional technology, and differences in native and non-native speakers' email communication. In her relatively sparse spare time, Dr. Biesenbach-Lucas enjoys exercising and going on long walks with her husband and dog.

Donette Brantner-Artenie holds an M.A. in Linguistics with an emphasis in TESOL from Ohio University. With undergraduate degrees in Elementary and Middle School Education, she taught EFL and trained teachers in the first group of U.S. Peace Corps Volunteers in Romania. Professor Brantner-Artenie has also taught in the intensive English programs at Ohio University and Ohio State University. Since 2000, she has been a faculty member in the intensive EFL program in the Center for Language Education and Development at Georgetown University, where she is a senior instructor and coordinator of the center's computer and digital language learning labs. She primarily teaches advanced level academic preparation and grammar courses. Outside of GU, Professor Brantner-Artenie has developed and conducted teacher training programs for the U.S. Department of State for teachers in Togo and Romania. Over the past 20 years, she has presented and conducted workshops at numerous local, regional, and international conferences. Her professional interests include English for Academic Purposes, Content Based Instruction, and Instructional Technologies.

Acknowledgements

The authors would like to thank the entire Pearson NGG team for its support and feedback. We would especially like to express our sincere appreciation to Massimo Rubini, who believed in our creative abilities, to Malgorzata Jaros-White, for her insightful feedback, and Ruth Voetmann, for pushing us to our creative limits. We would also like to thank the Administration of the Georgetown University Intensive English Program as well as our colleagues for their continued support, and our students for inspiring our work.

Dr. Biesenbach-Lucas would also like to thank her husband for his never-ending support and encouragement, and her two sons for their continued inspiration. Professor Brantner-Artenie would like to thank her family, especially her parents, for their constant support.

Reviewers

We are grateful to the following reviewers for their many helpful comments:

Yukiko Arita, Ibaraki University, Mito, Japan; **Asmaa Awad,** University of Sharjah, Sharjah, United Arab Emirates; **Kim Bayer,** Hunter College CUNY, New York, NY; **Michelle Bell,** University of South Florida, Tampa, FL; **Jeff Bette,** Westchester Community College SUNY, Valhalla, NY; **Leslie Biaggi,** Miami Dade College, Miami, FL; **Celina Costa,** George Brown College, Toronto, Ontario, Canada; **Eric Dury,** University of Sharjah, Sharjah, United Arab Emirates; **Katie Entigar,** Kaplan's English Scool, Boston, MA; **Margaret Eomurian,** Houston Community College, Central College, Houston, TX; **Liz Flynn,** San Diego Community College, San Diego, CA: **Ruth French,** Hunter College CUNY, New York, NY; **Jas Gill,** University of British Columbia, Vancouver, British Columbia, Canada; **Joanne Glaski,** Suffolk County Community College, Selden, NY; **Sandra Hartmann,** University of Houston, Houston, TX; **Cora Higgins,** Boston Academy of English, Boston, MA; **Carolyn Ho,** Lone Star College-Cyfair, Cypress, TX; **Gretchen Irwin-Arada,** Hunter College CUNY, New York, NY; **Bob Jester,** Hunter College CUNY, New York, NY; **Patricia Juza,** Baruch College CUNY, New York, NY; **Liz Kara,** Alberta College, Alberta, Canada; **Jessica March,** American University of Sharjah, Sharjah, United Arab Emirates; **Alison McAdams,** Approach International Student Center, Boston, MA; **Kathy Mehdi,** University of Sharjah, Sharjah, United Arab Emirates; **April Muchmore-Vokoun,** Hillsborough Community College, Dale Mabry Campus, Tampa, FL; **Forest Nelson,** Tokai University, Toyko, Japan; **Dina Paglia,** Hunter College CUNY, New York, NY; **DyAnne Philips,** Houston Community College, Southwest College, Gulfton Center, Houston, TX; **Russell Pickett,** Sam Houston State University, Huntsville, TX; **Peggy Porter,** Houston Community College, Northwest College, Houston, TX; **Tahani Qadri,** American University of Sharjah, Sharjah, United Arab Emirates; **Alison Rice,** Hunter College CUNY, New York, NY; **Kevin Ryan,** Showa Women's University, Tokyo, Japan; **Yasser Salem,** University of Sharjah, Sharjah, United Arab Emirates; **Janet Selitto,** Seminole State College of Florida, Sanford, FL; **Laura Sheehan,** Houston Community College, Southwest College, Stafford Campus, Houston, TX; **Barbara Smith-Palinkas,** Hillsborough Cummunity College, Dale Mabry Campus, Tampa, FL; **Maria Spelleri,** State College of Florida Manatee-Sarasota, Venice, FL; **Marjorie Stamberg,** Hunter College CUNY, New York, NY; **Gregory Strong,** Aoyama Gakuin University, Tokyo, Japan; **Fausto G. Vergara,** Houston Community College, Southeast College, Houston, TX; **Khristie Wills,** American University of Sharjah, Sharjah, United Arab Emirates; **Nancy Ramirez Wright,** Santa Ana College, Santa Ana, CA.

Business and the Economy

OUTCOMES

After completing this unit, I will be able to use these grammar points.

CHAPTER 1

Grammar Focus 1
Simple past and past progressive

Grammar Focus 2
Modals of advisability and suggestion

CHAPTER 2

Grammar Focus 1
Simple past and present perfect

Grammar Focus 2
Noun clauses with the subjunctive

MyEnglishLab

 What do you know?

CHAPTER 1 — Business in Economic Hard Times

Getting Started

A Read about SportSource, an outdoor sporting goods company. Then, read the issues and advice. Check (✓) the advice that you think will help SportSource.

Every company tries hard to make a profit. This becomes more difficult during an economic recession when people have less money to spend. SportSource sells clothing and equipment for outdoor activities such as camping, hiking, and rock climbing. Because profits have dropped, the company has hired a consultant to help plan new business strategies. The consultant has reviewed the last full year of sales.

Issues	*Advice*
Sales dropped 10 percent overall.	☐ SportSource should do a detailed market survey.
Equipment for hiking sold better than equipment for rock climbing.	☐ SportSource could market equipment for both activities together.
Camping gear was selling well in spring months, but it wasn't popular in summer.	☐ SportSource might hold a major summer sales event only for camping gear.
In May, SportSource was holding rock climbing classes in its stores when a competitor began holding free classes.	☐ SportSource should offer free classes at popular climbing areas.

B Write two other pieces of advice you would give SportSource. Explain why you would give this advice.

Advice 1: _____

_____

Advice 2: _____

_____

C Look back at Part A. Complete the tasks.

1. Underline **the simple past** verbs describing an activity or situation **completed in the past**.
2. Double-underline the **past progressive** verbs describing actions that are **in progress for a duration of time in the past**, or that are **interrupted by another action or event**.
3. **Modals** are verbs some of which indicate **advice**, **suggestion**, or **recommendations**. Circle the examples.
4. Complete the chart with verbs and modals. Then, compare your chart with a partner's chart.

Verb + -ed OR irregular form (simple past)	Be + verb + -ing (past progressive)	Modal + verb (advice / suggestion)

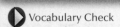
Reading

A WARM-UP Small, privately owned businesses often face unique challenges. With a partner, discuss three steps a business might take to stay successful during difficult economic times.

B SCANNING Scan the article from a business news website. Find three major changes that companies can make to maintain their business. Compare them with the steps that you suggested in Part A. Then, read the whole article.

---

ooo

Increasing Sales in a Recession:
Lessons Learned from Small Businesses

Expand Services or Products. In financially challenging times, small companies can expand the products or services they offer customers to maintain their business. In the 1990s, customers were lining up to schedule services from M & L Contractors, a snow removal company. Back then, the owners didn't worry about less business in the summer. This small company operates in the Northeast where winters are longer. However, mild weather resulted in less business in the past winter. "When I was contacting our regular customers to remind them about our services for next year, one of them asked me if we provided any lawn or landscaping services. They needed a new contractor to do the fall leaf removal and spring landscape care for their main office building," says Brad Madison, co-owner of M & L Contractors. Once they decided they wouldn't need to buy a lot of new equipment or hire many new employees, the company expanded their services. Madison believes that small firms should take risks to expand their potential markets in challenging economic times: "They had better try out new products or services, or they could end up losing their business."

Share Pay Cuts. When Jeff McConnell and Craig Spolsky bought UniCo, a uniform service, sales were declining and profits were shrinking. While the new owners were figuring out how to make the business profitable again, employees were planning for job losses. McConnell and Spolsky didn't want to lay off anyone from their small firm, but they needed to take drastic steps to save the business. After they looked at all their options, they decided to lower their employees' wages. They also took major pay cuts themselves. "Small businesses cannot afford to let employees go during hard times because they don't have enough staff to do so," says McConnell. In this case, business owners ought to consider reducing their personal earnings from the company when they cut employee wages. Employers also could use shared pay cuts to boost morale.

Build Partnerships. Small businesses could also combine forces to be able to compete with larger companies. Last year, Adware, Inc., an Internet marketing firm, started to share projects with Tech Smart, a technology support service. Because these two companies had staff with complementary skills, they were able to share portions of the work as well as costs and equipment. "Businesses should think carefully before they jump into a partnership, but with thoughtful planning, it can greatly benefit everyone involved," says Linda Beal of Adware, Inc. Firms who want to network with and combine their services with others might attend regional conferences to identify potential partners. They could also advertise for partners on business networking sites or in publications for small firms.

C UNDERSTANDING DETAILS Following the model below, describe a specific challenge that each company faced due to the nature of its business. Then, note what solution each one implemented to maintain its business.

Company	Company-specific situation	Solution

Grammar Focus 1 Simple past and past progressive

Examples	Language notes
(1) Last year, Adware, Inc. **started** to share projects with Tech Smart.	Use the **simple past** for actions or events that began and ended at a specific time in the past.
	Simple past sentences often include time expressions, such as *last year, in the past, in 2005, between 1995 and 2000.*
(2) During the late 1990s, customers **were lining up** to schedule services from M & L Contractors.	Use the **past progressive** for actions that were in progress for a period of time in the past or that were interrupted by another action or event.
	Past progressive sentences often include time expressions, such as *during the late 1990s, from April to June,* or *during the first / last few months of.*
(3) **When** Jeff McConnell and Craig Spolsky **bought** UniCo, sales **were declining** and profits **were shrinking**. Jeff McConnell and Craig Spolsky **bought** UniCo *while* sales **were declining** and profits **were shrinking**.	Use the simple past and the past progressive together to show how one action began earlier and was still happening when the second one occurred. Use **when** with the simple past to introduce an action that interrupted an earlier action or event, or use **while** with the past progressive. The action in the past progressive began first.
(4) *While* the new owners **were figuring out** how to make the business profitable again, employees **were planning** for job losses.	Use the adverbs of time **when** and **while** + **the past progressive** to show two actions in progress at the same time in the past. Use the past progressive in both the main clause and the subordinate clause.
	You can omit time expressions if the time reference (past or ongoing) is clear from the context.

Time expression	Subject	Simple past	Complement	Time expression
Last year,	Adware, Inc.	**started**	to share projects with Tech Smart.	
	Mild weather	**resulted**	in less business	in the past winter.
	They	**needed**	to find a new contractor.	

Time expression	Subject	Past progressive	Complement	Time expression
In the late 1990s,	customers	**were lining up**	to schedule services.	

Subordinate (Dependent) clause				Main (Independent) clause		
time expression	subject	simple past	complement	subject	past progressive	complement
When	they	**bought**	UniCo,	sales	**were declining**.	
time expression	subject	past progressive	complement	subject	past progressive	complement
While	the owners	**were trying**	to make profits,	employees	**were planning**	for job losses.

Grammar Practice

 A Complete the paragraphs with the simple past or past progressive forms of the verbs in parentheses.

Focus more on sales

    Increasing sales is always a goal for any business, but it becomes even more important during economic hard times. When the recession **1.** _____ (be) at its high point last year, sales **2.** _____ (drop) significantly for Home Grown Blooms, a small distributor of locally grown flowers. During that time, Diana Perez, founder and owner, **3.** _____ (search) for ways to increase sales. "Our traditional customers, small florist shops, **4.** _____ (experience) a drop in sales, too. So we **5.** _____ (know) we needed to look for other potential customers," says Perez. "We **6.** _____ (contact) gift shops, local grocers, and small specialty stores and **7.** _____ (bring) them free samples of our flowers to sell on a trial basis." An employee also **8.** _____ (come up with) the idea to do demonstrations for larger grocery chains in the area. More focus on product sales **9.** _____ (pay off) for Home Grown Blooms, and it **10.** _____ (be) able to grow its customer base. In difficult times, a small firm should ask all of its employees to find ways to increase sales.

Categorize customers

    A Capitol Cup, a local café in the busy downtown area of Washington, D.C., **1.** _____ (open) when gourmet coffee shops **2.** _____ (be) very popular. When the recession **3.** _____ (hit), it **4.** _____ (begin) to lose customers. Its regular customers **5.** _____ (start) looking for a less expensive cup of morning coffee on their way to work. While the café **6.** _____ (lose) customers, stores with cheaper coffee specialty drinks **7.** _____ (gain) them. A Capitol Cup **8.** _____ (be) unable to compete. The owners of the café **9.** _____ (decide) that they **10.** _____ (need) to attract their regular customers back to their business rather than attract new customers. They **11.** _____ (offer) "frequent customer" cards for a free drink for every ten drinks purchased. They also **12.** _____ (start) an email coupon service for regular customers. "Small business owners should treat their loyal customers differently and show them that their patronage is appreciated," says the co-owner of A Capitol Cup.

B Electronics Unlimited is a struggling Internet-based electronics company. On a separate sheet of paper, write a company scenario, using the background information with time expressions. Look at Part A as a guide. Use the simple past and past progressive.

Background	Time expressions
advertising is ineffective	between January and June of last year
company does not carry wide variety of brands	last month
customers complain about poor service	over the last year
sales decline	two years ago
young customers choose other companies	when
	while

Grammar Focus 2 Modals of advisability and suggestion

Examples	Language notes
(1) Small business owners **should consider** reducing their personal earnings from the company when they cut employee wages.	Modals are auxiliary verbs. The modals are *can*, *could*, *had better*, *may*, *might*, *must*, *ought to*, *should*, *will*, *would*. Modals do not change forms to agree with the subject, and they are followed by the base form of the verb. The modal auxiliary verbs show speakers' intentions. You can use modals to talk about necessity, obligation, advice, or suggestion.
(2) Small firms **should take** risks to expand their potential markets in challenging economic times. Small business owners **ought to consider** reducing their personal earnings. They **had better try out** new products or services, or they could end up losing their business. The company **had better not** avoid expanding its services.	Use the modal auxiliary verbs *should*, *ought to*, and *had better* to express advice. They mean "This is a good idea to . . ." or "It is important to . . .". *Should* and *ought to* have the same meaning. In questions and negatives, *should* is more common. *Had better* is close in meaning to *should* and *ought to*, but it is stronger. Use *had better* to express a warning about possible bad consequences. *Had better* can be contracted to *'d better*. The negative form is *had better not*.
(3) In addition to lowering costs, employers **could use** shared pay cuts to boost morale. Firms who want to network with and combine their services with others **might attend** regional conferences to identify potential partners.	Use *could* or *might* to make suggestions about the present or the future. *Could* and *might* have the same meaning when used to express suggestions. In other contexts, *could* and *might* are used to express different functions. (See Units 8 and 10.)

Subject	Modal auxiliary verb	Main verb (base form)	Complement
Firms	**should**	take	risks.
Business owners	**ought to**	consider	reducing their personal earnings.
They	**had better**	look for	other ways to increase sales.
Employers	**could**	use	shared pay cuts to boost morale.
Firms	**might**	attend	regional conferenes.

Grammar Practice

A Read each situation. Decide if the suggestion or advice that follows is appropriate. If it is not, decide if it is too strong or too weak. Write a new sentence using an appropriate modal verb. Discuss your answers with a partner.

1. A small computer store has lost a few of its business customers but continues to have strong sales to private customers.
   The store **had better** form a partnership with an office supply business.

   _____

   _____

2. Sales at a store that sells expensive clothing for women have dropped by 30 percent.
   The store **might** develop a less expensive clothing line to attract more customers.

   _____

   _____

3. Most of the customers at a florist shop come from the local neighborhood. Sales have slowed slightly in the past month.

The shop **ought to** invest part of its marketing budget in Internet advertising.

_____

_____

4. A grocery store has begun losing a lot of its fresh gourmet food items because customers are choosing the less expensive items. The result is not only a loss in profits but also a lot of wasted food.

The store **could** cut down the number of gourmet items it sells.

_____

_____

5. An ice cream shop has experienced a major drop in sales over the past year. A common customer complaint is that there aren't enough flavors to choose from.

The shop **had better** research its customers' preferences and make changes to its menu.

_____

_____

B Read the statements about work-related issues. Write a recommendation for each using modals of advisability or suggestion.

1. Phillip's supervisor thinks he dresses too casually at work.

_____

_____

2. Employees at UniCo complain that they are so busy that they often eat lunch at their desks.

_____

_____

3. Tina and Chen share an office. Tina likes to listen to music while she works, but the noise bothers Chen.

_____

_____

4. Several staff members at Electronics Unlimited have a team project to complete. Hans is often late to their meetings because he can never find a parking spot.

_____

_____

5. The manager at ABC Press is upset because several employees regularly complete projects late. This causes her to miss deadlines with her supervisors.

_____

_____

6. Many of Joel's colleagues are irritated with him because he often takes office supplies from their desks without permission.

_____

_____

7. Andrea frequently calls in sick and doesn't complete her work.

_____

_____

8. Tech Works office employees feel overwhelmed because they receive several interoffice memos in paper format every day. They also get a lot of email messages from upper management every day.

_____

_____

Listening

A BEFORE LISTENING Talk with a partner about where you live now. Describe your experience and talk about the pros and cons of living there.

B 🎧 UNDERSTANDING MAIN IDEAS Listen to students discuss their experience living in a university dormitory. List their four main complaints. Were all their complaints legitimate? Why or why not? Discuss with the class.

1. _____   3. _____

2. _____   4. _____

C 🎧 UNDERSTANDING DETAILS Listen again. List at least four suggestions the students discussed. Would you give the same advice? Why or why not?

1. _____   3. _____

2. _____   4. _____

Speaking

A You will participate in a student focus group to discuss positive and negative aspects of your experiences with the dining services on campus (or a popular place where many students eat). With a partner, identify issues you think need to be addressed and brainstorm possible suggestions for changes. Look at the model.

Potential Issues
limited choices or lack of variety of food
limited open hours
prices too high
unhealthy food (high-fat, high-calorie) and drinks (too much soda)
Other: _____

> *I thought there weren't enough choices. The cafeteria served only three types of dishes.*

> *I agree. They could serve a greater variety of dishes with the same or similar ingredients.*

B Work in groups of three or four students. Follow the steps.

1. Assign roles to group members: two or three as students and one or two as administrators who want to know about your experience with the dining services on campus. Discuss the issues you identified in Part A and your suggested changes. Try to use the grammar from the chapter. Look at the model.

> *What were your favorite kinds of food in the cafeteria last semester?*

> *I enjoyed most of the Italian dishes, especially the pizza. However, I thought that some of the dishes had too many calories. They could make low-fat versions of the same dishes for about the same cost.*

2. After the role play, share one or two of your ideas with the whole class. Decide as a class whose suggestions were the most helpful.

Writing

A Talk with a partner about an issue you want the Office of Dining Services on campus to address. Discuss specific details and offer concrete, reasonable suggestions for addressing the problem. Take notes.

B On a separate sheet of paper, write a complaint letter to the Office of Dining Services on campus about the issue. Use your notes from Part A. Try to use the grammar from the chapter. Use the following sample letter as a guide.

January 15, 2013

Miguel Rojas, Director of Dining Services
Central State University

Dear Mr. Rojas:

I am a student at Central State University. Last semester, I ate at Wilson Dining Hall because I was on a 19-meal plan. While most of my experiences eating at Wilson were positive, I often thought that the dining hall was not very clean. The tables were messy, and the floor had spills on it. Once when I was carrying my tray to a table, I slipped and fell. While I was trying not to drop my tray, I hit my arm on the floor and got injured.

I think that Dining Services should address this problem. Dining hall staff should mop the floor and clean the tables more often. Dining Services could assign an employee to monitor the dining area, or they could post signs to remind students to clean up after themselves. Students who currently eat at Wilson might have other helpful suggestions.

Thank you for your attention to this matter.

Sincerely,

Jennifer Lee

C Exchange letters with a partner. Discuss each other's letters. Did your partner follow the appropriate letter format? Did he or she include specific suggestions for addressing the problem? Can you offer additional suggestions to the problem?

CHAPTER 2 · Marketing Company Logos

Getting Started

A Look at the logos of two companies. Notice that the logos have changed since the companies were founded. Discuss the changes that you observe in these logos.

B Why do you think companies change their logos? Review the reasons below and check (✓) those with which you agree. Explain your answers.

☐ **1.** The company has changed design artists recently, and the new artist has suggested that the logo be more modern.

☐ **2.** The company has merged with another company, and the marketing department has recommended that both companies' logos become part of the new logo.

☐ **3.** The company did a lot to support the environment last year, and the company president advised that the company's logo show its concern for it.

☐ **4.** Since its founding, the company has changed its product lines several times, and the advertising manager suggests that a new logo reflect those changes.

☐ **5.** The company changed owners a few months ago, and the new owners recommend that a new logo represent new ownership.

☐ **6.** For many years, the company has had a complex logo with letters and images, and the board of directors advises that the logo have a more simple design.

C Look back at Part B. Complete the tasks.

1. Underline the **simple past** verbs describing an activity or situation **completed in the past**.
2. Double-underline the **present perfect** verbs referring to situations or activities that **have happened recently**.
3. Some **subjunctive verb forms follow verbs of advice, suggestions,** or **recommendations**. Circle the verbs that indicate **advice** and the verbs that follow in the **subordinate clause**.
4. Following the model, make a chart with examples. Then, compare your chart with a partner's chart.

Verb + *ed* OR irregular form (simple past)	*Have / has* + verb + *-ed* (present perfect)	Advice verb + *that* + subjunctive

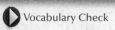
Reading

A WARM-UP Look at the old logos on the left and the updated logos on the right. With a partner, describe what the logos looked like in the past and how they have changed.

B SCANNING Scan the newspaper article to find answers to the following questions. Then, read the whole article.

1. What are the major changes that company logos have undergone?
2. Why have some companies begun to change their logos?
3. How is a logo important for a company / business? Why?

Warmer, Fuzzier: The Refreshed Logo

In recent years, many companies have updated their logos. The economy, environment, image repair—all are reasons for new designs. There are striking similarities among recent redesigns.

TONED-DOWN TYPE

In the past, company logos had bold, block capital letters. According to marketing consultants, it is important that new logos be mostly or completely lowercase to make them appear less serious and more like an informal chat. "Logos have become less official looking and more conversational," said Patti Williams, a professor of marketing at the University of Pennsylvania's Wharton School. "The old logos were yelling at people. Logos have become more neighborly." Many companies, such as Walmart and Stop & Shop, have replaced capital letters with lighter and rounder lowercase letters.

FRIENDLY FLOURISHES

Food companies have joined online stores and toy manufacturers and have adopted logos that "smile." Design experts recommend that, to lighten people's mood, tree branches and fountains appear on several big brands. A major image overhaul began a few years ago, and recently new logos have started to appear across the country. One design expert suggested that the military-style Walmart star change to a yellow sparkle. Walmart has created a new message: this is a company that cares, with fast and friendly service, and a fresh, new attitude.

HAPPIER COLORS

"The economy has been the number one influence for the past couple of years," said John H. Bredenfoerder, a designer who produced a new laundry detergent emblem a few years ago. He advised that a logo bring a little joy into people's lives during economic hard times. Therefore, since about 2010, color changes in logos have emphasized blue with accents in yellow, red, purple, orange, and green. Last year, many logos included green for the environment with images of leaves and flowers. Mr. Bredenfoerder also suggested that companies use blue to represent the environment (think of earth's blue globe as seen from space, or clear blue waters) as well as fresh optimism. As a result, companies like Sysco, which used dark navy blue in their logos in the past have changed the shade to a joyful sky blue.

C UNDERSTANDING DETAILS Make a list with at least three characteristics of the old logos and three characteristics of the new logos.

Grammar Focus 1 Simple past and present perfect

Examples	Language notes
(1) In the past, company logos **had** bold, block capital letters. A major image overhaul **began** a few years ago.	Use the **simple past** for actions or events that began and ended at a specific time in the past. Common time expressions with the simple past include: *in the past, last year, in 2005, between 1900 and 1930.*
(2) In recent years, many companies **have redesigned** their logos.	Use the **present perfect** for actions or events that began in the past but have an impact on the present time through clear results or are ongoing (unfinished) in the present. Common time expressions with the present perfect include: *in recent years, in the past few months, recently, since 2009.*
(3) *Since about 2010,* color changes in logos **have emphasized** blue with accents in yellow, red, purple, orange, and green. The economy **has been** the number one influence *for the past couple of years.*	Use *for* and *since* with the present perfect to talk about events that began in the past and continue in the present. Use *since + point of time* to show when the situation started. Use *for + a period of time* to show how long the situation has been true.
(4) Recently, new logos **have started** to appear across the country. For example, Walmart's star **has changed** to a yellow sparkle.	You can omit time expressions if the time reference (clearly past or clearly unfinished) is clear from the context.

Time expression	Subject	Simple past	Complement	Time expression
In the past,	company logos	**consisted** of	bold capital letters.	
	A major change	**began**		a few years ago.
Last year,	many logos	**included**	green for the environment.	

See Appendix A on page A-1 for a list of irregular verbs.

Time expression	Subject	Present perfect	Complement	Time expression
In recent years,	many companies	**have redesigned**	their logos.	
	Some food companies	**have adopted**	a logo that "smiles."	
In the past few years,	many logos	**have emphasized**	blue.	
	The economy	**has been**	the number one influence	**for** the past few years.
Since about 2010,	many logos	**have used**	blue with yellow accents.	

Grammar Practice

A Complete the sentences with the simple past tense or the present perfect tense of the verbs in parentheses.

1. An online store reports that its sales _____ (increase) 18 percent in the three months of last year, and sales in North America _____ (be) up 21 percent.

2. Membership at dating websites _____ (rise) almost 30 percent since March of last year. Last year, one of these websites _____ (have) its most profitable year in a long time.

3. Interest in the Peace Corps _____ (jump) 16 percent in the past two years. In the same time span, applications to other volunteer organizations in Europe and North America _____ (double), with more coming in each month.

4. Movie attendance _____ (decrease) nearly 9 percent a year ago compared with the same period the year before.

5. Early in this decade, many college athletic events _____ (set) new attendance records. Similarly, attendance at professional sports games _____ (rise) 57 percent since last April.

6. Between January and March of this year, sales of Blu-ray players in the United States _____ (grow) to more than 400,000 units; this _____ (be) an increase of 72 percent over the same period the year before.

7. Earlier this decade, Japanese car makers _____ (sell) 16.4 percent more used vehicles than in the late 1990s. Recently, sales _____ (stay) on track to increase an additional 15 percent.

8. In the past few years, memberships at some gyms and sports clubs _____ (go down) by as much as 26 percent. Many members _____ (have) to give up their membership at these clubs due to increased membership fees.

9. During the last economic downturn, sales of store-brand food products _____ (increase) significantly, and sales of name-brand products _____ (decrease).

10. Restaurant attendance at a popular restaurant _____ (remain) stable over the past several years. Since 1988, customers _____ (enjoy) good, hearty food in a relaxed and casual atmosphere.

B Look at the logo changes that two major companies have gone through. Complete the paragraphs with either the simple past or the present perfect form of the verb in parentheses. Then, work with a partner to discuss the questions. What verb forms did you use to answer the questions? Why?

A. *Starbucks*

In 1971, Starbuck's first logo **1.** _____ (show) a mermaid with two tails. The mermaid **2.** _____ (appear) in the middle of a round, brown logo. The words "Starbucks–Coffee–Tea–Spices" **3.** _____ (surround) the mermaid. Between 1987 and 2011, the logo **4.** _____ (undergo) two modifications: the color **5.** _____ (change) to green, and the image of the mermaid **6.** _____ (become) larger. Since 2011, the logo **7.** _____ (present) only the mermaid, without any words. The color green **8.** _____ (remain) the same.

- Why do you think Starbucks chose a mermaid for the center of its logo?
- Why do you think Starbucks changed the color from brown to green? Why did the company delete the words "tea" and "spices" in 1987?
- Why do you think Starbucks has omitted all words from its new logo?

B. *Nokia*

In its early years, Nokia **1.** _____ (be) not a company specializing in communications technology, but two Finnish companies that **2.** _____ (merge) to form one company. Before 1964, the Nokia logo **3.** _____ (undergo) one main change. The designers **4.** _____ (remove) the fish from the logo. Since 1965, the logo **5.** _____ (undergo) two more modifications. The color **6.** _____ (turn) into a shade of blue. Most recently, the designers **7.** _____ (add) the phrase "connecting people" under the Nokia logo.

- What did the original Nokia logo show? What animal did it show and why?
- Why do you think Nokia removed the fish? Do you think the new logos were improvements over the original one? Why or why not?
- Why do you think Nokia has chosen blue as the new color? Why has the company added the phrase?

Grammar Focus 2 Noun clauses with the subjunctive

Examples	Language notes
(1) Marketing consultants think **that new logos should look less serious**.	**Noun clauses** are dependent (subordinate) clauses. Subordinate clauses are not complete sentences, and they cannot stand by themselves. They must be connected to an independent clause. Noun clauses perform the same function as regular nouns. They can be subjects or objects. The word *that* often introduces noun clauses.
(2) Design experts recommend (that) a leaf **appear** on several big brands. Design experts recommended (that) a leaf **be** part of new logos of several big brands. *Incorrect:* Design experts recommend (that) a leaf **is** a part of new logos of several big brands.	The **subjunctive form** is a less common verb form in English. We see it in dependent (subordinate) noun clauses and mostly in formal written discourse. The word *that* introduces the subjunctive, and it can be omitted. The subjunctive is always the base form of the verb for both singular and plural and with all forms of the main verb.
(3) Marketing consultants *advise* that new logos **look** less serious.	The subjunctive verb forms appear in noun clauses following verbs of urgency, obligation, or advisability, such as: *recommend, advise, suggest, propose, urge.*
(4) According to marketing consultants, *it is important* that logos **be** lower case.	The subjunctive verb forms can also appear in noun clauses following adjectives of urgency, obligation, or advisability, such as *critical, crucial, essential, important, necessary.*
(5) Consumers agree that the new logos **are** less serious.	Noun clauses that follow verbs and adjectives that don't express urgency, obligation, or advisability don't need the subjunctive.

Advice / recommendation structure	Advice / recommendation clause			
	that	subject	subjunctive verb	complement
We recommend / advise / suggest	that	the new logo	**incorporate**	lowercase letters.
	that	the letters	**appear**	on a wavy line.
	that	the color	**be**	a blend of green and blue.
It is important / necessary	that	logos	**be**	lowercase.
	that	a logo	**look**	friendly.

See Appendix B on page A-6 for verbs and adjectives that are followed by the subjunctive.

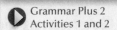

Grammar Practice

A Read the logo change recommendations for two companies. Find the recommendations that use modals. Then, write new sentences with the subjunctive. Use the verbs and adjectives in the list.

Verbs: advise, insist, propose, recommend, suggest

Adjectives: critical, crucial, essential, important, necessary

1. *Computer Gear*

The new company logo should incorporate lowercase letters. The letters could all be the same size on a straight line, and they should have friendly colors. The colors might be a blend of several rainbow colors. The type of the letters could be a youthful design: each letter might be elongated or tall. Also, the letters could cast a shadow behind them to look more three-dimensional.

Example: *We advise that the new company logo incorporate lowercase letters.*

_____

_____

_____

_____

_____

_____

2. *Village Mart*

The new logo should not be the same color as the old logo. The colors in the letters could also be a shade of green. The letters should be lowercase letters, and the type of the letters should be playful. They could arch alongside an image of a man and a woman pushing a shopping cart. The man and the woman could project the image of a family-friendly grocery store.

_____

_____

_____

_____

_____

B Match the companies on the left with appropriate recommendations on the right. Then, write the recommendations, using the subjunctive.

_f_ **1.** The Coffee Bean   **a.** offer a free card with every four purchased

____ **2.** Music-n-More   **b.** send a free bouquet to customers on their birthday

____ **3.** Star Appliances   **c.** add complimentary covers to protect against bad weather

____ **4.** Village Pastries   **d.** include manicure services

____ **5.** Uptown Florist   **e.** organize tastings of new cakes and cookies

____ **6.** Massage Madness   **f.** sell drinks at half price if customers bring their own cup

____ **7.** Send-A-Card   **g.** provide free repairs on kitchen electrical devices

____ **8.** Backyard Furniture   **h.** invite local artists for concerts

1. (recommend) _We recommend that The Coffee Bean sell drinks at half price if customers bring their own cup._

2. (important) _____

3. (advise) _____

4. (critical) _____

5. (suggest) _____

6. (necessary) _____

7. (advise) _____

8. (propose) _____

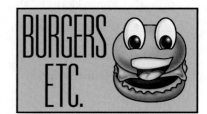

Speaking

 A During hard economic times, people tend to spend less money on food and entertainment, including restaurants. Read the information about *Burgers Etc.* Then, in small groups, discuss what you recommend Burgers Etc. do to attract customers and increase profit. Take notes. Try to use the grammar from the chapter.

Burgers Etc. is a small restaurant near a major metropolitan area. It did well in its first few months but has barely made ends meet since then.

- Opened last summer in busy business area close to downtown
- Off main road in building courtyard; not visible from street
- 20 sit-down spaces: tall tables with bar stools
- Fast food type restaurant: no waiters, customers wait in line for their food
- Fresh burgers with a variety of toppings
- Soft drinks and water
- Good lunch crowd; almost no dinner crowd
- "Classic rock" background music
- Paint and furnishings: brown tones
- Plastic plates and utensils

B With your group, present your recommendations to the class. Explain Burger Etc.'s situation and share your proposed solutions. Use your notes from Part A. Look at the model.

> Burger Etc. opened a year ago, but the location is not good. We suggest that the company search for a better restaurant space and . . .

Listening

 A BEFORE LISTENING Imagine that you are a marketing consultant for a small grocery store. In small groups, answer the questions.

1. What kinds of problems do you think small, local grocery stores might have?
2. What recommendations could you provide to the store owners to solve their problems? Complete the chart with your ideas.

Potential problems	Recommendations

B 🎧 UNDERSTANDING MAIN IDEAS Listen to a segment from a radio call-in show with an expert on marketing strategies. Then, read the statements about Zorelli's Market and the expert's recommendations. Check (✓) the statements and recommendations that are true, according to the listening.

Zorelli's Market's (ZM) situation	Phil Brickens's recommendations for ZM
☐ Traffic in the area has decreased. ☐ A major supermarket has opened near ZM. ☐ ZM doesn't sell any fresh produce. ☐ ZM has decided to sell fresh produce. ☐ The supermarket sells items at lower prices. ☐ ZM has focused on Italian food only. ☐ ZM has decided to sell bread. ☐ Customers have been able to buy the same items at the supermarket. ☐ The Zorellis have not sold any soda.	☐ Move the store to a different location. ☐ Have weekly sales on different items. ☐ Offer services that supermarkets do not offer. ☐ Sell Italian breads and desserts. ☐ Become an Italian specialty food store. ☐ Turn a section of the store into a restaurant. ☐ Hold cooking classes on Saturdays and Sundays. ☐ Teach customers how to cook Italian dishes. ☐ Enter a partnership with a candy company.

C ⌒ UNDERSTANDING DETAILS Listen to the radio segment again. Then, answer the questions.

1. Who started Zorelli's Market? When?
2. To whom is the store more important: Rita or her husband?
3. Why does Phil Brickens recommend focusing on Italian food?
4. Why does Phil Brickens recommend cooking classes on weekends?
5. What do Rita and her husband need to purchase if they start cooking classes?
6. Why do the Zorellis sell only six-packs of soda?
7. Why has Zorelli's Market not sold any other drinks?
8. What is special about the drinks from Nature's Naturals?
9. Does Phil Brickens recommend that Zorelli's Market continue to sell cards and candy? Why or why not?

Writing

A With a partner, select one company or store in your neighborhood or on campus. Brainstorm ideas about its current logo and your recommendations for a new logo. On a separate sheet of paper, draw the old logo and your new recommended logo.

B Write two paragraphs about the logos. In the first paragraph, describe the current logo. In the second paragraph, explain your recommendations for changes. Use your notes from Part A. Try to use the grammar from the chapter.

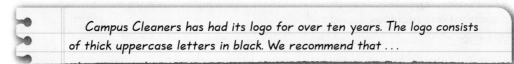

> *Campus Cleaners has had its logo for over ten years. The logo consists of thick uppercase letters in black. We recommend that . . .*

C Post your "before" and "after" pictures around the room. Vote with your class on the most innovative logo change.

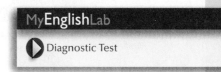

Grammar Summary

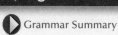
The simple past describes activities or situations completed in the past.

Simple past sentences usually include clear time expressions. The verbs in the simple past can be regular or irregular.	(1) Last year, the company changed its logo. (2) Between 1987 and 2011, the logo underwent two changes.

The past progressive describes actions that are in progress for a period of time in the past or that are interrupted by another action.

The past progressive can express: • an activity that took place over a period of time, with clear time expression; • an activity that was interrupted by another activity; • two activities occurring at the same time in the past.	(1) Over the course of last summer, the company was experiencing a slowdown. (2) When sales of sport utility vehicles were going well, a major recession hit and sales decreased. (3) While companies were closing, their employees were searching for new jobs.

The present perfect describes actions and events that began in the past, continue to the present, and may or may not continue to the future.

The present perfect can include clear time expressions. It can express actions that: began in the past but continue to the present or began in the past but have an effect on the present with visible result. Use *since* + point of time to show when the situation started. Use *for* + a period of time to show how long the situation has been true.	(1) In the past few months, sales have gone up. (2) Starbucks has changed its logo color from brown to green. (3) Since 2008, the restaurant business has experienced a downturn. (4) The company has been on the market for years.

Modals of advisability and suggestion are special verbs that express the speaker's intention. They are followed by the base form of the verb.

Modals *should, ought to,* and *had better* express advice. *Had better* is stronger than *should* and *ought to* and expresses a warning about possible bad consequences. *Should* and *ought to* have the same meaning, but *should* is more common in questions and negatives. *Could* and *might* express suggestions.	(1) The store had better hire a marketing consultant. (2) The company should lower its prices. (3) The company ought to consider price cuts. (4) The owners could take a pay cut. (5) The logo might include an earth-friendly image.

Noun clauses with the subjunctive use the base form of the verb for both singular and plural.

The subjunctive follows certain verbs of advice, urgency, or obligation. It consists of the base form of the verb. The word *that* introduces the subjunctive. It can be omitted.	(1) I advise that the company try a new strategy. (2) We recommend that the new logo color be green. (3) It is essential that the new logo color be green. (4) We urge (that) the company look into new ways of marketing their product.

Self-Assessment

A (7 points) Complete the paragraph with the simple past, past progressive, or present perfect forms of the verbs in parentheses.

Back in 1900, the first Shell logo **1.** _____ (be) a realistic scallop shell. Over the years, the logo **2.** _____ (evolve) into a bold, colorful, and much more basic shell. The evolution of the logo **3.** _____ (begin) after 1915, when designers **4.** _____ (experiment) with different images of the original shell. They **5.** _____ (add) the red and yellow colors to the symbol. Later, Raymond Loewy **6.** _____ (work) on a more memorable and recognizable logo. In 1971, he **7.** _____ (design) a very simple logo as compared to the earlier ones—the logo that is still used today.

B (5 points) Complete the sentences with the simple past or present perfect forms of the verbs in parentheses.

1. Over the past few months, sales of 3D television sets _____ (skyrocket).

2. During the 1990s, many people _____ (buy) second, or vacation, homes.

3. In April of last year, one local gas company _____ (lay off) half its workers.

4. Between May and April of last year, attendance at sporting events _____ (rise) significantly.

5. Since 2001, security at airports _____ (be) greater than before.

C (8 points) Write recommendations for increasing sales of two products. Use two modals and two subjunctive forms for each product.

Recommendations for special sales promotions for microwave ovens at a department store:

1. give away special microwave foods as incentives

_____

2. offer unique colors

_____

3. include special microwavable dishes at no charge

_____

4. offer free service for two years

_____

Recommendations for special sales promotions in a gourmet coffee shop:

5. offer free pastry with coffee drink

_____

6. have weekly coffee specials

_____

7. allow children to have a free drink

_____

8. offer "buy one, get one free" deals

_____

Unit Project: Recommendation report

 A You are going to examine how one specific company or business has responded to an economic crisis and recommend some best practices and innovative ideas. Follow the steps.

1. Work in teams of three or four students. Select a company that has had problems in the past few years. You can choose a large or a small company, such as a media or technology company, an airline, a restaurant, a retail store, or any business that interests you. Research specific information and statistics about the company's market performance. Your team can visit the business or do research online or in the library.

2. Research how the company or business has responded to the downturn. What strategies has the company used to improve its situation? Take notes.

3. As a team, make recommendations for this company to improve its situation. What could the company do to increase profits during economic hard times? Make a list. Keep in mind the ideas you have read about in this unit.

4. As a team, write a recommendation report for the company. Follow the model outline.

> **I. Overview of _____'s Market Performance**
>   A. Performance (give statistics)
>   B. What the company has done to combat recession
> **II. Recommendations** (provide details)
>   A. Recommendation #1
>   B. Recommendation #2
>   C. Recommendation #3
> **III. Conclusion** (summarize your three recommendations)

B Prepare a presentation based on your recommendation report. Follow the steps.

1. Follow the report outline and create a slide presentation for each point. Each slide should have no more than three sub-points.

2. Deliver the presentation to your class. Ask your classmates if they have questions or comments.

3. After all the teams have presented, vote on which team has provided the most innovative and feasible recommendations.

MyEnglishLab
▶ Unit Test

MyEnglishLab
▶ Search it!

UNIT 2

Psychology and Personality

OUTCOMES

After completing this unit, I will be able to use these grammar points.

CHAPTER 3

Grammar Focus 1
Adjectives and adverbs

Grammar Focus 2
Adjective clauses with subject relative pronouns

CHAPTER 4

Grammar Focus 1
Adjective clauses with object relative pronouns

Grammar Focus 2
Reducing adjective clauses to adjective phrases

CHAPTER 3 | Winning and Losing

Getting Started

A Think of an athlete or other person whom you consider to be a winner. Discuss the questions with a partner.

1. What does this person have that has made him or her victorious?
2. What does it take to be a winner?
3. Does being a winner always mean being in first place?

B In athletic competitions, some athletes seem to always win, some always lose, and some win against all odds. Read the statements about characteristics of winners and losers. With a partner, decide if you agree or disagree with the statements and explain why.

Winners

• Winners are exceptional athletes who expect to win.

• Winners are people whose talent is extraordinary.

• Winners have a positive attitude which is contagious.

• Winners are team players who unselfishly support their teammates.

• Winners constantly work to improve their skills.

• Winners thrive on extreme pressure.

Losers

• Losers are mediocre athletes who doubt their physical ability.

• Losers are people who lack motivation.

• Losers have an insecure attitude that becomes an obstacle to their success.

• Losers do not want to be part of a team that performs extremely poorly.

• Losers have extremely arrogant personalities.

• Losers get really nervous during competition.

C Look back at Part B. Complete the tasks.

1. **Adjectives** are words that **describe nouns**. Double-underline any examples.
2. Circle words that **describe verbs, adjectives, and other adverbs**.
3. Underline those parts of sentences that **describe a noun**.
4. Complete the chart with examples. Then, compare your chart with a partner's chart.

Adjectives	Adverbs	Adjective clauses
Before nouns	Before verbs	
After the verb *be*	Before adjectives	
	Before adverbs	

Reading

A WARM-UP With a partner, discuss the words and expressions below. What does each have to do with being a winner or loser?

comfort zone	egomaniac	phenomenal player	spotlight
concentration	intensity	respect for opponents	talent
crunch time	nervous	sneaker-endorsing	tattoo-covered

B SCANNING Scan the article for the attributes of winners. Then, read the whole article and explain each attribute in your own words.

Winners and Losers

Talent alone is not enough to be a winner. "Great players can have a great impact, but great players who have great attitudes have really great impacts," says Malik Rose, who won two national basketball titles. "When a phenomenal player spreads his intensity and desire to the other players, it's huge." Along with talent, there are other attributes that all winning teams (and winning players) have.

Humility: Professional sports are full of tattoo-covered, sneaker-endorsing, trash-talking athletes who are convinced they play unusually well. But those athletes who are truly exceptional are normally aware they will not always excel. "Humility leads to a deep realization that I'm not always the one who wins and that another person on any given day can win," says Wade Rowatt, who works as a social psychologist. "Really good athletes display this profound respect for opponents. If you have a player who regularly sees himself as better than everyone else and feels that he deserves truly special treatment, he'll never inspire

greatness—just the opposite. You need a player with a contagious approach, which is an example for overconfident teammates," says Rowatt.

Love of Pressure: Athletes whose incredibly strong desire to succeed pushes them out of their comfort zone prefer large performance venues, like national championships. These athletes are normally known for doing unusually well in crunch time. Football player Terry Bradshaw is an athlete who did extremely well when the spotlight was particularly bright. "It was unbelievably enjoyable playing hard in front of a huge crowd. So instead of becoming nervous, I got really excited. My level of concentration felt sky-high, and I truly excelled," says Bradshaw.

Selflessness: This trait is critically important, according to Leonard Zaichkowsky, a professor of sports psychology. "Athletes who can't control their huge egos successfully for the good of the team are only going to hurt things in the long run," says Zaichkowsky. The world of professional sports is full of egomaniacs whose need for publicity won't allow them to give up impressive personal statistics

and televised or published highlights in the name of victory. A clear exception was David Robinson, a basketball player who played extremely well for the San Antonio Spurs. Robinson, who had scored the most points for the team during one season, had given up his dominant position to focus on getting the ball back from the opponent, blocking shots, and leadership. "David took a big step back so that our team could take a huge step forward," says Malik Rose, who was Robinson's teammate, and whose admiration for Robinson seems obvious. "There are a ton of guys who wouldn't have done that. But David did. Why? The main reason is that David was more than just a great player. He was definitely a winner," says Rose.

C UNDERSTANDING DETAILS Match two behaviors on the right to each attribute on the left.

_____ 1. Humility

_____

_____ 2. Love of

_____ pressure

_____ 3. Selflessness

_____

a. athletes whose nervousness is transformed in front of spectators

b. an athlete who makes teammates stand in the spotlight

c. athletes with an attitude which acknowledges a competitor's strength

d. an athlete who recognizes his or her weaknesses

e. an athlete with exceptional ability to focus when it counts

f. an athlete that doesn't have an overly-inflated sense of self

Grammar Focus 1 Adjectives and adverbs

Examples	Language notes
(1) **Great** players can have a **great** impact. David Robinson was **exceptional**. His admiration for Robinson seems **obvious**. The **main** reason is that David Robinson was more than just a great player.	**Adjectives** describe or give more information about nouns. Adjectives can occur in two different positions. **Attributive adjectives** occur before the nouns. **Predicative adjectives** follow the nouns, the verb *be*, and linking verbs, such as: *feel, look, smell, sound, taste, appear, seem, become.* Some adjectives can only be in the attributive position, such as the adjective *main*. Some adjectives can occur only in the predicative position, such as the adjective *afraid*.
(2) All **winning** teams possess more than talent. Losers are **convinced** they are good. Egomaniacs are reluctant to give up impressive personal statistics and **televised** or **published** highlights. Professional sports is full of tattoo-**covered**, sneaker-**endorsing**, trash-**talking** athletes.	Some adjectives are derived from verbs and end in *-ing* (present participle) and *-ed* (past participle). These adjectives are called **participial adjectives**. The *-ing* forms modify nouns that are **the source** of an action or emotion. The *-ed* forms modify nouns that are **the receiver** of an action or emotion. Participial adjectives can attach to a noun to form a compound.
(3) Some players **regularly** see themselves as better than others. I played **hard** in front of a huge crowd. **Clearly**, Terry Bradshaw raised his game to new heights during competition. Many athletes can't control their egos **successfully**. He was **definitely** a winner. His heart beat **rapidly** in excitement.	**Adverbs** describe or give more information about verbs, adjectives, or other adverbs. Adverbs that modify verbs (actions) can describe frequency *(normally, regularly, occasionally, frequently)*, manner *(slowly, quietly, badly, rapidly, highly, hard)*, and certainty *(certainly, definitely, clearly, obviously, probably)*. Most adverbs can be placed before verbs or at the beginning or end of the sentence. The exceptions are the adverbs of manner and adverbs that modify the verb *be;* they must follow the verb.
(4) **Really** good athletes display respect for opponents. Great athletes like **extremely** large performance venues. Good athletes are known for doing **exceptionally** well in front of a crowd. Robinson played **extremely** well for the Spurs.	Adverbs that modify adjectives and other adverbs intensify the adjective or adverb and occur right before the adjective or adverb. Some common adverbs used to modify adjectives and adverbs include: *really, extremely, supremely, incredibly, well, critically, truly.* Most adverbs are formed by adding *-ly* to the adjective form. Exceptions: good → well fast → fast long → long hard → hard late → late

Grammar Practice

 Unscramble the sentences. Place the adjectives in the correct position in each sentence.

1. athletes / important / are / during / focused / successful / games
   Successful athletes are focused during important games.

2. a / is / persistent / does not / good / times / athlete / and / during / give up / tough
   _____

3. realistic / personal / goals / must be / athletes'
   _____

4. work ethic / exceptional / a / attitude / a winner / positive / and / has

_____

5. pictures / detailed / mental / these / winners / and / and / are / specific / create

_____

6. acknowledge / great / their opponent's strength / athletes / personal / and limitations

_____

B Rewrite the sentences using the adverbs in parentheses. Place the adverbs in the correct position in each sentence.

1. All good athletes are committed to their goals. (highly)

_____

2. It is a fact that successful athletes pursue excellence, not perfection. (regularly, extremely)

_____

3. A great athlete respects the sport as well as other competitors and coaches. (deeply, definitely)

_____

4. A superior athlete strives to perform during each competition. (well, consistently, extremely)

_____

5. A sign of many good athletes is that they focus on their teammates. (consistently, really, clearly)

_____

C The following passage describes another attribute of winners. Complete the passage with the appropriate adjectives or adverbs from the lists. Use each adjective and adverb only once. More than one answer may be possible.

Adjectives: critical, entire, great, hard, real, significant, strong, true, undefeated, wrong

Adverbs: constantly, directly, entirely, highly, really, truly, unfairly, very

Self-motivation: 1. _____ winners **2.** _____ motivate themselves. Sometimes this means recognizing that **3.** _____ times are about to happen. According to Dawn Staley, who turned the Temple University basketball program into a **4.** _____ **5.** _____ team, making yourself think that no one believes in you except you is **6.** _____ **7.** _____. It **8.** _____ motivates you to prove everyone **9.** _____. As Staley notes, the lives of **10.** _____ athletes are often based on overcoming obstacles, such as breaking a record or beating an **11.** _____ team. So when there is no **12.** _____ obstacle, athletes create their own. They convince themselves that they are **13.** _____ overlooked. They find a **14.** _____ **15.** _____ quote from an opponent and read it every day. "Success is **16.** _____ related to motivation," says one athlete. "When you believe it's you against the **17.** _____ world, it doubles your determination—even if it's not **18.** _____ true."

Grammar Focus 2 Adjective clauses with subject relative pronouns

Examples	Language notes
(1) Terry Bradshaw is an athlete *who* **did extremely well in championship games**. You need a player with an approach *which* **is an example for overconfident teammates**. There are other attributes *that* **are critical for winning teams**. Athletes *whose desire* **to succeed pushes them out of their comfort zone** prefer large performance venues.	**Adjective clauses** are dependent (subordinate) clauses. Dependent clauses are not complete sentences, and they cannot stand by themselves. They must be connected to an independent clause. Adjective clauses describe, identify, or give additional information about a noun or a pronoun in the independent clause. They come after the independent clause or inside it. Adjective clauses use **relative pronouns** as their subject to connect the independent clause to the dependent clause. Relative pronouns follow the noun or pronoun that they modify. Use *who* to refer to people. Use *which* to refer to things. Use *that* to refer to both people and things (*that* is slightly less formal when used with people). Use *whose* + noun to show possession and refer to both people and things.
(2) *Incorrect:* Terry Bradshaw is an athlete who he did extremely well in championship games.	The relative pronoun is the subject of the adjective clause. Do not use a double subject.
(3) Teams **whose players put their teammates first** tend to be successful. Great players **who have great attitudes** have really great impacts. A clear exception was David Robinson, **who played for the San Antonio Spurs**. Robinson, **who had scored the most points for the team during one season**, had given up his dominant position to focus on getting the ball back from the opponent, blocking shots, and leadership.	Subject adjective clauses can be **restrictive** or **non-restrictive**. **Restrictive** adjective clauses identify the noun which they follow and are essential for understanding the meaning. **Non-restrictive** adjective clauses provide extra information about the noun which they follow, and they are set off between commas. They are not essential for understanding the meaning. Do not use the pronoun *that* in non-restrictive clauses.

Main (Independent) clause	Adjective (Dependent) clause		
	relative pronoun (subject)	verb	complement
There are a lot of players	**who**	wouldn't have done	such a thing.
You need a player with an approach	**which / that**	is	an example for teammates.
The world of professional sports is full of egomaniacs	**whose need** for publicity	won't allow	them to give up impressive personal statistics.

Main clause subject	Adjective clause			Main clause complement
	relative pronoun (subject)	verb	complement	
Great players	**who**	have	great attitudes	have great impacts.
Other attributes	**which / that**	are	typical of winning teams	are humility and selflessness.
Teams	**whose players**	put	their teammates first	tend to be successful.

Grammar Practice

A Combine each set of sentences into one sentence with an adjective clause. Use *who, which, that,* and *whose* + noun as subjects of the adjective clauses.

1. The FC Bayern München is a legendary team in German soccer history. In the 1970s and 1980s, the team won most of its games.

   The FC Bayern München, which won most of its games in the 1970s and 1980s, is a legendary team in German soccer history.

2. However, one year during that time, the FC Bayern München was a mediocre team. That team was destined to fail.

3. The team's manager was a poor strategist. His approach required no discipline from the players.

4. The team's two young stars were having personal problems. The two stars were a goalkeeper and a forward.

5. As for experience under pressure, there were only two players. These two players had played in a national championship game before.

6. The FC Bayern München had a leader in Franz Beckenbauer. Beckenbauer refused to give up.

7. Beckenbauer was not the best player. His attitude conveyed that "special something."

8. Beckenbauer set a positive tone for the team. That tone had typically been absent.

9. Something about Beckenbauer inspired confidence. That confidence was contagious.

B Read the paragraph about another attribute of winners. Correct the 14 adjective clause errors.

   Work Ethic: "A winner is a player whose is constantly working to improve, that makes winning contagious," says Aimee Kimball who is the director of mental training at the University of Pittsburgh's Center for Sports Training. The winner doesn't just focus on a result who is impressive but also on improving and making the people which are around him or her great players, too. Players which see their teammate working hard feel motivated to do the same. In 1990, the Stanford University women's basketball team was an average group who had lost most of its games just four seasons earlier. But in 1990, the team won its first national championship behind Jennifer Azzi. She was a player who refused to skip a practice and who team spirit inspired all of her teammates. She talked to teammates which efforts were low and told them that they needed to do better. "When you have that one person who doesn't care about anything but winning, that's an amazingly powerful tool," says Dawn Staley who is Temple University's women's basketball coach and whose was a three-time Olympic gold medalist. "To have one person whose a winner and which can manage different personalities—I'll go to battle with him or her any day of the week. Sadly, those are the players which are hard to find," says Staley.

Listening

A BEFORE LISTENING List two individual sports and one team sport that you are familiar with. What are the three most significant characteristics that an athlete needs to have in order to be successful in these sports? Why? Complete the chart. Then, share your chart in small groups.

	Sport	Characteristics of success	Reasons
1.			
2.			
3.			

B 🎧 UNDERSTANDING MAIN IDEAS Listen to five athletes. All five athletes can be considered winners. Match each athlete with the appropriate attribute of success, and note each athlete's key characteristics that demonstrate the attribute. Then, compare your chart with a partner's chart.

Attributes: humility, love of pressure, selflessness, self-motivation, work ethic

Athlete	Attribute of success	Key characteristics
1.		
2.		
3.		
4.		
5.		

C 🎧 INFERRING INFORMATION Listen again and identify the sport each athlete is involved in. Write down a few clues that helped you decide. Compare your answers with a classmate's answers.

Sports: distance running, golf, skiing, soccer, swimming

	Athlete	Sport	Clues
1.			
2.			
3.			
4.			
5.			

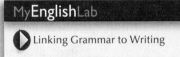
Speaking

A Work in small groups. Look back at the article on page 25 and discuss if there are any other attributes or behaviors that you think are important in being a winner. Give reasons for your choices.

Other "winner" attributes	Reason for importance

B Form new groups. Discuss which attributes of successful athletes might also be important for other people, such as students, professionals, military personnel, or another group. Select one group of people and complete the chart. Then, share your ideas with the class.

Who?	Which attributes?	Why important for success?

Writing

A Think about a sport you have been engaged in, or a job you have had or might like to have. What are the attributes that you have shown in your sport or your job? Or, what are the attributes you think you will need in that job? Brainstorm some ideas and take notes. Share your notes with a partner.

B Use your ideas from Part A to write a paragraph about the attributes you have shown in your sport or your job. Try to use the grammar from the chapter.

> Since I was 10 years old, I have played soccer. I've never won any medals, but I've always pushed myself extremely hard to improve . . .

> I have worked as a laboratory assistant in a hospital. Quite regularly, I was part of a team, and it was every team member's serious efforts that were important in each lab experiment . . .

C Share your paragraphs with the rest of the class. Give each other advice on what you can do to be a winner.

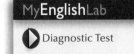

CHAPTER 4 Traits of Successful People

Getting Started

 A Work with a partner. Discuss the questions.

1. Have you ever set a goal to improve your performance at school or work?
2. What specific steps did you take to achieve that goal? How did you decide what to do?
3. Did you and your partner do similar things to reach your goals? What are they?

B Look at the following list of strategies commonly used by successful professionals. Put them in order with 1 being the most effective and 7 the least effective. Compare your answers with your partner's and discuss any differences in your answers.

Successful professionals . . .

_____ find mentors whom they can ask for guidance.

_____ devote their free time to activities they truly enjoy.

_____ study all of the policies presented in the company handbook.

_____ develop time management strategies that they use to optimize their work schedule.

_____ identify key skills which they need to develop.

_____ take opportunities to work with colleagues possessing different strengths.

_____ look for training programs that they can attend.

C Look back at the list of strategies in Part B. Complete the tasks.

1. Underline each **complete adjective clause**.
2. Put parentheses around **adjective clauses that contain a zero (Ø) relative pronoun**.
3. Double-underline **adjective clauses with a zero (Ø) relative pronoun and an -ed or -ing verb**.
4. Complete the chart with examples. Then, compare your chart with a partner's chart.

relative pronoun + subject + verb	Ø relative pronoun + subject + verb	Ø relative pronoun + -ed or -ing verb

Reading

A WARM-UP You will read an article by a business leader who specializes in customer service training programs. What kind of advice do you think such a person would offer to professionals who want to improve their work skills? Discuss three ideas with a partner.

B SKIMMING Skim the article and identify the main strategies for being successful at work. Then, read the whole article and verify the number of tips.

The Qualities of Successful People

John Tschohl, President of the Service Quality Institute, has written numerous articles and books on customer service and has developed over 26 customer service programs.

If you hope to succeed at your work, you must seek out all the training you can possibly get. The best jobs and the highest pay increases will go to those employees constantly learning how to do their jobs better. I offer the following suggestions.

Develop a sense of humor. A sense of humor is one of the qualities that high achievers have. Humor leads to a positive attitude, which others around you can benefit from. It can also promote collaboration and enhance alertness and mental efficiency expected in the workplace.

Set a goal. Once you identify what position you hope to attain, develop a plan that will help you achieve that goal. Training should be an integral part of the plan that you follow to become successful.

Identify what you need to know. Consult with your manager about what skills and training would help you get promoted. You could also talk to the person currently holding the job that you would someday like to have. What skills would you need in that position?

Look inside the company. Talk to representatives of the training department about what training is available through the company. If your company does not offer its own training program, check with human resources to see if there is a tuition reimbursement program offered to employees. These programs usually pay for part or all of the costs of training completed outside the company. More than 90 percent of employees who are eligible for company tuition reimbursement do not use it. Those are the employees whom you can leapfrog over on the way to a promotion.

Look outside the company. Local colleges, universities, and vocational-technical schools offer many educational opportunities that working people can take advantage of. There are various night and weekend classes as well as educational workshops and seminars that you can choose from.

Empower yourself. Take the initiative to improve yourself and to perform more effectively in your job. If you want to be creative and productive, set aside free time that you allot to activities that foster productivity and creativity. Empowered people become self-motivated people, and self-motivated people become successful.

Use your time effectively. Organize and execute around priorities. Identify what your most important or most difficult tasks are first. Group related and similar activities and work on them at the same time. Focus on activities which allow you to predict and prevent problems arising from a lack of foresight. When you prioritize, you are applying the Pareto principle: 80 percent of the results of your labors flow out of 20 percent of your activities. It is critical that you attain the highest possible quality production out of your time in order to succeed.

C UNDERSTANDING DETAILS Read the article again. Identify and underline at least one key detail for each of the major tips for success. Then, share your answers with the class.

Grammar Focus 1 Adjective clauses with object relative pronouns

Examples	Language notes

(1) Get advice from colleagues **whom you** *respect*.
Focus on skills **that you** *need* to get promoted.
Apply for job positions *in* **which you will learn new skills**.
You must seek out all the training (that / which) **you can possibly get**.
 	
Most Formal ↑
 	
   a. The supervisor **to whom** I spoke approved my training.
   b. The supervisor **whom** I spoke **to** approved my training.
   c. The supervisor **who** I spoke **to** approved my training.
   d. The supervisor **that** I spoke **to** approved my training.
   e. The supervisor I spoke **to** approved my training.
 	
↓ **Least Formal**
	The relative pronouns **who, whom, which,** and **that** can be the **object** of an adjective clause.
	
	They can also function as the object of a **preposition** in an adjective clause.
	
	You can omit the relative pronoun when it is the object of the adjective clause. This does not change the meaning of the clause. This is the zero (Ø) relative pronoun. Adjective clauses with the zero (Ø) relative pronoun are less formal.
	
	Examples a–e show the progression from most formal to least formal in object adjective clauses.

(2) *Incorrect:* The supervisor whom I consider ~~him~~ my mentor is going to retire soon.	A relative pronoun is the object of the adjective clause. Do not use a double object.
(3) Get advice from colleagues **(whom) you respect**. Leisure activities, **which many people dismiss as purely for "fun,"** provide an important balance to work.	Object adjective clauses can also be **restrictive** or **non-restrictive**. Restrictive adjective clauses identify the noun which they follow. They do **not** use commas. Non-restrictive adjective clauses provide extra information about the noun which they follow, and they are set off between commas. Do not use the pronoun **that** in non-restrictive clauses.
(4) *Incorrect:* Leisure activities, many people dismiss as purely for "fun," provide an important balance to work.	You can often omit an object relative pronoun in restrictive adjective clauses. You cannot omit the relative pronoun in non-restrictive adjective clauses.

Main (Independent) clause	Adjective (Dependent) clause			
	relative pronoun (object)	subject	verb	complement
Get advice from colleagues	**whom**	**you**	**respect.**	
Focus on skills	**which**	**you**	**need**	to get promoted.
Seek all the training	**(Ø)**	**you**	**can get.**	

Main clause subject	Adjective clause				Main clause complement
	relative pronoun (object)	subject	verb	complement	
Managers	**whom**	**employees**	**regard**	**as resources**	are more successful.
Training programs	**which**	**companies**	**offer**		are typically free.

Grammar Practice

A Read the numbered sentences. Then, decide if you agree with sentence A or B. Combine the sentence you chose with the main sentence, using appropriate object adjective clauses with *who(m), which, that,* and *Ø*. Note that you may need a preposition in some cases. Then, discuss your answers in small groups.

1. Knowing a foreign language is an important skill.
   A. People need this skill for most international companies.
   B. People need this skill to communicate with their international colleagues.

   _____

2. Time management represents a common problem.
   A. Both professionals and students struggle with this issue.
   B. Managers often address this issue with employees.

   _____

3. A mentor functions as a key person.
   A. New employees are often assigned to this person.
   B. Experienced employees can learn a lot from this person.

   _____

4. Managers are important sources of information.
   A. Employees should consult them about areas of weakness.
   B. Employees should ask them about other job opportunities.

   _____

B Complete the following passage with the correct object adjective clause from the list below. Write the letter of the phrase in the correct place in the passage.

a. in which you need the greatest improvement

b. with whom you share interests

c. whom several major companies have hired as a consultant

d. that you can realistically achieve

e. which you do on your days off

f. that you should make

Set a goal. What position do you hope to attain? Focus on a position **1.** _____.

Identify what you need to know. Ask your supervisor or manager to help you with this task. Together, identify the areas **2.** _____.

Develop a healthy self-image. Understand who you are and what you are capable of accomplishing. When you do, life is less threatening. Avoid comparing yourself and your performance with your co-workers'. The only meaningful comparison **3.** _____ is between what you are now and what you can become.

Develop fulfilling leisure activities. If you do not have fun in life, you will be bored. When you are bored, your bodily functions slow down and you feel sluggish, says Dr. Richard Barthol, **4.** _____. Develop a loose schedule of activities **5.** _____, so you do not lapse into passivity. Get involved in quality recreation, an activity fit for you and done just for the fun of it. Team up with co-workers **6.** _____.

Grammar Focus 2 Reducing adjective clauses to adjective phrases

Examples	Language notes
(1) Check with human resources to see if there is a tuition reimbursement program (that is) **offered to employees**.	Subject adjective clauses with the relative pronouns **who,** **which,** or **that** can often be reduced to **adjective phrases**. This is often helpful for making sentences more concise in writing, particularly if more than one adjective clause is used. Object adjective clauses **cannot** be reduced to adjective phrases.
(2) Talk to the **person who is currently holding your ideal job**. → Talk to the person **currently holding your ideal job**. It can promote collaboration and enhance the alertness and mental **efficiency that is expected in the workplace**. → It can promote collaboration and enhance the alertness and mental efficiency **expected in the workplace**. Sometimes the best opportunity to expand your training is a **program which is in your own company**. → Sometimes, the best opportunity to expand your training is a program **in your own company**. Julie Phillips, **who is the director of the human resources department**, conducts our computer training workshops. → Julie Phillips, **the director of the human resources department**, conducts our computer training workshops. A professional development plan **that consists of** specific goal statements is more useful for measuring progress. → A professional development plan **consisting of** specific goal statements is more useful for measuring progress. A professional development plan **that must be approved by your manager** is common at many companies. → *No reduction possible.*	There are two ways to reduce subject adjective clauses. a. Omit the subject relative pronoun and a *be* form of the verb. The clause cannot be reduced if *be* is followed by a single adjective. *(Last week's workshop, **which was successful**, will be held again next week. → ~~Last week's workshop, successful, will be held again next week.~~)* When the *be* form of the verb is followed by a noun phrase, only a non-restrictive adjective clause can be reduced to a phrase. This type of phrase is called an *appositive*. b. Omit the subject relative pronoun and change the verb to its **present participle form (-*ing*)** if there is no *be* verb in the adjective clause. The -*ing* form is typically used if the verb in the main clause is in present tense. Do not reduce the adjective clause if it contains a modal verb (*can, may, must, could, should,* etc.).

Grammar Practice

MyEnglishLab

Grammar Plus 2
Activities 1 and 2

A Read each of the following sentences and decide if the adjective clause can be reduced to an adjective phrase. If it can, put a check (✓) next to it and write the reduction above the sentence. If it can't, put an (X).

_____ **1.** People who set impossible goals for themselves often feel a sense of failure.

_____ **2.** The best way to expand your skills is to develop a plan that consists of very specific steps.

_____ **3.** Avoid negative people who might drain your energy by telling you what you can't do.

_____ **4.** Surround yourself with people who are willing to give you advice and support.

_____ **5.** Professionals who want to switch careers find it more difficult to attain success.

_____ **6.** Leaders who are inspirational make the best managers.

_____ **7.** Effective training programs which are offered by a company provide opportunities for self-reflection.

_____ **8.** The qualities of success in this article were outlined by John Tschohl, who is president of the Service Quality Institute.

B Read the paragraph about a successful person. Underline the adjective clauses and decide if they can be reduced. Write the reduction above the line.

J.K. ROWLING: A Wizard of Odds

Most people would think that it is very reckless to follow an artistic passion that does not provide a steady income if they are barely able to put food on the table. Also, most people would not take on a project which is complex and time-consuming during difficult financial times.  However, that is exactly what J.K. Rowling, who is the famous author of the *Harry Potter* series, did during the most challenging time of her life. As a newly single mother who was struggling to support her daughter, Rowling committed herself to her dream of becoming a novelist. "I was very low, and I had to achieve something that could change my life. Without the challenge, I would have gone mad," says Rowling. It was 1994, and when her baby daughter would fall asleep, Rowling would stroll her to a café that was close to her home. She would take the moments of peace to furiously scribble out tales of Harry Potter, who is known as the boy-wizard. The rest is literary history. Now that she has written the seventh volume, which is the final installment of Harry's saga, Rowling, who used to receive welfare payments, is now estimated to be a person who is richer than the Queen of England.

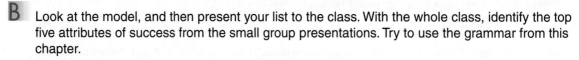

Speaking

A Work in a small group. Make a list of the characteristics of successful professionals that you learned from the reading and activities in this chapter. Then, decide if these characteristics apply to successful athletes. Discuss your ideas.

Characteristic	Applies	Does not apply	Why / Why not?
time management	✓		

B Look at the model, and then present your list to the class. With the whole class, identify the top five attributes of success from the small group presentations. Try to use the grammar from this chapter.

> *People who manage their time well are usually successful. Athletes also have to manage their time; they need to set priorities among activities they need to complete.*

Listening

A BEFORE LISTENING Do you know of a person in the public eye who has faced challenges before becoming famous? Answer the questions. Then, discuss your answers with a partner.

1. Who is he or she?
2. What was his or her challenge?
3. How has he or she overcome this challenge?
4. What is he or she doing now?

B ⌒ UNDERSTANDING MAIN IDEAS Listen to an excerpt from an interview with a psychologist who researched famous people and their paths to success. Then, work with a partner to answer the questions.

1. Who is the famous person being discussed?
2. What is the person's success?
3. What challenges did this person face?
4. How did the person overcome these challenges?

C 🎧 SYNTHESIZING INFORMATION Listen to the interview again. Check (✓) any stated or implied attributes or skills of success that are specific to this person. Give specific examples.

Attribute / Skill of success	Yes?	Example
Ability to balance work and leisure		
Ability to manage time		
Ability to set realistic goals		
Determination		
Humility		
Love of pressure		
Positive self-image		
Self-confidence		
Selflessness		
Self-motivation		
Sense of humor		
Work ethic		
Others		

Writing

MyEnglishLab

▶ Linking Grammar to Writing

A Think about the strategies and attributes of successful people from the reading and the listening in this unit. Brainstorm on the areas of your life (school or work) in which you feel you need improvement. Take notes on a separate sheet of paper.

> Time management: I never have enough time to complete all my tasks.

B Write a paragraph in which you describe your personal action plan for improving your performance either at school or at work. Use your notes from Part A. Try to use the grammar from this chapter.

> According to John Tschohl, an expert in customer service training, successful professionals are people who know how to manage their time effectively. This is one area of my life with which I have been struggling. I never seem to have enough time to complete all my tasks. I think this is because . . .

C Post your action plan around the room. Vote on who has the most effective and realistic plan for self-improvement.

MyEnglishLab

▶ Diagnostic Test

Grammar Summary

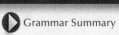

Adjectives and adverbs modify ideas in a sentence.

Adjectives can occur before a noun or after followed by *be*.	(1) Staley turned a bad team into a successful contender.
Some adjectives can be formed from present and past participle forms. These forms are often compound forms.	(2) The player's confidence was contagious. (3) In order to be successful, people need to be hard-working and self-motivated. (4) Normally, he has a winning attitude.
Adverbs can modify verbs and occur in different positions in the sentence.	(5) He is slowly moving across the field. (6) He examined his performance carefully. (7) She is a truly exceptional student.
Adverbs can also modify adjectives and other adverbs. They occur before the adjective or adverb they modify.	(8) Extremely successful people have a sense of discipline. (9) He works extremely hard at every practice.

Adjective clauses modify nouns and are introduced by relative pronouns: *who, whom, which, that, whose* + noun, or Ø.

Relative pronouns can function as subjects of adjective clauses.	(1) People who are self-motivated are usually successful.
Relative pronouns can function as objects of adjective clauses.	(2) Humor is one of the qualities that high achievers have.
Adjective clauses can be either restrictive (use of commas) or non-restrictive (no commas).	(3) There are other attributes that all winning teams possess. (4) Humor leads to a positive attitude, which others around you can benefit from.
Restrictive adjective clauses provide information necessary to identify the noun; non-restrictive adjective clauses provide extra information.	(5) Many employees who are eligible for company tuition reimbursement do not use it. (6) The person whom I talked to is my supervisor.
Who and *whom* are used for people.	(7) The attribute which is the most important in success is a solid work ethic.
Which and *that* are used for things.	(8) A person that works hard at all times is likely to be successful.
It is also acceptable to use *that* for people. *That* can be used only in restrictive adjective clauses to provide identifying information.	(9) She was a player whose team spirit inspired all of her teammates.
Whose must be followed by a *noun*.	

Adjective clauses can be shortened (reduced) in three ways.

If the relative pronoun is used as an object, the relative pronoun can be omitted. This is common in speech and less formal writing.	(1) You must seek out all the training (that) you can possibly get.
The relative pronoun and form of the verb *be* can be omitted if the past participle is followed by a prepositional phrase.	(2) Tuition reimbursement programs (which are) offered to employees can help defray the cost of education.
The relative pronoun can be omitted and the verb in the relative clause can be changed to a present participle (V + -*ing*) if the verb is in present tense.	(3) Employees (who are) looking for career advancement should talk to their supervisors.

Self-Assessment

A (6 points) Read the paragraph and decide if an adjective or an adverb should be used. Circle the correct word.

As a member of my college swim team, I must be able to relate **1. good / well** to each of my teammates. Even when I have not performed **2. outstanding / outstandingly**, it is **3. important / importantly** that I acknowledge the successes of others. I **4. regular / regularly** encourage my teammates, and I set an **5. excellent / excellently** example by working **6. hard / hardly** at practice and in competition.

B (4 points) Rewrite each sentence, using an appropriate adverb from the list. Use each adverb only once.

certainly	extremely	occasionally	really
exceptionally	normally	quickly	truly

1. People who put aside their personal ambitions for the sake of a greater good are remarkable.

_____

2. No matter what your job is, if you want to be successful, you have to work hard.

_____

3. For a runner, it is not important that he or she be fast but that he or she stay motivated.

_____

4. Successful people often thrive under pressure, which they find enjoyable.

_____

C (6 points) Complete the sentences with appropriate relative pronouns from the list. Some relative pronouns may be used more than once. More than one answer is possible.

who   whom   which   that   whose + noun   Ø (zero pronoun)

1. Success comes when you achieve the goals _____ you set for yourself.

2. Being with the people _____ matter to me every day is my benchmark of success.

3. When I have met all those people _____ I admire, then I have achieved success.

4. Employees _____ goal is to advance their position look for professional development opportunities.

5. Doug Doobey, _____ was my coach when I was a child, taught me to take responsibility for my actions.

6. Team spirit, _____ all coaches promote in their players, is a powerful motivational force.

D (4 points) Change the adjective clauses to adjective phrases. Cross out and change the appropriate words.

1. Employees who look for advancement opportunities within their own company should not be afraid of taking on extra projects.

2. Expectations for job duties are listed in employee handbooks that are given to new employees.

3. Many people who work with professional coaches consult them for on-the-job guidance.

4. People who are interested in moving up in their jobs should not be afraid to self-promote.

Unit Project: Group survey

 A You are going to conduct a survey to explore what people think are characteristics of successful people. Then you will write a report on your survey findings. Follow the steps.

1. Work in a group of three or four students. Each group member should survey **five** people. Follow the format below for each person you survey. Note some basic information about each respondent, his or her responses, and the reasons he or she gives.

   Survey questions: *Can you tell me three characteristics of successful people? Why do you think these three are important?*

male / female; approximate age: _____; student / professional / other: _____	
Success characteristic	Reasons

2. Once you complete your survey, tally the results with your group members. Make a chart with the three most commonly mentioned characteristics of successful people in the left column. Include the reasons that the respondents gave you in the right column.

Characteristic of Success	Reason

3. Write a report on your group's survey results. Divide the tasks evenly among your group's members. Follow the outline.

   ### Introduction
   Give a brief definition of "success" and/or "successful people." Include the three key characteristics from your survey.

   ### Body Paragraphs
   Write a paragraph on each success characteristic. Support your points with examples from the survey.

   ### Analysis Paragraph
   Compare the three characteristics to the attributes of successful people that you read about in this chapter. Are they similar or different? Why?

   ### Conclusion
   Summarize your points and give a final thought.

B Share your survey results with the class. Follow the steps.

1. Prepare an informal audio-visual aid to present the three characteristics.
2. As a class, discuss the similarities and differences among each team's survey findings.
3. Discuss which characteristics of success apply to you, and what you have learned in this unit.

MyEnglishLab
Unit Test

MyEnglishLab
Search it!

UNIT 3

Society, Conflict, and Justice

OUTCOMES

After completing this unit, I will be able to use these grammar points.

CHAPTER 5

Grammar Focus 1
Noun clauses as subjects, objects, and complements

Grammar Focus 2
Gerunds and infinitives as objects

CHAPTER 6

Grammar Focus 1
Quantifiers

Grammar Focus 2
Connecting structures for comparison and contrast

My**English**Lab

 What do you know?

CHAPTER 5 Conflict Resolution

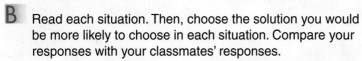

Getting Started

 A Discuss the questions in small groups.

1. Have you or anybody you know ever had a serious argument or dispute with someone? What was the dispute about?
2. How was the dispute resolved?
3. Would you resolve the disputes your classmates described in the same way or in a different way? Why?

B Read each situation. Then, choose the solution you would be more likely to choose in each situation. Compare your responses with your classmates' responses.

1. You have been searching for a parking space for over 20 minutes. You finally spot one, but as you get near, another driver swerves around you and right into the parking space.
   a. You think that this is unacceptable, and you proceed to yell at the other driver to move out of the way because you were there first.
   b. You believe that the other driver acted rudely, but you refrain from yelling at him or her and decide to drive on and look for another parking space.

2. You are working on a group project for one of your classes, but one group member refuses to do any work.
   a. The project evaluation depends on everyone's participation, so you decide to talk to your teacher and ask him or her not to give the group member any credit.
   b. That the project gets completed is important, so you and the other group members concentrate on working on it without the other person.

 C Look back at Part B. Complete the tasks.

1. Underline those parts of sentences with a **noun clause functioning as a subject**.
2. Double-underline those parts of sentences with a **noun clause functioning as an object**.
3. Circle verbs followed by **gerunds** (**verb** + **-ing**).
4. Draw a rectangle around verbs that are followed by **infinitives** (**to** + **verb**).
5. Complete the chart with examples. Then, compare your chart with a partner's chart.

Noun clauses as subjects	Noun clauses as objects	Verbs followed by gerunds (verb + -ing)	Verbs followed by infinitives (to + verb)

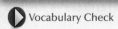
Reading

A WARM-UP On the playground, Jack, a small child, and Sam, a bigger boy, are fighting over a toy. In small groups, discuss how the two boys could resolve their conflict. Identify at least three options. Do you think that adults might solve conflicts in the same way? Why or why not?

B SCANNING Read the article and identify which of these three methods of conflict resolution is addressed in each paragraph: self-help (S), avoidance (A), negotiation (N). Write the correct letter on each blank in the article.

Lessons from the Playground: What We Can Learn from How Kids Resolve Their Disputes

Disputes and conflict are part of life. How to solve disputes requires knowing the best method of conflict resolution. Surprisingly, effective conflict resolution skills first develop on the playground, between young children. Experts explain that dispute resolution methods fall along a continuum from least to most confrontational. This can be illustrated by the most typical of all playground disputes—a fight over a toy.

_____ In the first method, one of the quarrelling people walks away from the dispute. Who decides to walk away is often a result of the relative power imbalance of the disputing parties. On the playground, this can be a smaller child (Jack) who chooses to permit a bigger child (Sam) to have the toy because Jack is afraid that Sam will harm him physically; this is a strategic decision. Conversely, the bigger child may decide that there are other exciting things to play with; again, this is a strategic decision. Adults also often make strategic decisions to avoid conflict. For example, a journalist believes that his idea for an article has been stolen, but he may choose to avoid initiating any dispute because it may prevent him from working with this or another newspaper in the future.

_____ The second method involves communicating about the dispute. Whether disputants want to compromise toward a win-win solution is important. Experts have found that both children and adults use this method most often. On the playground, this can take the form of the "bait and switch": two children want to play with the same toy. Sam realizes that another toy may be more attractive to Jack and offers it to him. An adult will likewise try to find win-win solutions and ask if both parties can work together to achieve an outcome that will work for everyone.

_____ The final method of conflict resolution is most extreme. It involves independent action by one of the parties. What is missing is communication between the parties, the ability to walk away, and most importantly, rules. On the playground, Sam neglects to use other methods and decides to resolve the dispute himself. He proceeds to rip the toy out of Jack's hands. He might not know that he has abused his power and used the most violent form of dispute resolution. Any teacher will confirm that a playground where all children resort to using this method will be utter chaos. Adults also frequently insist on taking matters into their own hands. The problem is that their actions could be illegal. A driver who commits road rage and enjoys causing harm to another driver or an angry neighbor who cuts down a 100-year-old tree and denies doing it are all examples of such behavior. Adults must learn that these acts of taking matters into one's own hands are rarely, if ever, acceptable means for conflict resolution.

C UNDERSTANDING DETAILS Following the model, make a chart comparing children's and adults' behavior for each conflict resolution method as described in the article.

Method	Children	Adults

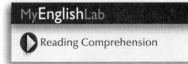

Examples	Language notes
(1) **What is important** is the disputants' desire to compromise.	**Noun clauses** are dependent (subordinate) clauses that function as nouns. Noun clauses can be the **subject** of a sentence.
(2) Experts explain **that dispute resolution methods fall along a continuum**.	Noun clauses can be the **object** of a sentence. Common verbs followed by object noun clauses are: *agree, believe, decide, discover, explain, feel, find out, forget, hear, hope, know, learn, notice, promise, questions (if / whether), read, remember, realize, say, tell someone, think, understand, wonder (if / whether).*
(3) *The problem* was **that Sam used violence to resolve the dispute.**	Noun clauses can be **subject complements**. They provide information about the subject of a sentence.
(4) Jack is *afraid* **that Sam will harm him physically.** *It is unquestionable* **that Jack made the right decision.**	Noun clauses can be **adjective complements**. They can follow certain predicative adjectives or *it is* + adjective patterns in adjective complement structures. Common adjectives followed by noun clauses are: *afraid, disappointed, happy, sad, sorry, sure, surprised.* Common *it is* + adjective structures are: *it is clear / unquestionable / certain / remarkable / doubtful.*
(5) He doesn't understand **(that) he has abused his power.** *The fact that* **conflict resolution skills develop in childhood** surprises many people.	The word *that* can introduce noun clauses. You can omit *that* when a noun clause functions as a direct object. You can use **the fact that** instead of *that* in subject noun clauses.
(6) An adult may ask **if / whether (or not) both parties can work together to find a win-win solution.** *Whether (or not)* **disputants want to compromise toward a win-win solution** is important. The question is **whether (or not) Sam's actions are illegal.** They are uncertain **whether (or not) they will reach an agreement.**	Noun clauses can include embedded questions (questions that are changed to noun clauses). Use noun clause markers *if* or **whether (or not)** to begin an embedded yes / no question. *If* and *whether* have the same meaning, but *if* cannot be used in a subject noun clause.
(7) *How* **people solve disputes** requires knowing the best method of conflict resolution. Sam doesn't understand **what he has done.** The issue is **how they will reach an agreement.** It is interesting **how children resolve conflicts.**	Use *wh-* **question words** to begin embedded *wh-*questions. *Wh-* words are: *what, when, where, why, how, who, whom, which, whose, whatever, whenever, wherever, however, whoever, whomever, whichever.*
(8) *Incorrect:* **How do people solve disputes** requires knowing the best method of conflict resolution. *Incorrect:* An adult may ask if ~~can both parties work together to find a win-win solution~~.	Use normal word order, not question word order, in embedded questions.

Noun clause = Subject	Verb	Complement
That Jack made the right decision	is	unquestionable.
Whether one should walk away or not	depends on	the situation.
Who decides to walk away	is	a result of the relative power imbalance of the disputing parties.

Subject	Verb	Noun clause = object
Jack	fears	**that the bigger child will harm him physically.**
An adult	will ask	**if both parties can influence each other in beneficial ways.**
Sam	doesn't know	**what Jack is going to do to get the toy.**

Subject	Verb	Noun clause = subject complement
The problem	was	**that Sam didn't want to negotiate.**
The question	is	**whether his actions are illegal.**

Subject + verb	Predicative adjective	Noun clause = adjective complement
It is	unquestionable	**that Jack made the right decision.**
Jack is	afraid	**that Sam will harm him physically.**

Grammar Practice

MyEnglishLab

▶ Grammar Plus 1
Activities 1 and 2

 A Form correct noun clauses with the statements, yes / no questions, and *wh*-questions in parentheses to complete the paragraph about another method of conflict resolution.

In another method of conflict resolution, the disputing parties recognize **1.** _____ _____ *(They should seek the intervention of a third party.)*. They also accept **2.** _____ *(Is this method informal or similar to a formal legal process?)* depends on the seriousness of the conflict. Through this process, the parties hope **3.** _____ *(They can achieve a quick resolution.)*. On the playground, **4.** _____ *(Who has to intervene?)* is often a mutual friend. The questions is **5.** _____ *(Can Sam and Jack resolve their dispute themselves?)*. Therefore, they ask a trusted friend **6.** _____ _____ *(Will he or she help them find a compromise?)*. It may be surprising **7.** _____ *(Why don't Sam and Jack ask a parent?)*, but there are times when children feel **8.** _____ _____ *(They need to consult someone who is their age.)*. Similarly, in the adult world it will be important to the outcome **9.** _____ *(Who will help to resolve the conflict?)*. Jack and Sam didn't know **10.** _____ _____ *(What decision would their friend make?)*, but they selected someone they trust. Likewise, adults need to feel **11.** _____ *(They select the right person.)* to listen to the evidence and make a fair decision.

What would you call this method of conflict resolution? Circle your answer.

mediation / arbitration / litigation

B Read the paragraph about another method of conflict resolution. Correct the nine errors in noun clause use.

In this method, a third party arranges the conflict resolution. This person does not order if the quarrellers should do; in other words, it is irrelevant what thinks this person the quarrelling parties should do. Instead, this person hears what are both sides of the dispute so that both parties achieve their own solution. How can this be resolved in the playground scenario is the following: Sam and Jack present their side of the story to Mom; they know that they must act in good faith and tell the truth. The fact is whether both children know Mom won't ultimately make any decision, but she may propose creative solutions to their dispute. Mom may ask what each child might be willing to play with the toy for ten minutes so that each has a turn. This solution allows both children to know that their side of the story has been told and that have they reached the ultimate resolution themselves. In the adult world, if or not both parties can maintain some control of their dispute is essential. This implies control of the costs, process, and outcome. However, both parties must realize they must be open and honest with the third party. Moreover, whom they concentrate on finding a compromise should be their main goal.

What would you call this method of conflict resolution? Circle your answer.
mediation / arbitration / litigation

Grammar Focus 2 Gerunds and infinitives as objects

Examples	Language notes
(1) Sam **avoids** *initiating* any dispute. Adults frequently **insist on** *taking* matters into their own hands. Mom **prevents the boys from** *hurting* each other.	A **gerund** is the **base verb + -ing**. Gerunds function as nouns. Gerunds can be the object in a sentence, following certain verbs or following certain verb + preposition combinations. Gerunds can also follow certain verb + noun / pronoun + preposition combinations.
(2) We should **all insist on** *not* taking matters into our own hands.	Add *not* before the gerund to form a negative statement.
(3) Sam and Jack often **go biking**.	We often use *go* + gerund to talk about recreational activities.
(4) Both parties **want** *to compromise* toward a win-win solution.	An **infinitive** is the word *to* + the base verb. Infinitives can also be the object in a sentence, following certain verbs.
(5) Jack **permits** *Sam* to have the toy.	Some verbs must be followed immediately by another object and then the infinitive.
(6) The parties **expect to find** a solution. (= *The parties think they will find a solution.*) The parties **expect** *the mediator* to find a solution. (= *The parties think the mediator will find a solution.*)	Some verbs can be followed by an optional object + an infinitive, depending on the meaning: *ask, expect, need, want, would like.*
(7) Sam did *not* **learn to take** matters into his own hands. (= *Sam did not learn that he could solve problems on his own.*) Sam **learned** *not* **to take** matters into his own hands. (= *Sam learned that he should let others solve his problems.*)	In the negative form, *not* can negate either the main verb or the infinitive, with a change in meaning.
(8) A third party **lets** both parties **reach** a compromise. Mom **helped** the boys **to resolve** their conflict. Mom **helped** the boys **resolve** their conflict.	The verb *let* is followed by an object and then the base verb. The verb *help* can be followed by either the infinitive or the base verb.
(9) Sam and Jack **continued fighting** over the toy. Sam and Jack **continued to fight** over the toy. The children **stopped arguing** over the toy. (= *They ended what they were doing.*) The children **stopped to argue** over the toy. (= *They interrupted another activity so that they could argue.*)	Some verbs can be followed by the gerund or the infinitive of a verb and the meaning is the same: *begin, continue, can't stand, dislike, hate, like, love, prefer, start.* Some verbs can be followed by the gerund or the infinitive form of a verb, but the meaning is different: *forget, regret, remember, stop.*

Subject	Verb	Noun / Pronoun	Preposition	Gerund = object = "something"
A reckless driver	may enjoy			**causing harm to another driver.**
The method	consists		of	**communicating about the dispute.**
Children	should not resort		to	**using "self-help."**
Mom	prevents	the boys / them	from	**hurting each other.**

Subject	Verb	Object	Infinitive = object = "something"
Two children	attempt		**to play with the same toy.**
Sam and Jack	decide		**to resolve the conflict themselves.**
Jack	permits	Sam	**to play with the toy.**

Common verbs followed by a gerund						
admit	consider	enjoy (less formal: feel like)	imagine	postpone	resent	risk
avoid	deny	finish	involve	practice	resist	suggest

Common verb + (noun / pronoun) + preposition combinations followed by a gerund			
accuse (someone) of	concentrate on	object to	thank (someone) for
approve of	discourage (someone) from	prevent (someone) from	think about
argue about	dream about	resort to	worry about
blame (someone) for	insist on	stop (someone) from	
complain about	look forward to	succeed in	

Common verbs followed by an infinitive					
agree	attempt	expect	intend	pretend	threaten
appear	choose	fail	neglect	promise	want
ask	dare	hope	offer	refuse	

Common verbs followed by another object and an infinitive					
advise	challenge	forbid	motivate	persuade	require
allow	encourage	force	order	promise	tell
ask	expect	instruct	permit	remind	want

See Appendix C on page A-6 for a complete list of verbs followed by gerunds and infinitives.

Grammar Practice

MyEnglishLab

Grammar Plus 2
Activities 1 and 2

 A Read the paragraph about another method of conflict resolution.
Correct the nine errors in the use of gerunds and infinitives.

    The sixth method generally takes place in the adult world. In this method, disputants arrange having a formal conflict resolution. However, even on the playground, Sam and Jack may insist to have a formal decision by the ultimate decision maker—Mom. She commands the boys following her verdict, but one of them might resent to give up the toy. For example, Mom decides letting Jack play with the toy. At first, Sam may refuse handing the toy to Jack and then complain about giving up the toy. Later, he may stop to argue but continue feeling that he has been treated unfairly. Sam may choose to hold resentment toward Jack. Now Jack worries about to lose a friend. In the adult world, disputants often insist on using this method as a legitimate and necessary resolution method, but parties cannot avoid to pay the costs (financial, physical, emotional, etc.).

What would you call this method of conflict resolution? Circle your answer.

    mediation / arbitration / litigation

B   Complete the paragraph with gerunds or infinitives. Use the verbs in parentheses.

Conflict resolution depends on **1.** _____ (understand) how culture influences the way we resolve conflict. In some cultures, disputants threaten **2.** _____ (hurt) each other. In other cultures, third parties encourage the disputants **3.** _____ (not take) out their anger on each other. In still other cultures, each disputant dislikes **4.** _____ (admit) that he or she might have been wrong. In Western cultures, such as Canada and the United States, successful conflict resolution usually involves **5.** _____ (foster) communication among disputants. People expect each other **6.** _____ (find) workable solutions. This approach concentrates on **7.** _____ (reach) agreements that meet both parties' needs. Westerners believe in **8.** _____ (create) win-win solutions. They avoid **9.** _____ (design) scenarios that are not mutually satisfying. In many non-Western cultures, such as Afghanistan, Vietnam, and China, people also prefer **10.** _____ (find) win-win solutions. However, the route to conflict resolution can be very different. Disputants do not want **11.** _____ (engage) in direct communication about the conflict. If one party chooses **12.** _____ (address) the issues directly, this behavior is perceived as rude, and the other party complains about **13.** _____ (be) treated unfairly. As a result, he or she may object to **14.** _____ (seek) any solution. Such attitudes promise **15.** _____ (make) the conflict worse and delay **16.** _____ (come) to a resolution. Rather, the disputants agree **17.** _____ (involve) religious leaders or community leaders. They offer **18.** _____ (communicate) through this third party, and they attempt **19.** _____ (make) suggestions indirectly through stories. In conflicts between members of different cultures, parties often fail **20.** _____ (resolve) the situation because the disputants expect each other **21.** _____ (act) and **22.** _____ (react) in ways that are consistent with their own culture. Consequently, there is much occasion for misunderstanding.

Which conflict resolution style that you have learned about in the chapter is used in many Western cultures? In many non-Western cultures?

Speaking

A Look at the pictures. With a partner, describe the conflict between the two donkeys and the way in which they manage to resolve their conflict. What strategy discussed in this chapter are they using?

B Now apply the situation from Part A to yourself and answer the questions. Share your answers with the whole class. Try to use the grammar from the chapter.

1. Have you ever had a similar conflict in which you and someone else had to work together to reach a solution? What happened? Did you resolve it in a similar or different way? How?
2. What guided your decision about which conflict resolution strategy you selected?

> *I remember that I had a dispute with my sister over the use of our family computer. We both wanted to use it for . . .*

Listening

A BEFORE LISTENING You will listen to an interview about research on how animals solve conflicts. Before you listen, discuss these the following questions with a partner.

1. Which animals do you think have been studied for their conflict resolution behavior? Why?
2. Why might researchers want to study animal conflict resolution in the first place?
3. How do you think researchers study human conflict resolution strategies?

B LISTENING FOR DETAILS Listen to a segment from a radio interview with a behavioral scientist. Then, read the statements. Write *T* for the true statements and *F* for the false statements. Correct any false statements.

_____ 1. We learn that research on animal conflict resolution has been done on dogs and cats.

_____ 2. It is true that conflict occurs regularly among primates.

_____ 3. Conflict appears to be very common among members of closely-knit groups.

_____ 4. Researchers have noticed that there are no conflicts between primate parents and their offspring.

_____ 5. Only 9 percent of conflicts among primates happen to result in a resolution.

_____ 6. After a conflict, many primate species avoid having contact with each other.

_____ 7. In experiments, researchers intentionally arrange to set up a conflict to study primate behavior.

_____ 8. There has been a lot of research that focuses on examining human conflict resolution.

_____ 9. Researchers approve of studying primate conflict resolution in the animals' natural habitat.

C CRITICAL THINKING Listen again. Discuss the questions in small groups.

1. How does reconciliation after a conflict help a species survive?
2. What are the challenges of observing what primates do in their natural habitat?
3. What is the benefit of choosing to conduct controlled experiments with primates?
4. How does the presence of the group influence conflict resolution in primates, and why?
5. Why do playgrounds offer good opportunities to research conflict resolution?
6. Why are researchers discouraged from studying conflict resolution in adults?
7. Why can researchers not depend on using people's own reports of conflicts and conflict resolution?
8. What can humans learn from the research on primate conflict resolution?

Writing

A Work with a partner. Complete the activities.

1. In this chapter, you have learned about the following six conflict resolution strategies: *arbitration, avoidance, litigation, mediation, negotiation, self-help*.
Place these strategies along a continuum, from least confrontational to most confrontational.

Least confrontational   Most confrontational

2. What types of conflicts might occur among people? Brainstorm examples of disputes that might occur between students, co-workers, neighbors, or even strangers.

B Select one of the scenarios below. Write about which of the six conflict resolution strategies you would recommend using and why. Try to use the grammar from the chapter.

Scenario A: Greg regularly stays up late to study in the room that he shares with his roommate, Alex. Alex prefers to go to bed by 10 P.M. because he has classes in the morning, but he can't sleep because of the light on Greg's desk and the music from his roommate's iPod. Alex is regularly tired and upset at his roommate. He thinks Greg should move out. Greg thinks Alex is the one who should move out.

Scenario B: Your neighbor's cat is often outdoors and roams throughout the neighborhood. You often see the cat in your yard. You have been angry about the mess the cat leaves. Recently, the cat attacked some baby birds in your tree. You have asked your neighbor many times to control her cat, but she has ignored your requests.

> In situation X, I advise the disputants to find a mediator. Both parties might refuse to compromise without a third party. The mediator could find out . . .

C Share your conflict scenarios and resolution options with the rest of the class. Compare the conflict resolution strategies that you and your classmates would adopt in these scenarios. Whose strategy is the fairest and the most practical?

Chapter 6   Alternative Forms of Justice

Getting Started

A   Think back to the situation between Sam and Jack in Chapter 5. They experienced a conflict typical for young children. Although teenagers also face conflicts with one another, as young people near adulthood, they can get into more serious situations. Working in small groups, discuss common examples of inappropriate behavior or trouble that teens get involved in.

B   Read the scenarios about teens who have had trouble with the law. None had been arrested before. Decide what punishment other than jail would be the most appropriate for each situation.

1. A boy "borrowed" a bicycle from his neighbor's yard. He knew the neighbor wouldn't approve, but he took it anyway, thinking that he would bring it back later. However, after two weeks had passed, the bike never reappeared, so the neighbor called the police. The bike was found in the boy's backyard.

Outcome/punishment: _____

2. Two friends went window shopping at the mall after school. Neither girl had any money with her. One of them saw a scarf that she liked and decided to put it into her handbag when the clerk wasn't looking. Likewise, her friend slipped some inexpensive jewelry in her own bag. The girls were stopped by an undercover security guard when they were leaving the store.

Outcome/punishment: _____

3. A number of high school students from two different schools got into an argument at a local park about a recent basketball game. While most of those involved were simply angry and doing a lot of yelling, a few of them escalated the argument and began pushing and hitting one another. Although very little physical contact occurred during the incident, someone called the police, who arrived to stop the fight.

Outcome/punishment: _____

C   Look back at Part B. Complete the tasks.

1. Underline words / phrases with **quantifiers** that show **quantities of count nouns**.
2. Circle words / phrases with **quantifiers** that show **quantities of non-count nouns**.
3. Put parentheses around words / phrases that show **similarities between ideas**.
4. Put a rectangle around words / phrases that show **differences between ideas**.
5. Following the model, make two charts with examples. Then, compare your charts with a partner's charts.

Quantifiers: count nouns	Quantifiers: non-count nouns

Comparison structures	Contrast structures

Reading

A WARM-UP Think of a court case you are familiar with or have seen in a movie or TV show. Describe what happened to a partner. Use words from the list in your description.

a defense attorney   a prosecutor   restitution   to hold accountable
a jail sentence   community service   to deliberate   to testify
a jury of peers   evidence

B SCANNING Scan the article on teen courts to identify the main requirements for young offenders to be referred to a peer court instead of a traditional court hearing. Who doesn't qualify for peer court? Then, read the whole article.

A Jury of Their Peers   Teen Courts Help Communities Get Smart about Being Tough

When teens commit a crime or show other problem behaviors, they might be referred to a youth court program. The goal is for them to learn a lot of valuable lessons and gain a great amount of responsibility. Youth courts hold teens accountable for their actions, yet they provide them with many important life skills in public speaking, problem solving, and critical thinking.

Communities that have teen court programs base them on the idea that young people make plenty of mistakes when they have their first taste of independence. "All of us did things at ages 14 or 15 that we are not proud of," says Police Chief Tim Roets. Chief Roets's Wisconsin agency began participating in teen court a few years ago. He believes that peer courts help correct some problem behaviors before they put youth at risk. "If you can correct a majority of these behaviors without a rigid fine or an offense that remains on their record throughout their teenage years, you will be successful," says Roets.

Unlike traditional court cases, almost all youth court hearings are run by teens. While a few key adults preside over the sessions for guidance, there is little involvement from other adults. The teens sit on the jury and act as

defense attorneys and prosecutors. Teens ask questions as the young defendant testifies. Also, both parents testify about the youth's character. Then, the jury leaves the room to deliberate. The jurors have plenty of time to reach a decision.

Youth court has two main goals: (1) Response to the behavior. This is an essential element of teen court. In a traditional courtroom, the judge hands down a sentence; in contrast, youth programs create a system of contractual relationships. Just as evidence is brought forth in a typical court, teen jurors base their decisions on the presented facts. Similar to typical court sentences, some of the consequences include restitution, community service, and personal restrictions, but the sentence does not include jail time. However, the program does have an implied threat—a youth who does not follow through faces further actions and severe consequences.

(2) Building responsibility. Community service, jury duty, and restitution teach youth about their responsibilities within the community. This allows a young person whose behaviors are inappropriate to develop a number of skills and tools that lead to appropriate behavior. Most importantly, youth court participation can be a mechanism for this to occur. Some of the best youth court ambassadors had committed a previous offense.

Although it has advantages, teen court isn't meant for all troubled teens. Youth courts meet the needs of a great number of low-risk kids committing first-time offenses, whereas teens with a second, third, or fourth offense go through the traditional court system instead. Very few teens with a police record are considered for teen court.

C UNDERSTANDING DETAILS Read the article again. Underline the specific roles teens play in peer court. Then, circle the potential outcomes that a youth in a peer court trial may receive.

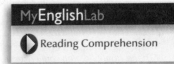

Grammar Focus 1 Quantifiers

Examples	Language notes
(1) The goal is for them to learn **a lot of** valuable *lessons*.	**Quantifiers** describe the quantity or amount of a noun or noun phrase. They answer the questions "How much?" or "How many?"
(2) **Each** *teen offender* is screened before he or she is referred to youth court. They provide them with **many** important life *skills*. **A few** key *adults* provide guidance. After **a great deal of** *time* had passed, the neighbor called the police. As young people receive their first taste of independence, they make **plenty of** *mistakes*. Jurors are given **plenty of** *time* to reach a decision.	Some quantifiers are used with only **singular count nouns**: *one, each, every, etc.* Some quantifiers are only used with **plural count nouns**: *two, both, many, few, a few, a number of, several, etc.* The most basic quantifiers are numbers. Other quantifiers are only used with **noncount nouns**: *little, a little, a great deal of, a great amount of, much, etc.* Some quantifiers can be used with **either plural count or noncount nouns**: *all, any, enough, most, plenty of, etc.*
(3) Very **few** *teens* with an established record are considered for teen court. (= *not many*) **A few** *adults* preside over the proceedings for guidance. (= *some, just enough*) There is **little** *similarity* to the adult court system. (= *not much*) There is **a little** *involvement* of adults in the process. (= *some, just enough*)	Quantifiers that emphasize **the lack of** a noun are negative. **Few** and **little** mean "not enough" or "not many / much". Note that *a few* and *a little* give a **positive sense** to a statement. They mean "some" or "just enough."
(4) **All** *teen offenders* are screened before they are referred to youth court. (*non-specific reference → teen offenders in general*) **All of** *the teen offenders* who take part in youth court receive a fair hearing with a jury of their peers. (*specific reference → a particular group of teen offenders*)	Use **of** with certain quantifiers to describe specific nouns. To make a reference to a count or non-count noun more specific, **of + the** can be used with quantifiers that also work without **of**. (See Unit 7 for more on articles.)

See Appendix D on page A-7 for a list of common noncount nouns.

< Quantifier + count noun		< Quantifier + noncount noun	
(almost / nearly) all		(almost / nearly) all	
most		most	
*a majority of			
*a lot of / lots of		*a lot of / lots of	
many		**much	
*a great / large number of		*a great / large amount of / a great deal of	
*a number of			
*plenty of	teens	*plenty of	responsibility
several			
some / **any		some / **any	
(very) few / a few		(very) little / a little	
hardly any		hardly any	
a couple of			
both / neither			
no / *none of the		no / *none of the	

*These quantifiers are only used with **of**.
**These quantifiers are only used in questions and negative constructions.*

Grammar Practice

A Complete each paragraph with a correct quantifier from the boxes below. You will not use all of the quantifiers, and some quantifiers may be used more than once. In some cases, more than one answer is possible.

many	nearly all	several	a number of
a majority of	a great deal of	little	

1. _____ successful youth programs bring together a different people to set

2. _____ common goals. They include 3. _____

professionals in law enforcement, probation, schools, and courts, but also members of civic groups.

These groups need to have 4. _____ opportunities to become involved and provide

5. _____ insight into what the program will include. Programs with

6. _____ community members as their supporters function more smoothly in the

long run.

all of	several	no
few	much	quite a few of

"I supervise the kids, but I have 7. _____ part in the decision," says

Jessica Breezer, a justice specialist with a teen court. She reminds jurors about 8. _____

the appropriate case details, but they decide the punishment, which can range from 9. _____

hours of community service to a class with a jail tour. 10. _____ the outcomes

include writing personal essay, apology letters, and more. "Teen court isn't easy, and I don't think it should

be," says Breezer.

very few	a majority of	hardly any	a lot of
several	little	a great deal of	many

Fifteen-year-old Lucy, who was sentenced by a teen court, says she learned 11. _____

lessons in the process, especially by completing 12. _____ hours of community

service and jury terms. She learned that her actions affected not only herself but also the people

around her. She also found she liked being noticed for the 13. _____ positive

things she was doing, such as tutoring younger students. Lucy's mother sees 14. _____

improvement in her daughter's behavior. "Before her teen court experience, Lucy put 15. _____

effort into helping others, and she had 16. _____ friends," she said. "Now she

spends 17. _____ time on volunteer activities and has made friends."

B Read the sentences. If the underlined quantifier is used correctly, write *C*. If it is used incorrectly, write the correct quantifier. More than one correction may be possible.

_____ 1. A majority of the time peer jurors spend deliberating a case is focused on the evidence.

_____ 2. Few adults realize that having peers judge teens' behaviors can have a powerful impact on these teens. However, research has shown the positive effects of peer courts.

_____ 3. An important piece in building a successful teen court also resides in a large number of responsible adult oversight from a parent, guardian, or other key adults.

_____ 4. Many of teens who volunteer in youth court juries once faced a jury in the past.

_____ 5. Training teen jurors how to deliberate is some of the essential components to successful youth court programs.

_____ 6. It is difficult to solve a social problem without a great deal of understanding and cooperation from the community.

_____ 7. Youth court does not always meet the needs of teen offenders. Some of teens have had previous trouble with the law and are referred to the regular court system.

_____ 8. Hardly any of the teens who find themselves in trouble with the law needed to learn more effective dispute resolution strategies when they were younger.

C Read the following sentences about peer mentoring, or teens supporting and guiding other teens. Rewrite each sentence using an appropriate quantifier from the list on page 56 to replace the underlined words or phrases. Try to keep the meaning the same.

1. A high percentage of teens who are at risk for getting in trouble with the law can benefit from a peer mentoring program.

_____

_____

2. Although some at-risk teens end up in court, most don't need a jail sentence to convince them to change their behavior.

_____

_____

3. Instead, having many positive experiences with another teen can help at-risk teens gain a lot of confidence and change their ways.

_____

_____

4. Nearly one hundred percent of the teens who want to be peer mentors undergo training at their schools, but a small number complete community training programs.

_____

_____

5. A number of the behaviors peer mentors help to change involve unhealthy habits like smoking, but some of them are related to crimes such as shoplifting.

_____

_____

6. Overall, a very small number of at-risks teens have negative experiences with peer mentoring, and a very high number of peer mentors say that they gained a lot of skills in the process.

_____

_____

Grammar Focus 2 Connecting structures for comparison and contrast

Examples	Language notes
	Use **connecting structures** to join ideas within sentences and between sentences. This chapter addresses these types of structures: **conjunctive adverbs**, **coordinating conjunctions**, and **subordinating conjunctions**, as well as **prepositions** and **phrasal prepositions**. You can use these structures to show **similarities** and **differences** between sentences or clauses.
(1) In the regular court system, a judge can rule on cases a jury can't agree on. **Similarly**, judges can make the final decision in peer court hearings. Attorneys in traditional courts are paid; **however**, teen court participants are often volunteers.	**Conjunctive adverbs** (also known as transitions or sentence connectors) connect ideas between sentences. They show similarities and differences between sentences. They are preceded by a period or semicolon and followed by a comma. Conjunctive adverbs of **similarity** include *similarly, likewise, also, in the same way.* Conjunctive adverbs of **contrast** include *however, on the other hand, in contrast, conversely.*
(2) Some teen courts use jury trials, **and** many adult courts do, **too**. Youth courts hold teens responsible for their actions, **yet** they provide them with many important life skills.	**Coordinating conjunctions** connect independent clauses. They are preceded by a comma. Coordinating conjunctions of **similarity** include the words *and . . . , too.* Coordinating conjunctions of **difference** include the words *but* and *yet*. Coordinating conjunctions and sentence connectors link ideas of **equal** importance.
(3) **Although** it has advantages, teen court isn't meant for all troubled teens.	**Subordinating conjunctions** connect dependent (subordinate) and independent clauses. If the dependent clause comes first in the sentence, it is followed by a comma. Subordinating conjunctions include *just as* for similarities, and words such as *although, even though, though, while,* and *whereas* for contrast (*although, though,* and *even though* indicate an unexpected outcome).
(4) **Like** typical court trials, teen court hearings have a judge who presides over the case.	Some **prepositions** and **phrasal prepositions** (*like, similar to, unlike*) can also be used to express similarities and differences. They are followed by a noun or noun phrase and connect to an independent clause. They are separated from the main clause by a comma. Subordinating conjunctions and these prepositions / phrasal prepositions link ideas of **unequal** importance; the idea in the main (independent) clause is emphasized.

Comparison Structures

Independent clause	Conjunctive adverb	Independent clause	
Judges hear trials in traditional courts.	Similarly, Likewise, Also, In the same way,	youth court judges can rule on cases.	

Independent clause	Coordinating conjunction (1)	Independent clause	Coordinating conjunction (2)
Judges hear trials in traditional courts,	**and**	youth court judges can rule on cases,	**too.**

Independent clause	Subordinating conjunction	Dependent clause	
Judges hear trials in traditional courts	**just as**	youth court judges can rule on cases.	

Phrase		Independent clause
preposition or phrasal preposition	noun or noun phrase	
Like, Similar to	judges in traditional courts,	youth court judges can rule on cases.

Contrast Structures

Independent clause	Conjunctive adverb	Independent clause
Attorneys in traditional courts are paid;	however, on the other hand, in contrast, conversely,	teen court participants are often volunteers.

Independent clause	Coordinating conjunction	Independent clause
Attorneys in traditional courts are paid,	but yet	teen court participants are often volunteers.

Independent clause	Subordinating conjunctions	Dependent clause
Attorneys in traditional courts are paid	while whereas although even though	teen court participants are often volunteers.

Phrase		Independent clause
preposition	noun or noun phrase	
Unlike	attorneys in traditional courts,	teen court participants are often volunteers.

 ## Grammar Practice

MyEnglishLab

Grammar Plus 2
Activities 1 and 2

A Choose the correct structure in parentheses to combine the clauses into complete sentences. Make necessary changes. Use correct punctuation.

1. some youth courts operate within local police agencies / other youth courts are run by the local school district (**whereas / similar to**)

_____

2. youths who have special skills can gain self-confidence by joining school teams or clubs / teens who don't have special talents build self-esteem through volunteer work in peer court (**likewise / in contrast**)

_____

3. adult judges in teen courts receive special training / teen judges also undergo training (**but / like**)

_____

4. some teens pressure their friends to engage in risky behaviors / teens who volunteer for youth court apply positive peer pressure (**yet / also**)

_____

5. peer court programs help first-time offenders change their attitudes / traditional justice programs focus primarily on punishing offenders (**just as / however**)

_____

6. youth court volunteers gain valuable knowledge and skills / defendants in youth court learn valuable lessons (**and . . . , too / while**)

_____

7. some teen court hearings are open to the general public / other teen court hearings are private public (**although / likewise**)

_____

8. sentences that require teens to make amends for their actions teach responsibility / sentences that have teens complete volunteer service in the community promote civic involvement (**even though / in the same way**)

_____

B Write sentences comparing or contrasting the two ideas in the clauses. Use the structures in parentheses. Decide which idea should be subordinated, or given less emphasis, by including it in the dependent clause.

1. an offender in a traditional court case could be sent to jail / a sentence in teen court does not include jail time (_a preposition or phrasal preposition_)

   Unlike in traditional court, a sentence in Teen Court does not include jail time.
   _____

2. schools have the responsibility to provide students with proper role models / parents must ensure that they model effective decision-making strategies for their children (_a preposition or phrasal preposition_)

   _____
   _____

3. many states continue to fund traditional youth justice programs that have not worked / research shows that treating teen offenders as adults is ineffective (_a subordinating conjunction_)

   _____
   _____

4. traditional methods of addressing juvenile crime are quite expensive / youth crime prevention programs can save states a great deal of money (_a preposition or phrasal preposition_)

   _____
   _____

5. juvenile justice programs that encourage family interactions are successful / youth justice programs that foster community support are effective (_subordinating conjunction_)

   _____
   _____

Speaking

 A Work in a group of three students. Discuss common policies a typical high school or university in your country has for student behavior. Choose the ideas from the box below or your own ideas. Use the questions to guide your discussion. Look at the model. Try to use the grammar from the chapter.

class attendance	completion of assignments
cheating on tests	independent vs. collaborative work
lateness	using school Internet or library resources
plagiarism	

1. What general rules must students follow?
2. What are the standards for academic honesty and ethical conduct?
3. What are the consequences for violating the policies?

> *In my high school, if students missed classes, they had to attend a meeting with their parents and the school director.*

B As a class, discuss the consequences for violating school policies that each group identified. What were the differences and similarities in the consequences for similar violations? Compare and contrast the ideas shared by each group.

Listening

A BEFORE LISTENING A university student was accused of committing plagiarism on an assignment. He had a hearing with the academic honor council at his university. With a partner, predict what may have been his punishment and his reaction to it. After you finish Parts B and C, check your predictions.

B 🎧 LISTENING FOR MAIN IDEAS Listen to an interview with a student who recently underwent a formal hearing with the academic honor council at his university for violating the school's honor code. Then, answer the questions.

1. How is an honor council or academic conduct board similar to a youth court?
2. How did Eric commit plagiarism?

C 🎧 LISTENING FOR DETAILS Listen to the interview again. Then, answer the questions.

1. What did the honor council require Eric to do for his punishment?
2. What did he learn from his experience?

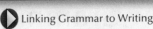
Writing

A Read the pairs of scenarios involving academic honesty issues. With a partner, discuss which scenario in each pair is an example of academic dishonesty and why.

> **1. a)** Juan and Abdul are both students in the English Reading and Writing class. They often meet to compare notes and check homework assignments together. When they have a particularly difficult assignment, they do it together, usually the night before the assignment is due. Afterwards, each makes his own copy and turns it in to the professor.
>
> **b)** Pavel and Takeshi are both students in the English Reading and Writing class. They often meet to compare their notes from the day's class. Each does his own homework assignments. When they have an especially difficult assignment, they meet a few days in advance to compare their answers. Each corrects or changes some of the answers in his work, and each turns in his own assignment.

> **2. a)** After Ji Yoon received her essay back from her professor in her English Composition class, she began planning how she would revise it. She wanted to make appropriate changes to the essay, so she scheduled an appointment to see a tutor at the Writing Center at her university. After receiving advice from the tutor, she went home, and rewrote the essay on her own. She read over it a couple days before it was due to check it one last time and turned it in on the due date.
>
> **b)** After Sara received her essay back from her professor in her English Composition class, she put it away for a few days. A day before the next draft was due, she began planning how she would revise it. She wasn't sure what changes she needed to make, so she asked a friend who was majoring in English to help her. Her friend checked the essay and corrected all the mistakes she found. Sara went home, rewrote the essay with her friend's corrections, and turned it in the next day.

B Write a short comparison / contrast paragraph for each set of situations in Part A. For each comparison / contrast, tell which scenario in Part A constituted the most serious violation of academic honesty policies and describe why. Try to use the grammar from the chapter.

> Like Juan and Abdul, Pavel and Takeshi are students in the English Reading and Writing class. Juan and Abdul often compare notes, and Pavel and Takeshi do, too. However, . . .

C Share your paragraphs in small groups. See if you agreed on the more serious violations and discuss what factors may have contributed to each violation.

MyEnglishLab
► Diagnostic Test

Grammar Summary

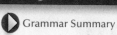

Noun clauses are dependent clauses and can function as the subject, object, or complement.

Noun clauses can function as the subject, object, or complement. Noun clauses can be formed from statements, yes / no questions, and *wh-* questions. They are introduced by noun clause markers. *That* can be omitted in informal contexts and in speech.	(1) What solution they select depends on the seriousness of the conflict. (2) The boys knew that they had to find a solution. (3) It is clear that Jack doesn't want Sam to hurt him. (4) The question is which conflict resolution method will work best for a given situation. (5) Sam hopes that his friend can solve the problem. (6) Jack wonders if Sam will be angry with him. (7) Sam asks Jack when he can play with the toy. (8) The boys promise (that) they will stop fighting.

Gerunds (verb + *-ing*) and infinitives (*to* + verb) are special verb forms and can function as objects.

Gerunds function like nouns and can function as the object of a sentence, following certain verbs and verb + preposition combinations. Similarly, infinitives can function as the object of a sentence, following certain verbs and verb + object combinations. Some verbs can be followed by either gerunds or infinitives without a change in meaning. Some verbs can be followed by gerunds or infinitives, but with a change in meaning.	(1) The boys admitted fighting over the toy. (2) They succeeded in finding a compromise. (3) Sam and Jack didn't hesitate to ask their a friend for advice. (4) Mom persuaded Sam to give the toy to Jack. (5) The children continued arguing over the toy. (6) The children continued to argue over the toy. (7) Sam and Jack remembered finding a compromise. (= *They recalled the action of finding a compromise.*) (8) They remembered to find a compromise. (= *They remembered it was their task to find a compromise.*)

Quantifiers describe the quantity or amount of a noun or noun phrase.

Some quantifiers can only be used with count nouns. Other quantifiers can only be used with noncount nouns. Some quantifiers can be used with both count and noncount nouns.	(1) Teens courts can successfully address a large number of behavioral problems in schools. (2) A great deal of crime occurs in major cities. (3) Some teens tend to get in trouble with the law. (4) Some intervention is necessary to reduce behavioral problems.

Connecting structures for comparison and contrast can be expressed with various structures. The type of structure affects punctuation.

Conjunctive adverbs join independent sentences and are preceded by a semicolon or period. Coordinating conjunctions join independent clauses within a sentence and are preceded by a comma. Subordinating conjunctions join dependent and independent clauses. Prepositions / phrasal prepositions + noun / noun phrase connect to an independent clause.	(1) Peer pressure can cause negative behavior; similarly, peer pressure can have a positive impact. (2) Teens tried in teen courts typically stay out of trouble, but teens tried in regular courts often become repeat offenders. (3) Just as peer pressure can cause negative behavior, peer pressure can have a positive impact. (4) Unlike teens tried in regular courts, teens tried in teen courts typically stay out of trouble.

Self-Assessment

A (5 points) Write appropriate noun clauses from the statements, yes / no questions, and *wh-* questions in parentheses. Add appropriate noun clause markers.

1. It is unquestionable _____.
   (People all over the world have conflicts with relatives, friends, and strangers.)

2. *(What strategy do people select to resolve their conflict?)* _____
   _____ depends on both their culture and the type of conflict.

3. People usually don't know _____.
   (How does culture influence conflict resolution strategies?)

4. They wonder _____.
   (Can the strategy that works in my country also work in another country?)

5. The question is _____.
   (Is the strategy successful in a given conflict?)

B (5 points) Complete the paragraph with appropriate forms of the verb in parentheses.

Early research on conflict concentrated on **1.** _____ (examine) disputes between

individuals who did not know each other. However, recent researchers have started **2.** _____

(analyze) conflict within a social context. Indeed, these researchers challenge us **3.** _____

(consider) conflict as a phenomenon that occurs mostly between people who know each other. In fact,

the researchers teach us **4.** _____ (see) conflict as an integral part of any relationship

with an interesting paradox: those who have a strong relationship are also the ones who can't help

5. _____ (argue) with one another.

C (6 points) Circle the correct quantifier to complete each sentence in the paragraph.

1. If **few / some** peer pressure among teenagers makes **2.** **many / a great deal of** teens engage in

dangerous or criminal behavior, peer pressure can also work to get **3.** **much / a lot of** teens to behave

positively. **4.** **Little / Few** teenagers really want to do bad things; in fact, **5.** **all / hardly any** teens thrive on

6. **much / plenty of** positive feedback and the feeling that they belong to a group.

D (4 points) Read each pair of sentences. Decide if they discuss something similar or something different. Then, on a separate piece of paper, combine the sentences with the type of comparison / contrast structure in parentheses.

1. In adult hearings, there are prosecutors and defense attorneys. In youth courts, adults do not usually serve as attorneys. (*subordinating conjunction*)
2. In regular court cases, the jury consists of twelve jurors. In most teen court cases, the jury is composed of twelve members. (*preposition or phrasal preposition*)
3. In some states, an adult performs the role of judge in serious cases. In cases with lesser offenses, a teen jury alone handles the cases. (*coordinating conjunction*)
4. Adult offenders are questioned during their court hearing. Youth offenders have to answer questions about their actions. (*conjunctive adverb*)

Unit Project: Mini-mock hearing

A You are going to participate in a mock academic honor council hearing. Work in groups of six or more. Complete the steps.

1. As a group, brainstorm a scenario involving a serious violation of an academic honesty policy in your school's official code of conduct or based on regulations with which you are familiar. Describe the specifics of what the student or students are accused of doing in a formal statement. (Refer back to the list of potential issues in Part A of the Speaking activity on page 62 for ideas, if necessary.)

2. Decide which roles will be included in your group's mock council hearing. A high school, college, or university honor council or academic conduct board hearing involves several people. Participants can include:
   • the accused student(s)
   • the accuser(s)
   • various honor council / academic conduct board members including:
      ◦ students from different grade levels (high school level)
      ◦ full- and / or part-time undergraduate and graduate students (college or university level)
      ◦ teachers, professors, teaching assistants
      ◦ administrators (the principal or dean of a school or other high-level administrator often has ultimate authority)
      ◦ school library staff members
      ◦ residence hall supervisors (college or university level)
      ◦ qualified members of the local community

Your group must include at least one accused student, one accuser, and two board members.

3. Decide what position each participant in the mock hearing will take. For example, decide if the accused student(s) will claim to be innocent and what kind of evidence the accuser(s) will bring to the hearing. In addition, decide what sanction(s) the accused will receive. Potential sanctions can include:
   • a letter or warning (less serious; sent to student directly)
   • a letter of reprimand (somewhat serious; placed in student's academic file)
   • suspension (serious)
   • dismissal (very serious)

4. Set up a space for each group to hold separate mock hearings. Set a time limit for the hearing within which each mock council should reach a decision on the recommended sanction(s).

B After the mock hearings have concluded, share your case facts and decisions with the class. Follow the steps.

1. Let each group present its case facts and decision.
2. Discuss the fairness of the sanctions decided by the mock council in each group.
3. Identify what the accused students in each case should do to avoid future violations of the honor code.

MyEnglishLab
▶ Unit Test

MyEnglishLab
▶ Search it!

UNIT 4

The Impact of Social Media

OUTCOMES

After completing this unit, I will be able to use these grammar points.

CHAPTER 7

Grammar Focus 1
Equatives

Grammar Focus 2
Comparatives and comparative clauses

Grammar Focus 3
Degree complements

CHAPTER 8

Grammar Focus 1
Present and future unreal conditionals

Grammar Focus 2
Reported speech

MyEnglishLab

 What do you know?

CHAPTER 7 | The Digital Gap

Getting Started

A Look at the three groups of people in the chart. Which type of online activities do you expect each group of people to engage in? Check (✓) all boxes that apply. Discuss reasons for your choices in small groups. Then, discuss the questions.

	Younger than 20	20-50	Older than 50
Send / Receive email			
Visit social networking sites			
Read news			
Read blogs			
Play games			
Watch videos			
Buy something			
Bank online			
Use search engines			

1. What other online activities might each group engage in? Why?
2. Which online activities do you engage in? Which online activities do your older relatives engage in? What are similarities and differences between your and your parents' online activities?

B Work with a partner. Decide if the following statements are true or false. Write *T* for the true statements and *F* for the false statements. Explain your reasons.

_____ 1. Internet use is as common among teenagers as it is among the elderly.

_____ 2. People in their 40s and 50s buy more products online than any other age group.

_____ 3. Online games are so popular among retirees that companies have to create new games.

_____ 4. For many older adults, Internet activities are too complicated to figure out how to use.

_____ 5. Most social networking sites are simple enough to use by elderly adults.

C Look back at Part B. Complete the tasks.

1. Underline those parts of sentences that express **equality between two items**.
2. Double-underline expressions that express **a difference between two items**.
3. Use a wavy underline for groups of words that **express ideas of "degree."**
4. Complete the chart with examples. Then, compare your chart with a partner's chart.

Equality between two items (equative structure)	Difference between two items (comparative structure)	Other ideas of "degree" (degree expression)

Reading

A WARM-UP Work with a partner and assign an age group to each of the generational labels. Then, discuss the meaning of each label.

_____ **1.** Teens   _64–72_ **2.** G.I. Generation   _____ **3.** Boomers

_____ **4.** Gen X   _____ **5.** Silent Generation   _____ **6.** Gen Y

B SKIMMING Skim the report and identify the main similarities and differences among older and younger Internet users. Then, read the whole report.

Old and Young Use Internet Differently

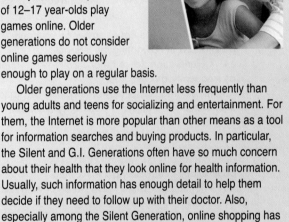

Today, larger percentages of middle and older generations are online than were in the past. They are also engaging in more activities online than they have in the past. While teens and Gen-Yers use more online applications for communicative, creative, and social uses than older adults do, more Gen-Xers and Boomers than other groups bank and shop online. Boomers and Gen-Xers make travel reservations as frequently as Gen-Yers do. Even older generations, the Silent Generation and the G.I. Generation, are as interested as the middle generations in email use. While instant messaging, social networking, and blogging have gained popularity as communications tools, they have not gained as much popularity as email, which is so easy to use that it is a very popular online activity, especially among the middle and older generations. In fact, the increase in Internet use among 70 to 75 year-olds has been so steep that it has doubled in the past 10 years, from 25 to 50 percent. However, email is not as popular as it used to be among teens: teen email use has declined from 89 to 70 percent due mainly to the availability of other media.

Teens and Gen-Yers use the Internet more regularly than other groups for entertainment and for communicating with friends and family. For these younger generations, the Internet offers activities that are too numerous to list here. Younger adults tend to be Internet-savvy enough to seek entertainment through online videos, online games, and downloaded music. These users also connect so closely with their peers that they read other people's blogs and write their own. They are also more likely than older generations to use social networking sites and to create profiles on those sites. Among teen Internet users, game playing is so popular that it is this age group's favorite online activity: almost 80 percent of 12–17 year-olds play games online. Older generations do not consider online games seriously enough to play on a regular basis.

Older generations use the Internet less frequently than young adults and teens for socializing and entertainment. For them, the Internet is more popular than other means as a tool for information searches and buying products. In particular, the Silent and G.I. Generations often have so much concern about their health that they look online for health information. Usually, such information has enough detail to help them decide if they need to follow up with their doctor. Also, especially among the Silent Generation, online shopping has developed too rapidly to dismiss: once the elderly master online navigation, they can manage online purchases easily enough to buy items without leaving the home.

Generational differences in online activities might continue to exist but might become increasingly blurred. With most adults having grown up in digital-only environments, there are likely to be fewer differences in generational online activities in years to come than exist today.

C UNDERSTANDING DETAILS Read the statements. Write *T* for the true statements and *F* for the false statements based on information in (or inferred in) the article. Correct any false statements.

_____ **1.** A woman in her sixties probably emails more frequently than a man in his early thirties.

_____ **2.** A man in his forties probably looks up less health information than a woman in her seventies.

_____ **3.** A teenager is probably less likely to use social media than a woman in her thirties.

_____ **4.** A woman in her seventies is probably familiar enough with the Internet to shop online.

_____ **5.** A man in his twenties probably plays as many online games as a teenager does.

Grammar Focus 1 Equatives

Examples	Language notes
(1) The Silent Generation is **as competitive as** younger generations when it comes to email.	**Equatives** compare two qualities, attributes, or quantities that are *equal*. In other words, they show how two things, people, or actions are similar.
(2) Teens are **as interested** in online videos **as** Gen-Yers.	We can form equative structures with adjectives. Use *as* + **adjective** + *as* to form the equative.
(3) Boomers make travel reservations **as frequently as** Gen-Yers do.	We can form equative structures with adverbs. Use *as* + **adverb** + *as* to form the equative.
(4) Teens spend **as <u>many</u> hours** on social networking sites **as** they spend on online games.	We can form equative structures with nouns. Use *as* + ***many / much*** + **noun** + *as* to form the equative. Follow the quantifier rules with nouns in Unit 3.
(5) Teens <u>are</u> **as interested** in online videos **as** Gen-Yers **<u>are</u>**. Boomers <u>make</u> travel reservations **as frequently as** Gen-Yers **<u>do</u>**. Teens <u>are</u> **as interested** in online videos **as** Gen-Yers **<u>(are)</u>**. Boomers <u>make</u> travel reservations **as frequently as** Gen-Yers **<u>(do)</u>**.	The verb in the clause following the equative is usually the auxiliary that agrees with the verb in the main clause. It is not necessary to mention the auxiliary if the meaning is clear.
(6) Older generations are **not as savvy as** younger generations in navigating the Internet. The G.I. Generation doesn't make travel reservations **as frequently as** Gen-Yers. Instant messaging, social networking, and blogging have **not** gained **as <u>much</u> popularity as** email.	Also use negative constructions to compare attributes that are not equal. Use *not as* + **adjective / adverb / noun** + *as* to show how two people, things, or actions are *not* similar. (Use *many / much* with nouns.) While this structure is equative, the meaning is, however, comparative.
(7) Older generations are **less savvy than** younger generations in navigating the Internet. Email is not **so popular as** it used to be among teens.	Particularly in speaking and informal writing, equatives are often used to avoid constructions with *less . . . than*. Also, in such genres, *as . . . as* is often replaced by *(not) so . . . as*.

Clause 1	Equative construction *as* + adj / adv / noun + *as*			Clause 2
The Silent Generation is	as	competitive	as	younger generations (are) when it comes to email.
Email is **not**	as	popular	as	it used to be among teens.
Boomers make travel reservations	as	frequently	as	Gen-Yers (do).
Boomers **don't** update their social networking sites	as	eagerly	as	younger Internet users (do).
Teens spend	as	many hours on networking sites	as	(they spend) on online games.
Blogging has **not** gained	as	much popularity	as	email (has).

Grammar Practice

A Combine the sentences, using equative constructions with an adjective, adverb, or noun, according to the prompts in parentheses. Some sentences need to be negative. Remember to add *many / much* with nouns.

1. social media close generational gaps easily / blogs can't close such gaps (easily)
   Blogs can't close generational gaps as easily as social media can.

2. searching for information about others has gained popularity among Gen-Yers / searching for information about themselves has gained popularity among teens (popularity)

   _____

3. Internet users over 50 have not found many friends online / Internet users under 50 have found many friends online (friends)

   _____

4. there are few other spaces—online or offline—where different generations naturally intersect / they intersect on social networking sites (naturally)

   _____

5. photos are valuable in providing a connection to family and friends / videos are valuable in providing a connection to family and friends (valuable)

   _____

6. social networking sites are useful for networking / face-to-face networking events are more useful for professional networking, and political participation (useful, not)

   _____

B Look at the information about other online activities people engage in. Use the information to create sentences using equative structures (affirmative and negative) that compare activities across groups as well as within groups.

	Teens	Gen-Y	Gen-X	Boomers	Silent Generation	G.I. Generation
Get job information	30%	65%	50%	40%	10%	10%
Visit a virtual world	10%	5%	5%	0%	0%	0%
Participate in a chat room	65%	65%	35%	20%	10%	5%
Visit government sites	0%	55%	65%	65%	60%	30%
Read news	65%	75%	75%	70%	55%	35%

1. *(adjective)* Gen-Yers are as interested in job information as they are in chat rooms.

2. *(adverb)* _____

3. *(noun)* _____

4. *(adjective)* _____

5. *(adverb)* _____

6. *(noun)* _____

7. *(adjective)* _____

Grammar Focus 2 Comparatives and comparative clauses

Examples	Language notes
(1) They are engaging in **more activities online than** <u>they have done in the past</u>. They are engaging in **more activities online than** <u>(they have done) in the past</u>.	Comparative clauses follow the comparison of two entities. The clause is often reduced with the subject and verb (or the verb) omitted.
(2) Internet games are **more popular** with teens **than** they are with older adults. [adjective] Young adults use the Internet **more frequently than** older adults. [adverb] Larger **percentages** of older generations are online **than** were in the past. [noun]	The comparative can be in the form of an adjective, adverb, or noun. Use **adjective / adverb + -er + than** for short adjectives and adverbs. For adjectives / adverbs ending in *y*, change *y* to *i* and add *-er*. Use **more / less + adjective + than** with adjectives / adverbs of two or more syllables. Some adjectives and adverbs are irregular: *good-better, bad-worse, far-farther, well-better, badly-worse.*
(3) Internet games are **less popular** with retirees **than** they are with teens. [adjective] Older generations use the Internet **less frequently than** young adults. [adverb] Teens and Gen-Yers embrace **more <u>online applications</u>** that enable communicative, creative, and social uses **than** older adults do. Boomers get **more <u>information</u>** online **than** they do through other means.	The opposite of **more** is **less** for both adjectives and adverbs. Use **more** with both plural count nouns and non-count nouns.
(4) Teens get **less <u>information</u> than** other groups from online sources. There are likely to be **fewer <u>differences</u>** in generational online activities in years to come **than** exist today.	Use **less** with non-count nouns, and **fewer** with plural count nouns.
(5) Teens and Gen-Yers are **more likely than** other groups to use the Internet for entertainment.	The word **likely** is an adjective. We often see it in comparisons of probability between two or more groups.
(6) Some groups are **not as likely as** teens and Gen-Yers to use the Internet for entertainment.	Equatives can also compare two qualities or attributes that are <u>unequal</u>, but in <u>negative</u> constructions.

	Clause 1	Comparative construction	Clause 2 (full vs. reduced)
Adjective	Internet games are	**trendier** with teens **than** **more popular** with teen **than**	(they are) with older adults.
	Internet games are	**less trendy** with older adults **than** **less popular** with older adults **than**	(they are) with teens.
Adverb	Young adults use the Internet	**more** frequently **than**	older adults do.
	Older adults use the Internet	**less** frequently **than**	young adults do.
Noun	They are engaging in	a **greater** variety of activities **than** **more** activities online **than**	(they have done) in the past.
	They are engaging in	**fewer** activities online **than**	(they have) in the past.
	They get	**less** information online **than**	other groups (do).

Grammar Practice

A Complete the excerpts about different groups' Internet use. Fill in the blanks with appropriate comparative clauses, using the clues in parentheses. Then, shorten comparative clauses where possible. (Note: ↑ = *more*; ↓ = *less / fewer*)

    Example: Several years ago, data showed that women were *less likely* than men ~~were~~ to use the Internet in the mid-1990s. (↓ likely)

1. While the gender gap in usage disappeared in the 2000s, women continued using the Internet _____ than men _____. (↓ frequently)

2. Recent research indicates that the gender gap in Internet use today is getting _____ than it _____ in the past. (↓ small)

3. Recent results have shown that _____ use the Internet for entertainment and leisure than females _____. (↑ males)

4. _____ use the Internet for interpersonal communication and educational assistance than women _____. (↓ men)

5. One study of email use showed that men express themselves _____ than women _____. (↑ aggressively)

6. Men used _____ in their messages than women _____. (↑ personal attacks and offensive remarks)

7. According to research, women are usually _____ than men _____ in their online messages. (↑ supportive)

8. Research also showed that women tended to be _____ than men _____. (↑ appreciative)

B Look again at the information about other online activities people engage in. Use the information to make sentences, using comparative clause structures. Compare activities across groups as well as within groups.

	Teens	Gen-Y	Gen-X	Boomers	Silent Generation	G.I. Generation
Get job information	30%	65%	50%	40%	10%	10%
Visit a virtual world	10%	5%	5%	0%	0%	0%
Participate in a chat room	65%	65%	35%	20%	10%	5%
Visit government sites	0%	55%	65%	65%	60%	30%
Read news	65%	75%	75%	70%	55%	35%

1. *(adjective)* Getting job information is more common with Boomers than with teens. _____

2. *(adverb)* _____

3. *(noun)* _____

4. *(adjective)* _____

5. *(adverb)* _____

6. *(noun)* _____

7. *(adjective)* _____

Grammar Focus 3 Degree complements

Examples	Language notes
(1) The increase in Internet use among 70 to 75 year-olds has been **so steep that** it has doubled in the past 10 years.	Degree complements are complement clauses that follow an adjective, adverb, or noun and express the degree or extent of a characteristic. Degree complements follow three typical structures. They cannot be reduced.

(2) Game playing is **so popular that** it is teens' favorite activity. [adjective]
These users connect **so closely** with their peers **that** they read other people's blogs. [adverb]
The Silent and G.I Generations often have **so much concern** about their health **that** they look online for health information. [noun]
	so . . . that:
	   so + adjective + *that* + clause
	   so + adverb + *that* + clause
	   so + *many* + count noun + *that* + *clause*
	   so + *much* + non-count noun + *that* + clause

(3) The Internet offers activities that are **too numerous to** list here. [adjective]
Online shopping has developed **too rapidly to** dismiss. [adverb]
For today's teens, there are **too many activities to** engage in. [noun]
	too . . . to:
	   too + adjective + *to*-clause
	   too + adverb + *to*-clause
	   too + *many* + count noun + *to*-clause
	   too + *much* + non-count noun + *to*-clause

(4) Younger adults tend to be **Internet-savvy enough to** seek entertainment through online videos. [adjective]
Older generations do not consider online games **seriously enough to** play on a regular basis. [adverb]
Such information has **enough detail to** help them decide if they need to follow up with their doctor. [noun]
	enough . . . to (note that *enough* follows the adjective and adverb, but it precedes the noun):
	   adjective + *enough* + *to*-clause
	   adverb + *enough* + *to*-clause
	   enough + noun + *to*-clause

	Clause 1	Degree expression	Degree complement
Adjective	Game playing is	**so** popular	that it is teens' favorite activity.
	Internet activities are	**too** numerous	to list here.
	Gen-Yers tend to be	tech-savvy **enough**	to seek online video entertainment.
Adverb	These users connect	**so** closely with peers	that they read other people's blogs.
	Online shopping has developed	**too** rapidly	to dismiss.
	Adults do not consider online games	seriously **enough**	to play on a regular basis.
Noun	Older people have	**so** much concern about their health	that they look for online health information.
	There are	**too** many activities	to engage in.
	Such information has	**enough** detail	to help them make a decision.

Grammar Practice

A Combine the sentences, using the word in parentheses. Remember to add *many / much* with nouns.

1. teens spend hours online / they often neglect their school work (so)

_____

2. older adults often don't have computer skills / they feel comfortable using online applications (enough)

_____

3. on the job, most people are usually busy / they visit social networking sites and update their profiles (too)

_____

4. many teens think that they send instant messages to their friends frequently / they maintain a good personal relationship (enough)

_____

5. Gen-Yers visit social networking sites regularly / they neglect physical exercise (so)

_____

6. social media provide information / people process that information (too)

_____

7. online health information tends to be clear / it answers someone's questions about a condition (enough)

_____

8. making online purchases has become easy / all age groups have done it at least once (so)

_____

9. many people do not research products and prices thoroughly / they make informed buying decisions (enough)

_____

B Complete the paragraph with appropriate degree expressions, the words in parentheses, and the degree complements.

In the past decade, social networking sites (SNSs) have grown **1.** *so extensively that* (extensively) they have reached over half a billion users worldwide. In 2011, social networking accounted for **2.** _____ (time) it began to interfere with some people's ability to manage their time properly. In fact, user figures have grown **3.** _____ (exponentially) keep accurate track of them. A research study in 2010 reported that the increase in time people spend on social networking sites was **4.** _____ (huge) researchers thought they had miscalculated the numbers. At that time, people all over the world spent **5.** _____ (time on SNSs) lose productive time each day. More specifically, two hours online per day is **6.** _____ (long) neglect other tasks. In 2010, some social media sites were visited **7.** _____ (frequently) they even became the common homepages for users. The same study found that 33 percent of adults posted on SNSs **8.** _____ (regularly) post an average of once a week. In addition, almost two-thirds of older adults felt that they were not **9.** _____ (old) maintain a profile on an SNS. A resulting question is the following: do people spend **10.** _____ (hours with online friends) have any real time for real friends?

Listening

A BEFORE LISTENING Work with a partner. Discuss the statements. Decide if you think they are true or false. Write *T* for the true statements and *F* for the false statements.

_____ **1.** The number of people who use social media is the same as the number of people who don't.

_____ **2.** People who spend a lot of time on social networking sites have fewer friends than those who don't.

_____ **3.** Social media users are closer to their online friends than their offline friends.

_____ **4.** Spending too many hours online detracts from other social activities.

_____ **5.** The average amount of time spent on online media is closer to two hours than it is to one hour.

B 🎧 LISTENING FOR MAIN IDEAS Listen to a news report on a study about the effects of online social networking on real-life relationships. Then, work with a partner to answer the questions.

1. The reporter mentions two groups with opposing views on the effect of social media on people's lives: cyber-optimists and cyber-pessimists. How are their views different?
2. Which group's view of social media is more strongly supported by the research? Why?
3. Would you change your answers to any of the statements in Part A? If so, how?
4. All research has potential limitations because the results may not be applicable to broader contexts. What are limitations of this study? Why are these limitations?

C 🎧 UNDERSTANDING DETAILS Listen to the news report again. Work with a partner. One of you completes the even-numbered items; the other completes the odd-numbered items with appropriate complements that are true based on the information you heard. Then, share your answers.

1. People are so inundated with online information _____

_____.

2. Cyber-optimists are (not) as convinced _____

_____.

3. Many people spend too many hours on social networking sites _____

_____.

4. Relationships are serious enough for social media users _____

_____.

5. Online relationships are (not) as meaningful _____

_____.

6. In the study, the researchers surveyed enough people _____

_____.

7. The survey may have had too many responses from Gen-Yers _____

_____.

8. In one's online and offline networks, some people are closer _____

_____.

9. The number of people who use social media is (not) as large _____

_____.

10. Respondents spent as many hours online _____

_____.

11. Respondents said they felt more close to offline contacts _____

_____.

12. Being online is not convenient enough _____

_____.

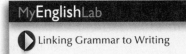
Speaking

A Work with a partner. Collect information among your classmates on their online activities. Write a check (✓) in the table to record each response.

	Send / Receive email	Visit SNS and update profile	Read news	Watch videos	Buy products	Play games	Make travel reservations
Number of classmates							
TOTAL							

B Work with the same partner. Show your findings as percentages in the table. Then, report your findings. Try to use the grammar from this chapter. Did your classmates have similar results?

> *Ninety percent of our classmates send and receive email regularly and visit social networking sites. This means that our classmates check email as . . .*

	Send / Receive email	Visit SNS and update profile	Read news	Watch videos	Buy products	Play games	Make travel reservations
Percentage							

Writing

A Work with a partner. Brainstorm ideas about the Internet. Put together an "Internet Use Fact Sheet" based on information you have learned from the reading and the exercises in this chapter.

> *More men than women engage in online gaming.*
> *Teens are not concerned enough about their health to find health information online.*

B Now select at least three facts and expand them into a brief news report. Try to use the grammar from the chapter.

> Teens are not concerned enough about their health to find health information online. However, even teens have health problems, and some problems might . . .

C Share your fact sheet and news report with the rest of the class. Then, discuss the questions.

1. Are there any facts on your classmates' fact sheets or in their reports with which you do not agree? If so, explain why and "correct" the fact.
2. Which facts do you expect to change in the coming years? How and why?

CHAPTER 8   Digital Footprints

Getting Started

A   With a partner, discuss your answers to the questions about personal information online.

1. If you did an online search of your full name . . .
   • on which social networking sites (SNS) do you think your name would appear?
   • what types of information about yourself would you find?
   • would you find any photos of yourself? If so, on which sites?
2. How would you react if you discovered personal information that you didn't know was online?

B   Match the clauses on the left with the most appropriate clauses on the right.

_____ **1.** I would check my personal email at work

_____ **2.** I wish

_____ **3.** The tech supervisor told the employees

_____ **4.** If users post inappropriate photos,

_____ **5.** The survey respondents said

_____ **6.** Most SNS users wish

_____ **7.** Teen Internet users report

_____ **8.** If frequent users wanted privacy,

a. that they distrust most social networking sites.

b. I could download music files from the Internet.

c. they might have to face consequences later.

d. that they were going to be more careful with personal information on the Internet.

e. they could use a screen name or post anonymously.

f. if it weren't against company policy.

g. that they needed to update their computer security.

h. that they wouldn't see so many ads on SNSs.

C   Look back at Part B. Complete the tasks. Be sure to note the verb tenses in your examples.

1. Circle conditional clauses that show **unreal or imagined ideas** in the present or future.
2. Underline clauses that **report something someone said or wrote**.
3. Complete the chart with examples. Then, compare your chart with a partner's chart.

Verb phrases in present / future unreal conditionals / tenses	Verb phrases in reported speech / tenses

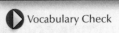
Reading

A WARM-UP With a partner, discuss the meanings of the reporting verbs in the list. How do you decide which reporting verbs to use when describing information from an outside source? Do you know other reporting verbs?

affirmed	indicated	pointed out	said
confirmed	noted	reported	stated

B SKIMMING Skim the report to find to the answer the question. Then, read the whole report. What is online reputation management? Describe the term in your own words.

Trends in Online Reputation Management

According to a recent survey by the Pew Research Center, reputation management has become a critical issue for many Internet users. Although more users overall are careful about their online image, many are still quite casual about the information they post. Increased use of blogs, greater complexity of social media, and the effectiveness of search engines have led to more vigilant use of security settings and more careful sharing of information. Sheila Connelly, who studies online behavior in social networking sites (SNSs), commented on the Pew report. She pointed out that there were changes in what kinds of information users share. "We are seeing a shift," Connelly stated. "When it becomes clear just how much information one can collect from SNS posts, users often wish that there were easier ways to control such information."

Interestingly, the Pew study revealed that users aged 18-29 are more likely to customize the information they share online and choose with whom they share it. Connelly noted that many users in this age group had reported a greater caution of social media services and that they were more likely to delete unwanted comments. "If there were stricter security settings in social media, I think most young people would use them," she contended. "I wish that older users were as savvy about their digital footprints as younger users."

This increased awareness of reputation management has significantly impacted online behavior. Nearly 60 percent of adults in the survey stated that they used search engines to find information about themselves, and 27 percent of employed Internet users affirmed that their employer had policies about how they present themselves online. The study also found that 41 percent of users employ multiple online identities and that many avoid using their real names.

Connelly's own research shows an increased awareness of "online persona" among SNS users, especially those who must follow work policies. "Most people make an effort to follow their work rules," said Connelly. "If my employer didn't have an official policy, I would still be careful about what I posted," many reported. Some indicated that they were confused about their employers' policies. "I wish that my employer had explicit guidelines about what I can and cannot post online" and "If my employer had an official Internet policy, I could make better decisions about what I post online" were typical comments.

Connelly's study also addressed potential job seekers. Recent university graduates said that they would ask about Internet policies in future job interviews.

As technology and online behavior continue to evolve, perceptions about what is safe and appropriate for users to put on the Internet will, too.

C UNDERSTANDING DETAILS Read the report again. Find three ways Internet users manage their online reputation and underline them in the report.

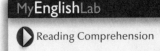

Grammar Focus 1 Present and future unreal conditionals

Examples	Language notes
(1) **If** Internet security policies **were stricter**, online activities **would be** safer. (= *Internet security policies aren't stricter.*)	**Unreal conditionals** describe hypothetical situations—something that is unreal, imagined, unlikely, or untrue in the present or future. Unreal conditionals have two clauses: The dependent (subordinate) clause [*if*-clause] contains the condition, and the main clause contains the result of this condition.
(2) Employees **could make** better decisions about online posting **if** companies **had** clear Internet policies. **If** companies **had** clear Internet policies, employees **could make** better decisions about online postings.	To form present or future unreal conditionals, use: *would / could / might* + base verb [main clause] + a *simple past verb* [*if*-clause]. When the subordinate clause comes first in the sentence, it is followed by a comma.
(3) Social media users often **wish that** they **had** easier ways to control the information they post online. (= *Social media users don't have easier ways to control the information they post online.*) He **wishes (that)** he **could** find a safer program to use.	The other type of conditional uses the verb **wish**. Sentences with *wish* show a regret or desire for a different situation in the present (or in the future). In sentences with *wish*, use the simple present of **wish** + **noun clause** [*that*-clause]. The past form in the *that*-clause shows that the situation is untrue. Use **the simple past, the past progressive,** *could* or *would* in the *that*-clause. In conversation or informal writing, **that** can be omitted in constructions with *wish*. (See Unit 3 for noun clauses.)
(4) I would think about the consequences if I **were going to post** personal details on a social networking site. I wish that I **were able to change** the way social networking sites work.	The verb **be** in conditional constructions is **were** with all subjects.

If-clause: past tense verb	Main clause: *would / could / might* + verb
If Internet security policies **were** stricter,	online activities **could be** safer.
If my employer **didn't have** an official policy,	I **would** still **be** careful about what I posted.

Main clause: *would / could / might* + verb	*If*-clause: past tense verb
Employees **could make** better decisions	if companies **had** clear Internet policies.
Older SNS users **would post** less personal information	if they **were** more wary of such sites.

Subject	Verb (*wish*)	Noun clause
I	**wish**	(that) my employer **made** explicit guidelines.
He	**wishes**	(that) he **could find** a safer program to use.

Grammar Practice

A Complete the paragraph with unreal conditionals or *wish* constructions. Use the words in parentheses.

According to a recent survey, 12 percent of employed Internet users are "public personae," and younger adults aged 18–29 are more likely to have a job that requires them to promote themselves online. If the professionals in this group of unique users **1.** _____ (not, monitor) search results connected to their names, their reputations **2.** _____ (can be) damaged and they **3.** _____ (may lose) work opportunities. People in this group are also more likely to use social media. They frequently update their status and use their profiles to market their skills. However, many wish that they **4.** _____ (have) quicker access to online tools. Blogging is another common activity for public personae. Respondents in this group noted that it is more difficult to self-monitor in blog writing. However, they also said, "We **5.** _____ (not, reach) so many readers if we **6.** _____ (not, post) to their blog on a regular basis." This group of users also routinely deletes things that others have posted about them, including photos and videos. They see this as crucial to maintaining their online reputation. "If there **7.** _____ (be) a more effective way to manage what others post about me," most respondents said, "I **8.** _____ (find) it much easier to monitor my online identity." Many say they wish that they **9.** _____ (can intervene) in what others post about them and that their friends **10.** _____ (possess) more common sense about posting insensitive material.

B Read the statements. Then, based on the implied meaning of the statement, write a new sentence that includes an unreal conditional or a *wish* construction. Follow the verb tense in the original statement.

1. We don't have a way to work online in a completely secure manner. (wish)

We wish that we had a way to work online in a completely secure manner.

2. A lot of teens maintain multiple online identities. They can make anonymous posts. (if)

_____

3. Younger SNS users post photos of themselves. They have a bigger digital footprint than older users. (if)

_____

4. Some professionals have a strong Internet presence. (wish)

_____

5. Many Internet users don't know whether their email address is online for others to use. (wish)

_____

6. Our department manager has training in information security. She is able to keep our online work secure. (if)

_____

7. Employees don't know about their employers' ability to monitor online activities. Many employees spend time at work on non-work-related Internet activities. (if)

_____

8. Many managers have to spend significant resources on Internet security and training. (wish)

_____

Grammar Focus 2 Reported speech

Examples	Language notes
(1) She said, "Internet users reported changes in their behavior." She **said** that Internet users had reported changes in their behavior.	**Reported speech** (also called **indirect speech**) describes something someone said or wrote without using the person's exact words. This information is included in a **noun clause** that follows a **reporting verb**, such as *say, tell,* or *ask*. The word ***that*** can introduce a reported statement. It can be omitted in conversation or informal writing. If you report a question, the noun clause is introduced by words *if, whether,* or a *wh-* word.
(2) A survey respondent said, "I never **discuss** my job online." → A survey respondent **said** (that) he never discussed his job online.	If the original idea (in direct speech) is expressed in the simple present, **the reporting verb** is in the **simple past**. This signals that the subject of the sentence is not the original speaker or writer.
(3) He **said**, "I never **discussed** my job online." → He **said** (that) he **had** never **discussed** his job online. She said, "I **will request** a copy of the guidelines." → She **said** (that) she **would request** a copy of the guidelines.	When the **reporting verb** is in **the simple past**, the verb in the reported speech "shifts back" to a past viewpoint—present becomes past, and past becomes past perfect. Certain time and place words also change.
(4) He said, "The college **might** change its rules." → He said that the college **might** change its rules.	These modal verbs <u>do not shift</u>: *should, ought to,* and *might*.
(5) My mom often says, "You need to change your password regularly." → My mom often **says** (that) I **need** to change my password regularly.	If the **reporting verb** is **simple present, present perfect**, or **future**, the noun clause verb does <u>not</u> change.
(6) She asked, "Did you post the photos?" → She asked **if / whether (or not)** I had posted the photos. He asked, "What did you post online?" → He asked **what** I had posted online. My boss told me, "Read the list of Internet policies." → My boss told <u>me</u> **to read** the list of Internet policies.	Use ***if / whether (or not)*** to introduce reported **yes / no questions**. Use ***wh- words*** to introduce reported **wh- questions**. Use an **infinitive** to report **imperatives (commands)**. You need to include the object in this form of reported speech.
(7) ***Incorrect:*** She asked what ~~had I posted online~~. She asked what I had posted online.	Do not use question word order in reported speech. Use statement word order.

See Appendix E on page A-5 for a complete list of tense and place / time shifts.

Subject	Verb *(reporting)*	Noun clause in reported speech
Original: He said, "I never **discuss** my job online."		
→ He	said	*that* he never **discussed** his job online.
Original: The teens in the study stated, "We **have posted** anonymously on SNSs many times."		
→ The teens in the study	stated	*that* they **had posted** anonymously on SNSs many times.
Original: Some respondents indicated, "We **would be** surprised if online security improved."		
→ Some respondents	indicated	*that* they **would be** surprised if online security improved.
Original: She asked, "**Did** you **post** the photos online?"		
→ She	asked	*if / whether* I **had posted** the photos online.
Original: She asked, "What **did** you **post** online?"		
→ She	asked	*what* I **had posted** online.
Original: The supervisor told <u>me</u>, "Read the list of Internet policies."		
→ The supervisor	told <u>me</u>	*to read* the list of Internet policies.
Original: He **says**, "I never **discuss** my job online."		
→ He	says	*that* he never **discusses** his job online.

Grammar Practice

A Read the sentences. If the sentence is correct, write *C*. If it is incorrect, write *I* and correct the error.

_____ 1. About one-third of the respondents said that details about the groups they belong to were available for others to see online.

_____ 2. Gen-Yers reported that they have the biggest digital footprint of all the age groups.

_____ 3. Older Internet users indicated that they won't post their birth dates for others to see.

_____ 4. Younger users said that they post their cell phone numbers in their profiles but not their home addresses.

_____ 5. Highly active users stated that they received frequent contacts by people from their past.

_____ 6. Fewer people reported that they are concerned about how much information about them is available online.

_____ 7. The researchers in the study asked younger adults whether they limit their personal information online.

_____ 8. A fairly high percentage of Internet users over 65 said that they weren't very concerned about their online identity.

_____ 9. Many Boomers indicated that in the last few months they have updated their profiles mostly on professional networking sites.

_____ 10. The researchers in the study told respondents don't use their real names online.

B Rewrite each statement in reported speech, making necessary changes in the verb tense, time / place, and pronoun.

1. Sixty-five percent of adult social networking users said, "I've changed my privacy settings to limit what I share online."

_____

2. Seven percent of employed women say, "My job requires me to self-promote online."

_____

3. Connelly always asks study participants, "Have you ever shared personal details online that you regretted later?"

_____

4. Connelly told study participants, "Read the questionnaire and then fill it out."

_____

5. Over half of social networking users report, "I delete contacts when my networks become too large."

_____

6. Researchers asked study participants, "What details do you want others to know about you?"

_____

7. One-third of employed Internet users confirm, "I have searched online for information about my co-workers."

_____

8. Connelly explains, "A lack of concern about online reputation may show a lack of awareness."

_____

9. A survey respondent noted, "The information we post today might affect us next year."

_____

10. A majority of Boomers indicated, "I must update my professional SNS often because it might lead to a new opportunity."

_____

Listening

A BEFORE LISTENING You will listen to three people from different contexts as they discuss Internet use policies in their school or workplace. With a partner, discuss your answers to the questions.

| a government employee | a university student | an employee at a small graphics design firm |

1. Who do you think will report that he or she follows highly detailed and strictly enforced Internet use policies? Why?

   Speaker: _____

   Reason: _____

2. Who do you think will say that he or she doesn't really have an official policy? Why?

   Speaker: _____

   Reason: _____

3. Who do you think might indicate that he or she dislikes the policies that he or she has to follow? Why?

   Speaker: _____

   Reason: _____

B 🎧 LISTENING FOR MAIN IDEAS Listen to a panel discussion on Internet use policies. Then, answer the questions. Compare your answers in small groups.

1. What was the common element of the policies that were discussed?

   _____

2. What change did most of the speakers feel needed to be made to their policies?

   _____

3. What did the speakers say were benefits of having a detailed Internet use policy? Describe one.

   _____

C 🎧 LISTENING FOR INFERENCES Listen to the panel discussion again. Then, answer the questions with your partner.

1. Whose school or workplace Internet use policy seems to be the strictest? Why?

   Speaker: _____

   Reason: _____

2. Who seemed to be the *most* satisfied with the policies that he or she had to follow? Why?

   Speaker: _____

   Reason: _____

3. Who seemed to be the *least* satisfied with the policies that he or she had to follow? Why?

   Speaker: _____

   Reason: _____

Speaking

A Work with a partner. Use the model below, and write three questions to ask a classmate about his or her own online reputation management. Try to use the grammar from the chapter.

> *If your favorite social networking site designed stronger security settings, what would you change? What information do you wish you could keep off the Internet?*

Survey questions
Q1.
Q2.
Q3.

B Switch partners. Ask the questions from Part A and following the model, take notes on your partner's responses. Then, tell your classmates what your partner told you. Use reported speech.

Partner's responses
Q1.
Q2.
Q3.

Writing

A The technology support staff at your school wants to create a new academic networking site for students. With a partner, brainstorm features that you think the site should include. Consider the questions.

1. Who would have access to the site?
2. How could students and faculty use it?
3. What learning tools could be available?
4. What social aspects would it include?

B Work with your partner to write a paragraph summarizing your ideas for the technology support staff. Use your ideas from Part A. Try to use the grammar from the chapter.

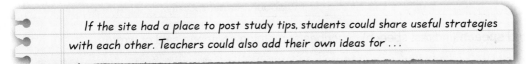

> *If the site had a place to post study tips, students could share useful strategies with each other. Teachers could also add their own ideas for . . .*

C Share your summary with the rest of the class. Generate a class "top ten" list of ideas for the academic networking site. Then, discuss the questions with the whole class.

1. Which suggested features seemed to be the most useful or interesting?
2. Would you use such a website if your school had one? Why or why not?

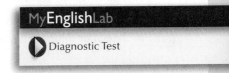

Grammar Summary

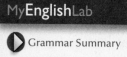
Equatives compare two things with respect to being, having, or doing something.

Equative structures can be formed with adjectives, adverbs, and nouns. The verb in the clause after the equative tends to be an auxiliary that agrees with the main clause verb. The clause after the equative is often reduced. In the negative form, equatives compare two things that are unequal.	(1) Cell phone use is **as** *typical* of teens **as** it is of adults. (2) Teens use cell phones **as** *frequently* **as** adults do. (3) **As** many *teens* **as** adults use cell phones. (4) Teens *use* cell phones **as** *frequently* **as** adults *do*. (5) Teens use cell phones **as** *frequently* **as** adults. (6) The G.I. Generation does *not* use cell phones **as** frequently as teens **do**.

Comparative clauses also compare two things with respect to being, having, or doing something.

The comparative can be in the form of an adjective, adverb, or noun. Comparative clauses follow the comparison of two things. The clause is often reduced.	(1) Teens are more **interested** in SNSs than adults are. (2) Teens visit SNSs more **regularly** than adults do. (3) Fewer **adults** than teens visit SNSs. (4) Teens are more **interested** in SNSs than adults are. (5) Teens visit SNSs more **regularly** than adults do.

Degree complements follow expressions that express the degree or extent of a characteristic.

Degree complements follow three typical structures. They cannot be reduced. Each structure can be used with an adjective, adverb, or noun.	(1) Teens are **so** *iPod-focused* **that** they ignore their surroundings. (2) Teens often listen **too** *intently* to their iPods **to** be able to focus on their surroundings. (3) Teens think that they don't spend **enough** *time* on SNSs **to** be informed about their friends' lives.

Unreal conditionals describe imagined, or untrue, information or wishes in the present or future.

The verb form in the *if*-clause is the simple past (if the verb is *be*, its form is *were*); the verb form in the main clause is *would / could / might* + verb. When the *if*-clause comes first, it is followed by a comma. A clause with *wish* is followed by a *that*-clause (a noun clause), in which the verb takes past tense forms. If that verb is *be, were* is used. *That* can be omitted in speech or informal writing.	(1) If I knew a site's security features, I might not post to a SNS. (2) I would not post to a SNS if I knew a site's security features. (3) If I were more knowledgeable about Internet security, I could avoid many mistakes in my Internet use. (4) I wish I knew more about Internet security. (5) He wishes he could remove some personal information. (6) She wishes (that) she were more knowledgeable about Internet security.

Reported speech (indirect speech) describes something someone said or wrote.

A reported utterance or quote is presented in a noun clause and preceded by a reporting verb, such as *say, state, question, ask, request, tell*. When the reporting verb is in the simple past, the verb in the reported clause "shifts back" to a viewpoint, as do certain time and place words. Certain modals don't shift. *That* can be omitted in speech or informal writing.	(1) She said, "I have posted a picture online." → She said that she had posted a picture online. (2) She asked, "Do you have any personal past information online?" → She asked if I had any personal information online. (3) "You should remove your address," he said. → He said (that) I should remove my address. (4) He told me, "Take your pictures off the Internet tomorrow." → He told me to take my pictures off the next day.

Self-Assessment

A (7 points) Complete the paragraph with equative or comparative structures, using the clues in parentheses. Add *many / much* with nouns.

In a 2007 study on gender and cultural differences in Internet use, researchers found that European students were **1.** _____ (*equative:* Asian students, likely) were to own computers. However, European students used computers **2.** _____ (*comparative:* Asian students, ↓ frequently) did. Nevertheless, European students did not feel **3.** _____ (*equative:* Asian students, self-confident about their computer skills) did. Both European and Asian males spent **4.** _____ (*comparative:* their female counterparts, ↑ time online) did. More specifically, the men played computer games **5.** _____ (*comparative:* women, ↑ frequently) played such games, and women were **6.** _____ (*comparative:* men, ↑ active in chat rooms) were. Interestingly, the gender gap was not **7.** _____ (*equative:* in the Asian group, great) it was in the European group.

B (3 points) Complete the degree expressions with a word that makes sense.

1. Between home and work, it is surprising that people still find enough _____ (work / time; to / that) update their social networking profiles each day.

2. Some people among the older generation are so _____ (intimidated / excited; to / that) they refuse to go online at all.

3. Today, news tends to be broadcast too _____ (rarely / frequently; to / that) be verified in all details.

C (5 points) Complete the unreal conditionals and wishes.

If employees **1.** _____ (know) that employers have the capability to check their computers, they **2.** _____ (not, update) their social media sites while at work, and they **3.** _____ (be) more careful about what they post about their company. Many employees wish that they **4.** _____ (can, reverse) reverse earlier decisions. There are also those who wish their employers **5.** _____ (have) more lenient policies.

D (5 points) Report this Gen-Xer's experience. Add appropriate reporting verbs in the past and reported speech clauses with proper verb forms.

1. "Posting photos or careless remarks on the Internet today can have an effect on you later in life."
The Gen-Xer _____ that _____.
_____.

2. "People might ruin their chances to get a job they really want."
The Gen-Xer _____ that _____.
_____.

3. "Are people really not aware of the consequences of careless online posting?"
The Gen-Xer _____ if _____.
_____.

4. "It is difficult for public figures to recover from the scandal of careless online posting."
The Gen-Xer _____ that _____.
_____.

5. "Don't have an expectation of privacy for voluntary postings on social media sites."
The Gen-Xer _____ his friend _____.
_____.

Unit Project: Group survey

A You are going to survey people from three different age groups about Internet use and security. Follow the steps.

1. Work in teams of three students. Decide which three age groups your team will survey.
2. Following the model below, make a chart in which you will write survey questions and responses. Create questions on two or three ideas from Chapter 7 (The Digital Gap) and two or three ideas from Chapter 8 (Digital Footprints). You will need to use the chart model for each person you survey.

Survey questions	Responses for age group
Unit 7: The Digital Gap	Person:
Unit 8: Digital Footprints	

3. Conduct the survey. Each team member should survey five people from one age group, so the team has information about three different age groups. Use your best guess about which age category respondents belong to. Do not ask about age!
4. With your team, review your findings and identify the most common responses. Then, present them in the form of the model table. Finally, prepare an oral summary of your findings.

	Question	Age group 1	Age group 2	Age group 3
The Digital Gap				
Digital Foot- prints				

5. At the end of your presentation, state if any of the responses confirmed the information from the readings in this unit. Were any of the responses surprising? Which ones, and why?

> *We reported that all of the respondents in age group X used the Internet frequently. The finding did not support the information from this unit. This surprised us.*

B After each group's presentation, discuss the questions with the whole class.

1. What were the greatest similarities among the different categories of users?
2. What were the greatest differences?
3. What conclusions can you draw about the unit topics and your survey findings? What predictions can you make?

MyEnglishLab
▶ Unit Test

MyEnglishLab
▶ Search it!

UNIT 5

Planning Public Spaces

OUTCOMES

After completing this unit, I will be able to use these grammar points.

CHAPTER 9

Grammar Focus 1
Stative passives

Grammar Focus 2
Adjective clauses with *where, when,* and *why*

Grammar Focus 3
Adjective clauses with quantifiers

CHAPTER 10

Grammar Focus 1
Subject-verb agreement

Grammar Focus 2
Dynamic passives

MyEnglishLab

 What do you know?

CHAPTER 9 The Role of Public Spaces in Communities

Getting Started

 A Work in small groups. Discuss the questions.

1. What famous places are there in your country? Have any of your classmates visited these places?
2. What famous places in other countries do you know? Which of these have you visited?
3. Why are these places famous?
4. While they are all different, what do they have in common?

B Read the facts about some famous places in the world. Locate them on the map. What else do you know about them? What do these places have in common? What do they have in common with the places you discussed in Part A?

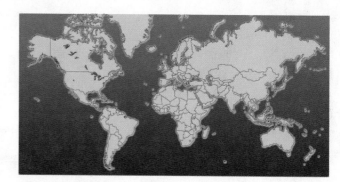

1. The Pyramids in Egypt are known as gigantic tombs where deceased pharaohs were connected with the heavens.
2. The Taj Mahal is located in Northern India and is dedicated to the memory of Emperor Shah Jahan's wife.
3. The Great Wall of China dates back to around 220 B.C.E., when there were separate Chinese states, many of which were concerned about intruders.
4. Stonehenge in England is recognized as a megalithic monument where an ancient civilization performed astronomical observations and ritual activities, some of which are still mysterious.
5. The reason why Machu Picchu was built in Peru was most likely due to its geographical features, the majority of which were considered sacred in Inca culture.

C Look back at Part B. Complete the tasks.

1. **Stative passives** are *be* + **past participle** + **preposition** combinations. Circle any examples.
2. Underline any **adjective clauses** that begin with *where / when / why*.
3. Double-underline those **clauses that begin with quantifiers**.
4. Complete the chart with examples. Then, compare your chart with a partner's chart.

Stative passives	Adjective clauses with *where / when / why*	Adjective clauses with quantitiers

Reading

A WARM-UP Look at the list of four different places. Which of these places have you heard of? What do you think they have in common? List at least three ideas. Share your ideas in small groups.

1. Central Park in New York City

2. Union Station in Washington, D.C.

3. Santa Monica State Beach in Santa Monica, California

4. Mellon Square in Pittsburgh, Pennsylvania

B SKIMMING Skim the article on urban planning and identify the key characteristics of great public spaces. Then, read the whole article.

GREAT PUBLIC SPACES

Think of communities that are known as good places to live, and public spaces inevitably come to mind. Public spaces, where people gather to shop, socialize, or relax, are like glue that binds communities together. Such spaces, all of which are associated with key public areas, are so important that they often come to symbolize the very cities where they are located.

The beginning of great public spaces goes back to early American history, when the first important act in creating plans for an American town was devoted to establishing key public spaces. In 1683, William Penn created plans for the city of Philadelphia, one of which designated several public squares. This early plan already recognized the importance of public spaces.

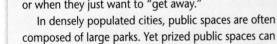

Great spaces come in all sizes, types, and forms, some of which can be village greens, urban plazas, or parks. They are located in small towns and large cities, and they are not limited to one particular area. Each public space can have a different function (such as to provide a shopping area or a place where people can gather), much of which is the result of variations in size, climate, and location. However, they all have one common element: they are regularly crowded with people at all times of day, when they want to socialize or when they just want to "get away."

In densely populated cities, public spaces are often composed of large parks. Yet prized public spaces can also be modest in size if they draw their distinction from the way they are related to surrounding buildings and connected to specific land uses. For example, space near a body of water can be converted into a waterfront park. Many treasured public spaces in American cities are enclosed within buildings. During the first half of the twentieth century, when railway transportation expanded, railroad stations performed many of the same functions as public squares. They were sometimes equipped with monumental public spaces, a few of whose designs have survived until today. Likewise, many American cities have public indoor marketplaces where people can shop and interact with others. The reason why people are drawn to these markets is that these places remind their visitors what a special place is composed of: its climate, culture, economy, tastes, and values.

Creating and maintaining successful public spaces is a critical part of the challenge that urban planners, many of whom are award-winning architects, are dedicated to when designing great communities. To underscore that point, each year the American Planning Association's Great Places in America Program chooses its top ten Great Public Spaces, all ten of which exemplify exceptional character and highlight the role planners and planning play in creating communities of lasting value.

C APPLYING INFORMATION Answer the questions, based on the information in the article.

1. Why do you think the four places mentioned in Part A are considered great public spaces?
2. Describe another great public space. What makes it a great public space?
3. Why might Niagara Falls in the United States *not* be considered as great public spaces?
4. Why might the Pyramids of Egypt *not* be associated with great public spaces?

Grammar Focus 1 Stative passives

Examples	Language notes
(1) Public spaces are busy. Public spaces are busy places. Public spaces are crowded places. Public spaces **are crowded**. *Incorrect:* Public spaces are crowded ~~by people~~.	**Stative passive** constructions describe the status, condition, or quality of a noun. To form the stative passive, use **be + the past participle** of the main verb. The characteristics of the stative passive include: • The status or condition may continue over time, but no action takes place. • The past participle functions as an adjective. • There is no *by*-phrase.
(2) Public spaces **are crowded with** people. Some communities **are known as** good places to live. Public spaces **are located in** many cities. Public spaces **are** often **made of** large parks. Public spaces **are not limited to** rich areas. Public spaces **are equipped with** monumental places. Typically, open public spaces **are surrounded by** buildings and landscaping.	Stative passive constructions do not have "agents"; instead, they are typically followed by **prepositions**, such as *about, against, as, for, from, in, with, of, to, by*.
(3) Communities <u>(that are)</u> <u>known as</u> good places to live also typically have great public spaces.	In reduced relative clauses, the form of *be* can be omitted. (See Unit 2.)

See Appendix F on page A-9 for a list of common stative passive + preposition combinations.

Subject	Verb: *be* + past participle	Preposition	Complement
Many public spaces	**are crowded.**		
The government act	**was devoted**	to	key public spaces.
People	**may not be pleased**	with	all public spaces.

Grammar Practice

MyEnglishLab

▶ Grammar Plus 1
Activities 1 and 2

 A Complete the paragraph with the stative passive forms of the verbs in parentheses and any appropriate prepositions. Be sure to use the correct tense.

Union Station in Washington, D.C., **1.** _____ (know) one of the greatest public spaces in America. It **2.** _____ (locate) over 200 acres, but many visitors **3.** _____ (impress) not only its massive scale but also by its architectural detail and the volume of the spaces that **4.** _____ (enclose) it that make it a great place to be. The exterior **5.** _____ (compose) gigantic white stonework that **6.** _____ (finish) classic Roman columns and arches. Within the station, spacious squares with vaulted ceilings **7.** _____ (connect) each other. For more than 50 years, Union Station **8.** _____ (recognize) the major gateway into and out of Washington. However, in the 1950s and 1960s, people **9.** _____ as _____ (not, interest) train travel as before, and rail ridership **10.** _____ (limit) those without cars. Over the years, the building fell steadily into disrepair. In 1978, a portion of the roof collapsed and the station's interior **11.** _____ (cover) "No Trespassing" signs. In 1981, the U.S. Congress **12.** _____ (commit) redeveloping Union Station. A total of $160 million **13.** _____ (dedicate) the station's restoration. Now, Union Station is a point of arrival and departure for thousands of passengers traveling on commuter and subway trains with a major station that **14.** _____ (locate) the building itself. But Union Station **15.** _____ (not, limit) being just a busy train station. It is an exciting space that **16.** _____ (fill) people meeting, dining, shopping, seeing an exhibit or a movie, hearing music, or simply watching the passing scene. Today, Union Station **17.** _____ (regard) a great public space.

B Complete the paragraph with appropriate verbs from the list in the stative passive form. Be sure to use the correct tense.

connect	distinguish	reflect	tie
dedicate	divide	root	know
designate	organize	~~situate~~	

Savannah
BURIAL GROUND
Savannah River
Hutchinson Island

Savannah, Georgia, **1.** _____ *is situated on* _____ on a cliff overlooking the Savannah River. Savannah **2.** _____ for its urban planning because its squares allow for more open space in Savannah than in any city layout in history. Savannah's remarkable city plan **3.** _____ from those of previous colonial towns through its repeated pattern of neighborhoods, squares, and streets that **4.** _____ to each other. Streets and building lots **5.** _____ as a central open space or square. The streets outside each city unit **6.** _____ for uninterrupted movement of traffic, and internal streets were open to citizens to create a pedestrian-friendly atmosphere. The resulting city blocks **7.** _____ into lots with subdivisions, which create a diverse pattern of building sizes and types. The political and organizational considerations of Savannah's early days **8.** _____ in the plan. City blocks **9.** _____ to a larger regional plan of garden and farm lots. The repetitive non-hierarchal sequence of city blocks and squares points out that the original colony **10.** _____ to utopian ideals. To this day, Savannah has remained an exemplary model of city planning: many other cities' blueprints **11.** _____ in Savannah's design.

Grammar Focus 2 Adjective clauses with *where, when,* and *why*

Examples	Language notes
(1) Public spaces often come to symbolize the very cities **where they are located.** This was a time **when railways expanded.** The reasons **why public spaces attract people** are many.	Adjective clauses with **where, when,** and **why** add explanatory, descriptive information about a place, time, or reason.

(2) Public spaces **where people gather** are connected to culture.
Public spaces **in which people gather** are connected to culture.
 	
Most Formal
↑
    a. Public places symbolize the cities **in which** they are located.
    b. Public places symbolize the cities **where** they are located.
    c. Public places symbolize the cities **which** they are located **in.**
    d. Public places symbolize the cities **that** they are located **in.**
    e. Public places symbolize the cities **Ø** they are located **in.**
↓
Least Formal
	Use **where** to form an adjective clause that **modifies a place.** You can replace *where* with *in which, at which,* or *on which. Where* can also be replaced with *which* or *that* + preposition *in, on,* or *at.* In this type of adjective clause, you can omit *which / that.*
	
	In examples a–e, note the progression from most formal to least formal in adjective clauses with *where.*

(3) This was a time **when / that public transportation via railways expanded.**
This was a time **during which public transportation via railways expanded.**
 	
Most Formal
↑
    a. This is a time of day **at which** people want to socialize.
    b. This is a time of day **when** people want to socialize.
    c. This is a time of day **which** people want to socialize **at.**
    d. This is a time of day **that** people want to socialize **(at).**
    e. This is a time of day **Ø** people want to socialize **(at).**
↓
Least Formal
	Use **when / that** to form an adjective clause that **modifies a noun of time.** You can also replace *when* with *during which, in which, at which,* or *on which.* You can omit *when / that.*
	
	In examples a–e, note the progression from most formal to least formal in adjective clauses with *when.*

(4) The reasons **why public spaces attract people** are many.	Use **why** to express a reason. *Why* goes only with the word *reason.*
(5) Public spaces often come to symbolize the very cities **where they are located.** This was a time **when public transportation via railways expanded.** Public spaces, **where people gather to shop, socialize, or relax,** are like glue that binds communities together. The establishment of great public spaces goes back to early American history, **when the plan for a typical American town was created.** The reason **why people are drawn to markets** is that the markets remind them of the past.	Adjective clauses with *where* and *when* can be **restrictive** (no commas) or **non-restrictive** (with commas). Adjective clauses with *why* occur only in restrictive form.

Main clause	Adjective clause with *where / when / why*	
Many cities have *great public spaces*	**where**	**people come to socialize.**
Those were *the decades*	**when**	**public transportation expanded.**
The association with culture is *the reason*	**why**	**public spaces are so popular.**

Main clause subject	Adjective clause with *where / when / why*		Main clause complement
Public spaces,	**where**	**people come to socialize,**	are located in most cities.
The decades	**when**	**public transportation expanded**	were the heydays of railroad stations.
The reason	**why**	**railways lost ridership**	is related to a boom in the automobile industry.

Grammar Practice

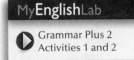
MyEnglishLab

Grammar Plus 2
Activities 1 and 2

 A Read the sentences. Add commas where necessary in the non-restrictive adjective clauses.

1. The area where three rivers come together in Providence, Rhode Island, is known as Waterplace Park.
2. The Yavapai County Courthouse in Arizona was dedicated to its city in 1916 when it replaced an earlier courthouse.
3. Santa Monica State Beach is located between Santa Monica and Venice where visitors can enjoy not only sand and water but also a park-like atmosphere among native plants and trees.
4. Lancaster Park in Pennsylvania where residents do as much socializing as they do shopping originated in 1730.
5. In the early 2000s when commercial structures took over the downtown area the city of Keene in New Hampshire established architectural guidelines and required new structures to be consistent with traditional building designs.
6. Keeping Chicago's lakefront free of development was a major reason why a string of parks was situated on the banks of Lake Michigan.

B Combine the sentences with *where, when,* or *why.* Add commas where necessary.

> In 1853, a New York commission selected a stretch of swampy, rocky terrain in Manhattan. Central Park is now located there.
>
> In 1853, a New York commission selected a stretch of swampy, rocky terrain in Manhattan where Central Park is now located.

1. Cleveland's West Side Market dates to 1912. Citizens were looking for a central marketplace then.

_____

2. Burlington, Vermont, created a pedestrian mall. Stimulating sidewalk activity was the reason.

_____

3. Portland, Oregon's Courthouse Square is referred to as the city's living room. There, people can feel "at home."

_____

_____

4. Charleston, South Carolina, constructed its Waterfront Park. Meeting the needs of both citizens and visitors was the reason.

_____

_____

5. In the 1980s, the U.S. Congress decided to redevelop Union Station in Washington, D.C. At that time, the place had deteriorated.

_____

_____

C Replace *where / when* with appropriate preposition + *which* constructions.

1. Minneapolis's Grand Rounds is a 50-mile stretch of land where visitors can enjoy trails, lakes, parks, and recreational facilities.

_____

_____

2. During the Revolutionary War, when General George Washington addressed the local soldiers, the New Haven Green in Connecticut served as a marketplace with a meeting house at the center.

_____

_____

3. Savannah's squares, where architecture and landscape mirror each neighborhood's unique character, help reduce traffic and make the streets safer for pedestrians and bicyclists.

_____

_____

4. The address where both residents and tourists like to gather in Virginia Beach is the city's restored boardwalk.

_____

_____

5. The place where Delaware became the first state to approve the U.S. Constitution in 1787 is the Golden Fleece Tavern in Dover.

_____

_____

6. The history of East Park on Round Lake in Charlevoix, Michigan, dates back to the year 1925, when a waterfront building burned down.

_____

_____

Grammar Focus 3 Adjective clauses with quantifiers

Examples	Language notes
(1) Great spaces come in all sizes, types, and forms, **some of which** can be village greens, urban plazas, or parks.	Adjective clauses can have an expression of quantity. They follow the pattern **quantifier + of + relative pronoun.** They modify a preceding noun. Quantifiers occur only in clauses with *whom, which,* and *whose.* (For rules on quantifier use with count and non-count nouns, refer to Unit 3.)
(2) Urban planners, **some of whom** are award-winning architects, are dedicated to designing great communities. Great public spaces, **all of which** are associated with key public areas, are very important to their cities. William Penn created plans for the city of Philadelphia, **one of which** designated several public squares. William Cullen Bryant and Andrew Jackson Downing, **both of whose names** are associated with Central Park, were instrumental in designing the New York City landscape. Railroad stations can be monumental public spaces, **a few of whose designs** have survived until today.	Use **quantifier + of + whom** with people; Use **quantifier + of + which** with things; Use **quantifier + of + whose + noun** with people and things, but this pattern is rare. Adjective clauses with quantifiers are always **non-restrictive.** (They need commas.) This pattern is formal and more common in writing than in speaking.

Main clause	Adjective clause			
	quantifier	of	relative pronoun	complement
Designing great communities is a challenge for urban planners,	all most a majority a lot		whom	are award-winning architects.
Public spaces have different functions,	many a (large) number	of	which	are the result of variations in size, climate, and location.
Most railway stations in large cities were designed by teams of architects,	plenty several some (a) few [number] a couple both [if two] neither [if two]		whose designs	have survived until today.
Each space has a different function,	much each one none	of	which	is the result of variations in size, climate, and location.

Grammar Practice

 A Combine the sentences. Use the second sentence as an adjective clause with a quantifier.

1. *Public spaces in Philadelphia were a challenge for many designers, one of whom, William Penn, brought together Philadelphia's southwest quadrant in Rittenhouse Square.*

2. Rittenhouse Square is a vibrant neighborhood. Much of the neighborhood consists of shops, office, homes, schools, hotels, and cultural institutions.

3. This mixture of uses and the surrounding buildings provides a constant source of people. Many people use the square throughout the day and evening.

4. The square dates back to William Penn's original designs for Philadelphia. Many of the old designs are no longer recognizable.

5. The area was originally used as an animal pasture. Most of the pasture turned into a fashionable backyard for wealthy Philadelphians in the late 1900s.

6. In 1913, private citizens hired an architect to transform the square into a combination of sidewalks. A number of sidewalks cut across stretches of grass.

7. The diagonal sidewalks give the square the appearance of multiple mazes. The large number of mazes makes the square look larger than it is.

8. The square is surrounded by city streets. Four of the streets are separated from the square through ornate iron fences.

9. Over the years, urban construction has threatened the square in the eyes of many Philadelphians. Some Philadelphians have strongly opposed plans for parking garages and huge buildings.

10. Rittenhouse Square has survived as a green city oasis for over 300 years for several reasons. One reason is Philadelphia's engaged community and its pride in "Philadelphia's living room."

B Read the paragraph about choosing a college. Correct the nine errors in the use of adjective clauses with quantifiers.

Choosing the Right College

When choosing a college, students usually look at a variety of factors, some of whom have to do with academics, neither of which have to do with extracurricular offerings, and a number which have to with finances. Location, however, should also be a consideration for students, many of whom overlook a critical factor: quality of life. College selection should include several goals, one of which is to understand the importance of the learning environment of the selected school. Every year, surveys about the best college campus are conducted among recent college graduates, the majority of which stress the importance of the campus setting and location. Students who study on beautiful campuses typically report higher satisfaction with their college experience and motivation for studying, much of whom can influence how well students might do in school. The Best Colleges survey has identified the 50 most beautiful college campuses, all of which stand out among the rest. Scripps College in California is a private college for students, all of which are women. The campus features green areas, most of whom include tulip trees, sycamores, almond, and orange trees. Gettysburg College, adjacent to the Gettysburg National Military Park in Pennsylvania, pays homage to battles in U.S. history, one of whom was the famous Battle of Gettysburg. The Stine Lake area is the most popular among students, of whom do not know that it was never actually a lake. Elon University in North Carolina is considered an aesthetic and educational resource, all three of which contribute to student satisfaction. The area around Elon has been used as the setting for several movies, some of which were actually filmed on campus grounds.

Listening

A BEFORE LISTENING What features would you expect the following three types of spaces to have? Discuss your ideas with a partner.

B 🎧 UNDERSTANDING MAIN IDEAS Listen to descriptions of three public spaces. Their names are not mentioned in the listening. Based on the details in the listening, decide the order in which you hear about each space. Number them from 1 to 3. What clues in the listening helped you?

_____ Waterplace Park　　_____ Yavapai County Courthouse Plaza　　_____ Church Street Marketplace

C 🎧 UNDERSTANDING DETAILS Listen again. Check (✓) the features that are true for each public space. Then, discuss the questions with a partner.

	Waterplace Park	Yavapai County Courthouse Plaza	Church Street Marketplace
Constructed before 1950			
Constructed after 1950			
Situated in downtown area			
Located near a body of water			
Adjacent to a government building			
Gives priority to pedestrians over cars			
Place for people to socialize, shop, eat			
Place for businesses			
Decorated with trees and or statues			
A place for performances			
Original function of the space changed			
Space has metaphorical name			

1. Did your predictions from Part A confirm what you heard? How so, or how not?

2. Which place would you most like to visit? Why?

3. Is there a public space in your country that is similar to one of these three spaces?

Speaking

A Work in groups of three students. Choose a public space near where you live. Discuss its use. Answer the questions and take notes. Try to use the grammar from the chapter.

1. How is the space designed? How is it currently used?

2. Is this a reasonable use of the space? Why or why not?

3. How could the current space be turned into a better public space?

> In my neighborhood, there are several small shopping centers, all of which have a fast food restaurant, a drycleaner, and a convenience store. In the middle is a huge parking lot, most of which is covered with asphalt . . .

B Present your ideas to the class. Use your notes from Part A. Try to use the grammar from the chapter. After all teams have presented, discuss the questions.

1. Which team has the best analysis of the current use of a public space? Why?
2. Which team has the best ideas for possible redesigning of this public space? Why?
3. What can citizens do to encourage the best use of a public space?

Writing

MyEnglishLab
▶ Linking Grammar to Writing

A Work with a partner. Brainstorm ideas about a public space in your community that you think should be redesigned. Discuss specific details and offer concrete, reasonable suggestions for addressing the problem. Take notes.

B Write a petition letter to the neighborhood association of your community about the use of a space in your area. Use your notes from Part A and the grammar from the chapter. Use the sample letter as a guide.

June 9, 2013

Naomi Lamas
East Village Community Office

Dear Ms. Lamas:

    I am a resident in East Village. I am petitioning to consider a redesign of the empty, unused lot that is located on Gerard Street. Among residents, the lot is known as "the Junkyard" because it is unsightly, it has been overgrown with grass, it is littered with trash, and it is cluttered with all sorts of debris. It is also often filled with for-sale cars, many of whose owners apparently think that residents are pleased with an outdoor "showroom."

    The reason why I am petitioning a restoration of the Gerard Street lot is because I feel that it could become a place where residents could gather—to hear a speaker or a music group, to have lunch, or just to socialize in a beautiful outdoor setting that is protected from noise and traffic. I have conducted a survey among current residents, most of whom wish that the community had a site where they could enjoy being outside at times when they need a break. The residents are also willing to be dedicated to the continual upkeep of the new space on a rotating basis.

    I look forward to hearing from you.

Sincerely,

Hasan Hamani

C Post your letters around the classroom. Which letter addresses the most serious public space problem? Which letter offers the most reasonable suggestion for redesigning the public space?

MyEnglishLab
▶ Diagnostic Test

CHAPTER 10

The Role of Public Spaces on Campuses

Getting Started

 A Work with a partner. Think about your school's library or another important building on your campus. Discuss the questions.

1. How is the interior of the building arranged?
2. What purposes do the rooms or areas in the rooms serve?
3. What criteria do you think the administration used to design and arrange the rooms or areas? Consider these factors:
   • purpose of each space and characteristics of users
   • types of materials, facilities, or equipment required for each space
   • physical space limitations
4. What do spaces on campus have in common with community spaces?

B Read the statements. Decide whether you agree, disagree, or are not sure. Mark each response with a check (✓).

	Agree	*Disagree*	*Not sure*
1. School libraries should only be designed for students' needs.	☐	☐	☐
2. Most of the buildings on our school campus are used as they were intended by the original planners.	☐	☐	☐
3. All of the equipment in our school contributes to our learning in some way.	☐	☐	☐
4. The library is the place where a lot of socializing takes place.	☐	☐	☐
5. If school campuses were designed by students, they would include more social spaces.	☐	☐	☐
6. At least 80% of students are happy with the design of our campus.	☐	☐	☐
7. A number of factors are considered when a campus is designed.	☐	☐	☐
8. Every school has to make difficult decisions about how space is used.	☐	☐	☐

C Look back at Part B. Complete the tasks.
1. In English, verbs must **agree in number** with their subjects. Underline the **subject(s) of each clause**.
2. Double-underline the **verb(s) in each clause**.
3. Circle each passive construction that **includes a *by*-phrase**.
4. Put a rectangle around each passive construction that **does not include a *by*-phrase**.
5. Following the model, make a chart with examples. Then, compare your chart with a partner's chart.

Subjects and verbs	Passives without a *by*-phrase	Passives with a *by*-phrase

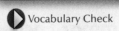
Reading

A WARM-UP This article from a university's student newspaper describes a study that is being conducted to investigate how patrons use specific areas inside the library. The results of the study will be used to make improvements to the library. Answer the questions. Then, discuss your answers with the class.

1. What areas inside the library do you think researchers would focus on? Why?
2. What types of "user" behaviors or habits do you think would be of interest to the researchers?
3. How do you think the researchers would conduct this kind of study?

B SCANNING Scan the article to find answers to the questions in Part A. Were your answers correct? Then, read the whole article.

Library Examines Space, Socialization

An ongoing study is allowing university researchers to examine Lauinger Library through a new lens.

The library's administration has commissioned a group of staff members to document the activity on the building's second and third floors through photographs. Photographs are taken hourly on two randomly chosen days of the month. Various areas of the library have been selected by the administration for the study. The images are taken in these specifically marked areas so that researchers can track the use of those areas over the next few months.

The study will allow the staff to suggest improvements to the library, which will then likely be implemented fairly soon. According to Stephanie Clark, the director of Planning and Assessment, administrators are trying to determine the best use of the space, and the photo study research is helping them to decide what gradual improvements they can make. There are several potential changes that could be made as a result of the study. These changes range from rearranging books or periodicals to adding significant amounts of seating. All of the information from the study is being evaluated by the appointed staff as they draft recommendations.

Clark added that researchers are using the photographs to observe how much time people spend in certain parts of the library, as well as the ways in which they utilize library resources. She said the data collected from the photo study is being examined alongside the results from past surveys. "The purpose of this project is to document how specific spaces in Lauinger are being used at different times of the day as well as different times during the semester," Clark said.

Leaders of the study are particularly interested in the second and third floors of the library. The building's main entrance opens onto the third floor, which also houses the reference stacks and circulation and reserves desk. On the second floor, patrons access bound periodicals, theses, and newspapers. Both levels feature quiet areas, group meeting rooms, and technological resources to assist students.

By examining the variety of space available on these two floors, researchers can rearrange the layout of the library in general. The study is not officially connected with the structural renovations that were proposed a few years ago. In 2008, a group of professional advisors and architects was employed by the library to study the possibility of adding physical space to the building.

However, the goal of the new study is not only to determine how students study inside the walls of Lauinger but also how they socialize inside it. Clark said that the photographs from the second floor, where the student-run coffee shop, The Midnight Mug, is located, are being used to see how students interact. Although photographs are not being taken inside The Midnight Mug itself, the sitting area outside its doors is being documented on film.

C APPLYING INFORMATION Discuss the questions with a partner.

1. How can the ideas behind planning for public spaces influence the design of campus spaces?
2. What role does aesthetics (artistic qualities, beauty) play in the design of *internal* school spaces, such as a library?

Grammar Focus 1 Subject-verb agreement

Examples	Language notes
(1) Our **library conducts** surveys on its design. [singular subject + singular verb] The **librarians conduct** the surveys. [plural subject + plural verb]	In English, verbs **must agree in number** with their subjects. This is especially important in present tenses.
(2) A quiet **atmosphere is** important in study spaces. The new **furniture** in the study lounge **is** more comfortable. The research **committee is** planning to make several recommendations.	Noncount nouns* as subjects take a **singular** verb. These include **abstract nouns** (things a person can't physically interact with), **mass nouns** (substances or things that can't be counted), and **collective nouns** (nouns that define a group).
(3) The **results** of the study **and feedback** from students **are** helping the library make decisions.	Subjects that consist of multiple count or noncount nouns are connected by **and**, and must take a **plural** verb.
(4) There **are** dining **areas** in the student center. There **is** a small grocery **store** on campus.	In sentences beginning with **there + be**, the "true" subject follows the verb *be* and must agree with it.
(5) **Every student and professor was** asked to express his or her opinion.	Quantifiers **every** and **each** always take a singular noun, followed by a singular verb, even if there are multiple nouns connected by *and* in the subject.
(6) **Two weeks was** not enough to finish the project. **Twenty-thousand dollars is** too much to pay for a study. **Fifty feet is** being added to the library.	Words that show **plural** units of time, money, and distance take a **singular** verb.
(7) **That students' opinions about their campus are important is** clear. **Socializing is** a common but little-examined activity in the library.	Noun clauses and gerunds and infinitives as subjects also take a **singular** verb. (See Unit 3 for noun clauses and gerund and infinitive forms.)
(8) **Eighty percent** of the **study is** completed. Only **half** of the **students report** that they use this resource. **Some** of the **survey was** conducted last year. **One of the plans includes** redesigning the second floor. **A lot of** the **committee are focusing** on computer use. **A number of items** on the survey **have been changed**. [quantifier] *The* **number of items** on the survey **has expanded**. [subject]	In expressions with fractions, percentages, and quantifiers with the word *of*, the noun that follows determines whether the verb is singular or plural. Exceptions: • Quantifiers **one of, each of,** and **every one of** always take a singular verb, even if the noun is plural. • **Collective nouns** after the quantifiers *a lot of* and *many* take a plural verb. • *A number of* as a quantifier takes a plural noun and verb. As a subject of a sentence, it is followed by a singular noun and verb.
(9) **The goal** of the **researchers was** to complete the study by the end of the year. (*The head noun comes before the prepositional phrase.*)	In complex subjects, find the **head noun** (the main noun) and separate it from the information that comes between it and the verb. Look for modifiers such as prepositional phrases, compound prepositional phrases, negative noun phrases (*not* + noun phrase), and adjective clauses (with *who, which, that,* and *whose*). The head noun comes before these modifiers.

See Appendix D on page A-7 for a list of other common noncount nouns.

Finding the **head noun** in a long subject:

Full subject		Verb	Complement
head noun (in italics) = main subject	modifying information		
Surveys	on campus exercise facilities (prepositional phrase)	have guided	new purchases of equipment.
The library's **director**,	together with the staff, (compound prepositional phrase)	has drafted	a proposal for changes.
The planning **director**,	not the consultants, (negative noun phrase)	was asked	to write the proposal.
A campus **study**	that examined technology issues (adjective clause)	was done	last year.

Grammar Practice

MyEnglishLab

Grammar Plus 1
Activities 1 and 2

A Match the subjects on the left with the correct verbs and complements on the right.

_____ 1. Many undergraduate students

_____ 2. The current planning committee

_____ 3. Over half of the space for books

_____ 4. Changing the way people use shared spaces

_____ 5. Their criteria for making changes to the space

_____ 6. The underlying philosophy of the center's design

_____ 7. The lighting and temperature

_____ 8. Each desk and table

a. was evident in the open feeling it conveyed.

b. is measured before it is moved into the library.

c. are important factors in an effective study area.

d. is comprised of both faculty and students.

e. is often difficult to do.

f. like to study and socialize in the library.

g. were based on student input.

h. has been reduced to make room for other items.

B Read each sentence and underline the full subject in each. Then, circle the head noun and put parentheses around all modifying information. Finally, write an appropriate, logical form and tense of the verb in parentheses.

1. Designing an effective study of how students use a space on campus _____ (be, not) as easy as it sounds.

2. Grant money for renovation projects _____ (be) often difficult to get.

3. Furthermore, few administrators _____ (want) to give up financial resources for such projects.

4. Organizers of campus projects _____ (have) many factors to consider.

5. One of the most important factors in planning a renovation _____ (be) who will use the space.

6. In the past few years, the number of libraries with a traditional design _____ (decrease).

7. Universities that have traditional libraries often _____ (reevaluate) how patrons are using these facilities nowadays.

8. That the needs of patrons have greatly changed _____ (become) clear to many universities planning to update their libraries.

C Read the article about libraries. Correct the 10 subject-verb agreement errors.

The Changing Role of Libraries

Academic libraries are facing numerous changes. Their budgets are decreasing even as the cost of buying and storing information and materials are rising. Search engines has replaced librarians as the source of information, and students headed to the library are more likely to search for a cup of coffee than a book. At Johns Hopkins University in Baltimore, students and faculty members in the schools of medicine, nursing, and public health has no need to go to a library building at all. The library, through specialists known as "informationists," comes to them.

Today, many or most of the resources needed for teaching and research doesn't require a physical library. Journal articles and research papers come in digital form, and the medical library buy fewer and fewer print books. Patrons' changing habits and the digitization of research materials has also contributed to this decreased appeal of the older library building. The administration are currently planning to close the old library building in the near future.

At the moment, the informationist program include 10 library specialists. Six of them serve about 10 departments in the Schools of Medicine and Nursing, while the other four works with the departments of the School of Public Health and the basic science departments. However, one thing hasn't changed; like librarians everywhere, the Hopkins informationists also has a more basic mission: to teach patrons how to find and use information.

Grammar Focus 2 Dynamic passives

Examples	Language notes
(1) *Active:* Staff members <u>take</u> photos in selected areas. *Passive:* Photos <u>**are taken**</u> **by** staff members in selected areas.	In **passive** sentences, the **object** of a sentence (receiver of action) is in the **subject** position. The subject of the active sentence is the **agent** ("performer") of the action and becomes the complement of the passive sentence. It may or may not be shown in a **by-phrase.**
(2) All of the information from the study **is being evaluated** by the appointed staff. Professional advisors and architects **were employed** by the library. There are several potential changes that **could be made** as a result of the study. The results of the study **will not be published** immediately.	The form of the passive is **be + past participle.** Passive sentences can occur in the present, past, and future forms. They can also be used with modals. To make the passive sentence negative, use *not* after the first verb.
(3) Numerous problems **occurred** during the last renovation.	Only **transitive verbs** (verbs with a direct object) can be used in the passive. **Intransitive verbs*** (verbs that cannot be followed by a direct object) cannot be made passive.
(4) **The science building was renovated** last year. [passive] **A "green" construction firm renovated** the science building last year. [active] **School campuses are used** for a variety of purposes. **People use** school campuses for a variety of purposes. [passive]	Passive constructions are more common in formal, academic writing. They focus attention on what *happens to* the subject while active forms focus on what the subject *does.* Passives also bring a more impersonal, objective tone to sentences and help to avoid vague subjects such as "you" or "people."

a. **Students were asked** to answer the survey (by the researchers).
   b. **An anonymous donation was sent** to the university (by someone).
   c. **Several names were** accidentally **left off** of the list of donors (by someone in the publicity office).
   d. The new media room **will be designed** by a student.
   e. Changes to the lab **were determined** by the results of a year-long study.
   f. The results **are being analyzed** by the staff.
	Omit the **by-phrase** when
	   a) the agent is obvious or less important than the receiver.
	   b) you don't know who performed the action.
	   c) you want to avoid mentioning the agent, often to avoid blame.
	
	Use the **by-phrase** when
	   d) the agent is important or surprising.
	   e) the agent is "non-human"—an idea, result, or process.
	   f) you want to emphasize the agent or introduce new information about it.

(5) **It is believed that** aesthetics plays a key role in the design of classrooms. [passive] People **believe** that aesthetics plays a key role in the design of classrooms. [active] He **is believed** to be an advocate of multi-purpose spaces. [passive] People **believe** that he is an advocate of multi-purpose spaces. [active]	In formal language, passives without *by*-phrases are used to report ideas or state opinions. Specifically, they convey observations, judgments, and expectations. These structures are typically formed in two ways: **it + passive verb + *that* + noun clause,** or **subject + passive verb + infinitive.** Constructions of the second type are less common because they can be awkward and difficult to understand.

*See Appendix G on page A-9 for a list of common intransitive verbs.

Subject (receiver)	Verb: *be* + past participle		*by-phrase* (agent)	Complement
The science building	**was**	**renovated**		last year.
The results	**are being**	**analyzed**	by the staff.	
Changes	**should be**	**made**		to the layout of the library.

Common verb tenses used in passives		
verb tense	active form	passive form
simple present	The staff **conducts** the study.	The study **is conducted** by the staff.
present progressive	The staff **is conducting** the study.	The study **is being conducted** by the staff.
simple past	The staff **conducted** the study.	The study **was conducted** by the staff.
past progressive	The staff **was conducting** the study.	The study **was being conducted** by the staff.
simple future	The staff **will conduct** the study.	The study **will be conducted** by the staff.
be going to (future)	The staff **is going to conduct** the study.	The study **is going to be conducted** by the staff.
present perfect	The staff **has conducted** the study.	The study **has been conducted** by the staff.
past perfect	The staff **had conducted** the study.	The study **had been conducted** by the staff.
future perfect	The staff **will have conducted** the study.	The study **will have been conducted** by the staff.
simple modal	The staff **should conduct** the study.	The study **should be conducted** by the staff.
past modal	The staff **should have conducted** the study.	The study **should have been conducted** by the staff.

Grammar Practice

MyEnglishLab

▶ Grammar Plus 2
Activities 1 and 2

 A Read the sentences. Underline each verb. Mark each sentence as *A* (active) or *P* (passive). Then, if possible, circle the agent of the action and double-underline the receiver of the action.

_____ 1. The cost of making structural changes to the building has been enormous.

_____ 2. Committee members are appointed by the president of the university.

_____ 3. The need for printed books should decline as digital media become less expensive.

_____ 4. Our recommendations must be submitted to the coordinator by Monday.

_____ 5. Library budgets have been hurt by the economic downturn.

_____ 6. Traditional libraries of the past will become obsolete in the near future.

_____ 7. The survey was conducted in both English and Spanish.

_____ 8. Some facilities inside our student center are considered to be outdated.

B Read each sentence. Identify the underlined verbs as *T* (transitive) or *I* (intransitive). Rewrite each sentence that has a transitive verb to make it passive. Keep the verb tense the same. Decide whether a *by*-phrase is necessary.

1. The two universities in the area <u>have made</u> major changes to their campuses in the past few years.

_____

_____

2. If the market <u>drops</u>, investors won't have the finances to support the renovations.

_____

_____

3. A firm specializing in eco-friendly construction <u>rebuilt</u> the damaged building.

_____

_____

4. Some schools <u>publish</u> articles about their campus renovation experiences in various journals.

_____

_____

5. Student organizations <u>should contact</u> the administration to discuss the project.

_____

_____

6. The campus police <u>may have rejected</u> the proposal for security reasons.

_____

_____

7. The university <u>asked</u> students to post comments about the new student center.

_____

_____

8. It <u>appears</u> that the newly reconfigured group study rooms are quite popular.

_____

_____

C Rewrite each sentence in the passive form using a subject with *it* or another appropriate subject from the sentence. Be sure to put the verb in the correct tense.

1. People believe that the purpose of libraries will always change with the times.
   It is believed that the purpose of libraries will always change with the times.

_____

2. The media reported that Johns Hopkins University has closed its old library.

_____

_____

3. We assume that community colleges face similar issues with space.

_____

_____

4. People think that students can offer objective feedback about changes to their campus.

_____

_____

5. Research has shown that university student centers can serve a great variety of needs.

_____

_____

6. Schools know that academic libraries are important places of learning and socializing.

_____

_____

Speaking

 A Work with a partner to complete the activity. Follow the steps. Try to use the grammar from the chapter.

1. Think about your school library, student center, or another multifunctional building on your school campus. Discuss who uses this building, the key areas inside it, and the ways in which they are used. You can use the verbs in the box help you. Take notes.

| access | complete [tasks] | eat/drink | plan | study | use |
| buy | discuss | meet | print | type | |

Typical users	Important internal spaces / areas	Common uses

2. Now discuss helpful changes that could be made to the building you selected. Look at the model below, and then use the verbs in the box to help you.

| add | change | eliminate | include | move | redesign |
| adjust | divide | enlarge/expand | modify | reconfigure | reorganize |

> *Our cafeteria should be redesigned because it doesn't meet all of our needs. For example, the tables and chairs take up too much space. Smaller . . .*

B Share your ideas with the class and get other suggestions. Then, as a class, decide which ideas overall were the best and why.

Listening

 A BEFORE LISTENING You will listen to a university radio station report on the construction of a "bookless" learning center. Make predictions about what will be reported for each aspect of the center.

Kind of building: _____

Intended patrons: _____

Types of furniture and other materials / equipment: _____

Technology resources: _____

Specific areas in the center: _____

B 🎧 LISTENING FOR DETAILS Listen to the student reporter as she describes the learning center project and talks about it with an administrator and a student. Next, fill in the chart with information from the listening. Compare your notes with your predictions in Part A.

Why the new center was built	How it is designed	Who is served by the center

C 🎧 LISTENING FOR OPINIONS Listen again. As you listen, focus on the speakers' specific reactions to the center. Then, answer the questions with your partner.

1. Which feature of the new center did Jason Reed say was the most useful? Why?
   Feature: _____ Key comments: _____
2. What two activities did Gina Rossi say she enjoyed doing in the center? Why?
   Activities: _____ Key comments: _____
3. What area of the center did Karen Herrera say was useful for faculty and staff? Why?
   Area: _____ Key comments: _____

Writing

MyEnglishLab
Linking Grammar to Writing

A Work in small groups. Choose a space or a building on your school campus that you think should be redesigned. Discuss its specific uses and decide whether it is being used to its full potential. Brainstorm concrete suggestions for change. Take notes.

B Write an email to the editor of the school paper about the use of a building on your campus. Use your notes from Part A. Try to use the grammar from the chapter. Use the sample letter as a guide.

Dear Editor:

As concerned students at Branson University, we would like to suggest a potential renovation project on our campus. A number of our classes are held in Fillmore Hall. We have noticed that half of the classrooms on the bottom floor of this building are not used by faculty on a regular basis. Many of our assignments have to be completed collaboratively, in and out of class. It is difficult to find spaces where we can meet and use computers. It has been reported that a new campus plan is being developed. On behalf of our fellow students, we would like to suggest that those classrooms be converted into group study rooms with technology resources. Our class would be happy to share fundraising ideas for the project with university administrators.

The Students of Advanced English

C Post your emails around the room. Discuss with the whole class which message contains the most interesting or effective suggestions for change.

MyEnglishLab
Diagnostic Test

Grammar Summary

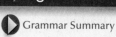

Stative passives describe the status, condition, or quality of a noun.

This condition may be permanent or continue for some time. Stative passives are formed with *be* + past participle. They are also typically followed prepositions, such as *about, in, to, with*.	(1) The Seaside Garden is filled with exotic plants. (2) The Garden's origin is rooted in Japanese culture. (3) Citizens have been committed to the Garden's maintenance.

Adjective clauses with *where, when,* and *why* describe a place, time, or reason.

Clauses with *where* and *when* can be restrictive or non-restrictive (without or with commas). Clauses with *why*-clauses can be restrictive only. The words *in / at / on which* can replace *where*. The words *during / in / at / on* can replace *when*.	(1) The Quad, where most students like to gather, is a popular place. (2) The year when the Quad was equipped with benches was 2000. (3) The reason why students like the Quad is because of its central campus location. (4) The place in which most students like to gather is the Quad. (5) The year in which the Quad was equipped with benches was 2000.

Adjective clauses with quantifiers focus on the number / amount of a preceding noun.

These clauses follow three patterns and are always non-restrictive (they are enclosed in commas): *quantifier + of + whom* describes people; *quantifier + of + which* describes things; and *quantifier + of + whose + noun* describes people and things.	(1) The Seaside Garden was designed by a team of urban planners, two of whom have won awards for their community designs. (2) The Garden is filled with exotic plants, a large number of which are native to Pacific islands. (3) The Garden is supported by the community, many of whose residents work to protect it from vandals.

Subject-verb agreement requires that verbs must agree in number with their subjects.

Non-count and collective nouns take a singular verb. Plural units of time, money, and distance take a singular verb. With fractions, percentages, and quantifiers, it is the following noun that determines the verb. In long, complex subjects, the head noun determines the verb.	(1) Functionality was a consideration in the design of the Quad. (2) The soccer team usually meets on the Quad. (3) Six months is the estimated time for renovation. (4) Ten thousand dollars was donated to the project. (5) A third of those funds come from students. (6) The number one concern of many current and former students was the deterioration of the Quad.

Dynamic passives permit a different sentence focus.

In passive sentences, the object of an active sentence becomes the subject, and the subject becomes a *by*-phrase, or is omitted. The *by*-phrase tends to be omitted when the doer of the action is not important, not known, or is concealed (often to avoid blame). The *by*-phrase is used when the doer of the action is important, surprising, or non-human. Passives can also convey ideas and opinions.	(1) The renovation was led by a team of architects. (2) The renovation was approved by the trustees. (3) In 2000, the Quad's benches were added. (4) In 2004, the Quad's benches were vandalized. (5) During restoration, a lot of grass was destroyed. (6) Funding was provided by students. (7) It was thought that the vandals were strangers.

Self-Assessment

A (5 points) Complete the paragraph with the stative passive form of the verbs in the list and the correct prepositions. Use each verb only once.

compose	protect	reserve	situate	surround

The campus of the University of California at Santa Barbara is **1.** _____ a cliff, and it **2.** _____ the Pacific Ocean on three sides. One part of the campus **3.** _____ a lagoon and restored marshland. One area of the lagoon **4.** _____ tanks that are filled with marine life that students can research. In the tanks, the fish and plants **5.** _____ potentially harmful elements in the open ocean.

B (3 points) Combine the sentences using *where, when,* or *why.* Add commas where necessary.

1. The town council approved the restoration of the old railroad station last month. A contractor submitted a feasible proposal then.

_____

2. The citizens petitioned for a restoration of the railroad station. They wanted to get rid of an ugly place. That was the reason.

_____

3. The new railroad station will be a popular place. People can gather, have dinner, and go shopping there.

_____

C (4 points) Circle the correct phrase to complete the paragraph.

We are petitioning to restore the area surrounding Cedar Lake, **1. a few of which / much of which** is bordered by tall grass and overgrown shrubs. The residents of the adjacent town homes, **2. many of which / many of whom** offer a view of the lake, cannot enjoy the lake because they look out over a wilderness of plants. The Community Association should hire the local team of planners, **3. two of whose members / two of which** won awards last year for restoring a similar outdoor space. Once the area has been restored, the lake could be used as a true recreation space by the residents, **4. a great number of which / most of whom** would be willing to contribute to the project.

D (5 points) Complete the paragraph with the singular or plural form of the verbs in parentheses.

A central idea of achieving a unified campus design **1.** _____ (be) the need to develop ties between new and existing buildings. There **2.** _____ (be) visual and functional ties. About 80 percent of the visual ties **3.** _____ (involve) building form, with respect to size, shape, color, or texture. New architecture **4.** _____ (contribute) to the visual unity of the campus. On a unified campus, the landscapes of knowledge, buildings, and grounds **5.** _____ (meet) synergistically.

E (3 points) Rewrite the sentence in the passive. Omit the *by*-phrase where possible.

1. Architects give campus design much more thought and planning than students often believe.

_____

2. Research has suggested that students feel happier on beautifully designed campuses.

_____

3. Students and faculty are submitting suggestions for campus improvement.

_____

Unit Project: Group observation report

A You will plan and carry out an observation of a popular public space in your community or on your campus. Follow the steps.

1. Work in groups of three or four students. Select a popular public space in your community or on your campus that people use for various purposes. Make a list of questions about people's behaviors and other factors in the space that you want to investigate.

   Example: What types of activities are done in the Sports and Recreation Center? How do men and women exercise differently?

2. Set hypotheses about what you expect to find.

   Example: It is predicted that the most popular activities are exercising and practicing team sports.
   It is expected that men do more strength training and women do more aerobic exercise.

3. Make a plan for observing that space (time, day, time interval) and team member responsibilities. Which specific activity will each member observe? Where and when? Who will serve as the group leader? Which parts of the presentation will each member deliver?

4. Carry out your observation and collect your data (use a notepad to record your observations).

5. Synthesize and analyze your information.

   Example: Our results show that the most common activities are exercising and practicing individual sports. We observed 25 men, 80 percent of whom were doing strength training, and 16 women, half of whom were also doing aerobic workouts.

6. Optional: Create a chart, graph, or table to depict your findings visually.

7. Interpret your findings and determine if your hypotheses were accurate.

   Example: Our hypothesis about the most popular activities was proven incorrect. It is assumed that individual sports were more popular than team sports because our school has strong long-distance running and tennis programs.

8. Prepare a presentation of your observation results and analysis to your class. Include these parts in your presentation:

   • Topic and observation questions (what you wanted to find out)
   • Hypotheses (what you expected)
   • Methods (what you did)
   • Results with visual (what you found)
   • Interpretation / Conclusions (what you think about the results)

B After each group's presentation, discuss the questions with the whole class.

1. Did you observe any unexpected behaviors in your selected space? If yes, why were they surprising?

2. Did you identify any aspects of your selected space that could be improved? If yes, how?

MyEnglishLab
▶ Unit Test

MyEnglishLab
▶ Search It!

UNIT 6

Public Health: Pandemics

OUTCOMES

After completing this unit, I will be able to use these grammar points.

CHAPTER 11

Grammar Focus 1
Coordinating conjunctions

Grammar Focus 2
Adverbial time clauses and time phrases

CHAPTER 12

Grammar Focus 1
Past perfect and past perfect progressive

Grammar Focus 2
Past unreal conditionals

CHAPTER 11 | Current Virus Threats

Getting Started

A In what places are people exposed to the most viruses and bacteria? Why? Discuss your ideas with your partner and make a list of the top five "germiest" places.

B Read the sentences about the spread and prevention of infections. Write *T* if you think the statement is true and *F* if you think it is false. Compare your answers with your partner's.

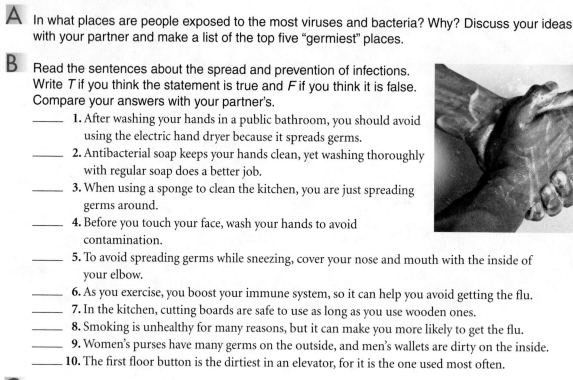

_____ 1. After washing your hands in a public bathroom, you should avoid using the electric hand dryer because it spreads germs.

_____ 2. Antibacterial soap keeps your hands clean, yet washing thoroughly with regular soap does a better job.

_____ 3. When using a sponge to clean the kitchen, you are just spreading germs around.

_____ 4. Before you touch your face, wash your hands to avoid contamination.

_____ 5. To avoid spreading germs while sneezing, cover your nose and mouth with the inside of your elbow.

_____ 6. As you exercise, you boost your immune system, so it can help you avoid getting the flu.

_____ 7. In the kitchen, cutting boards are safe to use as long as you use wooden ones.

_____ 8. Smoking is unhealthy for many reasons, but it can make you more likely to get the flu.

_____ 9. Women's purses have many germs on the outside, and men's wallets are dirty on the inside.

_____ 10. The first floor button is the dirtiest in an elevator, for it is the one used most often.

C Look back at Part B. Complete the tasks.

1. Circle the **coordinating conjunctions** that join **two independent clauses**.
2. Underline the **adverbial time clauses** and double-underline the **main clauses**.
3. Put parentheses around the **adverbial time phrases that modify main clauses**; double-underline the **main clauses**.
4. Complete the chart with examples. Then, compare your chart with a partner's chart.

Coordinating conjunctions	Adverbial time clauses	Adverbial time phrases

Reading

A WARM-UP What do you know about the science behind the cause and spread of major diseases? Discuss your ideas with your partner. Use some of the words from the box.

bacteria	influenza	mortality rates	pandemic	viruses
germs	inoculate	mutate	transmission	virus strain
infect	microbes	outbreaks	vaccines	

B SCANNING Scan the article to identify the two viruses that are described. Which virus is the greater threat to human populations? Why? Then, read the whole article.

Pandemic Challenges of Today

Our globalized world is the stage for innumerable interactions between animals, humans, and microbes such as bacteria and viruses. Most of these interactions are harmless, but when human activity combines with a mutating microbe, some result in the emergence of a health threat that can travel rapidly within and between continents.

Flu viruses are among the most genetically unstable viruses, for they mutate easily and, when certain conditions are present, they can exchange genetic material with other influenza viruses. Most flu viruses that infect humans are believed to have originated in avian (bird) species. Some viruses have combined with swine (pig) viruses or with both avian and swine. When infecting humans, some cause mild symptoms, yet others lead to severe illness. This ability to mutate and exchange genetic material makes these infections difficult to treat. After eventually identifying the origin and genetic makeup of a virus, researchers work to develop a vaccine to inoculate the public against further outbreaks.

Once a disease spreads rapidly and results in high rates of infection and mortality, it is labeled a "pandemic." In 2009, the World Health Organization designated the H1N1, or swine flu, virus as a pandemic. The H1N1 virus, which combines wild bird, domestic pig, and human virus strains, is the result of human and animal interaction. As the number of large industrial farms grows, contact with animal populations and their diseases increases, too. This process provides germs like

flu viruses new opportunities to evolve, mutate, and spread.

Prior to 2009, scientists were concerned about the spread of the H5N1 avian virus, which had infected chickens in many parts of the world. The H5N1 virus rarely passes from human to human, but it can spread from domestic birds to humans, often causing severe and highly fatal disease. As long as it continues on this course, it won't reach pandemic levels. However, the possibility of H5N1 spreading through human-to-human contact greatly concerns scientists.

All recognized strains share a characteristic: they are first identified in humans, and the animals that carry and transmit them to humans are eventually found and the risks assessed. To improve this process, specialists are working to first identify the infections as soon as they appear in animals, evaluate the risks of transmission to humans, and then better manage these risks.

By the time H1N1 reached post-pandemic status in August 2010, it was clear that the outbreak had resulted in much lower mortality rates than anticipated. However, the potential for a virus of this type to evolve into something much more lethal still exists. Improved understanding of the risks of viruses in animal populations and their interactions with human virus strains may help us to avoid future pandemic diseases.

C UNDERSTANDING DETAILS Read the article again. Then, draw a flow chart based on the reading of the possible emergence, transmission, and treatment of pandemic flu viruses.

virus emerges in an animal	→		→		→		→	

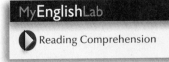

Grammar Focus 1 Coordinating conjunctions

Examples	Language notes
(1) Animals can infect humans with disease, **and** humans can transmit disease to animals.	As you learned in Unit 3, **coordinating conjunctions** join **independent clauses** and connect ideas of **equal** importance in compound sentences. All are preceded by a **comma**. These connectors are sometimes called "FANBOYS" as a way to remember them: *for, and, nor, but, or, yet,* and *so.*
(2) Flu viruses are difficult to manage, **for** they mutate easily.	**For** shows **causes** or **reasons** and is used in formal language. **For** is different than other coordinating conjunctions because the clause that follows **for** receives less emphasis than the clause before it.
(3) Germs can spread from continent to continent, **and** they can result in high rates of infection and mortality. We *don't* always know the origin of new viruses, **nor do** we understand their transmission.	**And** and **nor** are used to show **additional** ideas. **Nor** is only used to connect **negative** ideas, and the auxiliary verb is added and inverted. If the main verb is a form of *be*, it is also inverted.
(4) The H5N1 virus rarely passes from human to human, **but** it can spread from domestic birds to humans. A health crisis was avoided, **yet** the potential still exists.	**But** and **yet** connect **contrasting** ideas. **Yet** is used to show a **concession**, or an **unexpected contrast**: "X is true, yet . . ."
(5) A flu virus can spread from one animal to another, **or** it can move from an animal to a human.	**Or** connects **alternative** ideas.
(6) Researchers identified the genetic structure of the virus, **so** they were able to make a vaccine.	**So** expresses **results**. It shows the idea in the second clause is the outcome of the first idea.
(7) Some viruses have not "jumped" to humans. **So,** we don't consider them global health threats yet.	It is not common in formal, academic writing to begin a sentence with a conjunction, but in informal writing or conversation, *and, but,* and *so* can be used to show additional, contrasting, or resulting ideas.

Independent clause	Coordinating conjunction	Independent clause
Many viruses don't become pandemic,	**for**	they are less dangerous and easier to treat.
Health agencies monitor virus outbreaks,	**and**	they develop methods of treating them.
The virus **isn't** new,	***nor**	**is it** dangerous.
Some human activities lead to infection,	**but** **yet**	these activities continue.
A flu virus can evolve on its own,	**or**	it can trade genetic material with other viruses.
The virus spread throughout the area,	**so**	officials issued a quarantine.

*Nor *joins only negative ideas*

Grammar Practice

A Read each pair of sentences and decide what kind of relationship they have (additional, contrasting, alternative or resulting idea, or cause / reason). Then, choose the best conjunction from the box to connect the two ideas in a new sentence. Be sure to put the clauses in a logical order.

| and | but | for | nor | or | so | yet |

1. Viruses have existed for millions of years.
   Viruses can be found in any plant or animal host.

   _____

2. Flu viruses are hard to identify.
   Flu viruses frequently change their genetic makeup.

   _____

3. The outbreaks of Ebola and Lassa viruses caused high rates of mortality in infected areas.
   These outbreaks have not become pandemic.

   _____

4. The 2009 H1N1 virus did not have the traits of a highly dangerous disease.
   The 2009 outbreak didn't cause as many deaths as expected.

   _____

5. Viruses can change suddenly in a process called reassortment.
   Viruses can change over a longer period of time by mutating to adapt to different host species.

   _____

6. Public health interventions could not stop virus outbreaks.
   Public health interventions have slowed down pandemic virus outbreaks.

   _____

7. World health officials believed that the avian H5N1 virus was a major threat.
   World health officials updated preparedness systems in anticipation of a pandemic.

   _____

8. More research on the transmission of virus among species is necessary.
   Health officials must find ways to improve detection and treatment of viruses.

   _____

B Read the paragraph about influenza viruses. Correct the five errors in coordinating conjunctions.

Influenza viruses are grouped into three types: A, B, and C. C-type viruses are quite common, for they are not dangerous. They usually cause no symptoms or only very mild respiratory illness, nor they are not considered a public health concern. Type B viruses cause sporadic outbreaks of more severe respiratory disease, particularly among young children in school settings. Both B and C viruses are essentially human viruses. C viruses are stable, for A and B viruses are prone to mutation. The influenza A viruses cause the most concerns. These viruses mutate much more rapidly than type B viruses, or this gives them great flexibility. In addition to humans, they infect pigs, horses, sea mammals, and birds. Their unique features enable them to cause seasonal epidemics in humans that result in high infection and death rates. Influenza A viruses cause recurring pandemics, so the pandemics are unpredictable.

Grammar Focus 2 Adverbial time clauses and time phrases

Examples	Language notes
(1) **When a new virus appears,** experts work to identify its origins.	**Adverbial clauses** are dependent (subordinate) clauses. They show relationships between ideas in terms of *time, cause and effect, contrast,* and *condition.* They begin with **subordinators,** which can be single adverbs or phrases. This chapter focuses on **adverbial time clauses.**
(2) Scientists work to identify a virus **before it spreads through populations.** **Once a strain has been identified,** specialists work to develop a vaccine for it. The strain, **once it is identified,** is then studied and assessed.	Subordinators that begin time clauses include *after, before, when, while / as, *by the time, since, until, as soon as / once, as / so long as,* and *whenever.* Most time clauses can come before or after the main clause. If placed before the main clause, they are followed by a comma. Some adverb clauses come inside independent clauses. They are placed between commas. (*By the time will also be addressed in Chapter 12.)
(3) The report <u>will be released</u> **when the testing <u>is</u> done.** Viruses have infected animals and plants **since they have been in existence.**	When describing future ideas with **when** and **until,** use the simple present in the time clause. In time clauses with **since,** use the present perfect in the main clause.
(4) **When <u>they are</u> working on a vaccine,** specialists consider many factors. → **When <u>working</u> on a vaccine,** specialists consider many factors. Diseases impact age groups differently **after <u>they infect</u> a region.** → Diseases impact age groups differently **after <u>infecting</u> a region.** *Incorrect:* **While searching for the origin,** <u>the disease</u> continued to spread. → **While <u>researchers</u> were searching for the origin,** <u>the disease</u> continued to spread.	Adverbial time clauses can also be **reduced** to **adverbial time phrases** with the subordinators **before, after, when, while,** and **since.** Time phrases can come before or after the main clause. If there is an auxiliary form of **be** in the clause, the subject and *be* are omitted (e.g., in progressives or passives). If there is no *be* form, omit the subject and change the verb to its *-ing* form. This is possible <u>only</u> if the subjects of both clauses are the same. If a time clause with a subject that is different than the subject of the main clause is reduced, it results in a **"dangling modifier" error.** (The modifier does not have the proper subject to modify.)

Time clause (Dependent)	Main clause (Independent)	Meaning
<u>When</u> a new virus appears,	experts work to identify its origins.	*at that time*
<u>Once</u> / <u>As soon as</u> a strain is identified,	specialists develop a vaccine for it.	*when X happens, Y happens soon after*
<u>As</u> / <u>while</u> specialists work on a vaccine,	officials put out health warnings.	*during that time*
<u>Before</u> the H1N1 virus appeared,	the H5N1 virus was a concern.	*prior to*

Main clause (Independent)	Time clause (Dependent)	Meaning
Diseases impact age groups differently	<u>after</u> they infect a region.	*following*
Outbreaks don't spread easily	<u>so/as long as</u> they remain in animals.	*during all that time*
Viruses have infected animals	<u>since</u> they have been in existence.	*from that time to now*
Research will continue	<u>until</u> an effective vaccine is found.	*to that point and then no longer*
Outbreaks of disease bring panic	<u>whenever</u> officials are slow to respond.	*every time*

Time phrase	Main clause (Independent)
When <u>working</u> on a vaccine,	specialists consider many factors.

Grammar Practice

A Read the clauses that refer to myths about the H1N1 outbreak or pandemic viruses in general. Match each clause on the left with its appropriate main clause on the right. Then, write sentences combining the clauses.

_____ 1. when people get the swine flu

_____ 2. until it "jumps species"

_____ 3. since the disease first struck

_____ 4. by the time a pandemic reaches it peak

_____ 5. once a pandemic is over

_____ 6. as long as they are strong and healthy

a. the danger of new infections occurring is small

b. it won't be back for decades

c. people won't get infected

d. a virus shouldn't be a concern to researchers

e. only the very young or old have been infected

f. their symptoms are just like those for seasonal flu

1. _____

2. _____

3. _____

4. _____

5. _____

6. _____

B Read the sentences. Change the adverb clauses to adverbial phrases if possible. If it is not possible, write *no change*.

1. Since the rate of meat consumption increased worldwide, more industrial farms have been built.

_____

2. While they are working on industrial farms, many migrant workers are exposed to sick animals.

_____

3. When the animals are crowded together in large farms, they exchange more viruses with their human handlers.

_____

4. After they enter the middle class, poorer segments of the population will add to the global demand for meat.

_____

5. By the time we reach the year 2020, the United Nations estimates that world consumption could top 386 million tons of meat.

_____

6. Government officials create economic hardship when they mistakenly ban meat products from infected regions.

_____

7. Until changes are made, the ecological conditions that promote viral evolution will continue to worsen.

_____

8. As long as we use the same methods of raising animals, we will continue creating the conditions for another severe global pandemic.

_____

Speaking

A In small groups, discuss what you typically do to avoid getting a seasonal cold or the flu. Decide what approaches might be the most helpful and why. Report your top three tips to the class. Look at the model below, and try to use the grammar from the chapter.

> *When there is a flu virus going around, I drink a lot of fluids, but I don't drink sodas.*

B About 100 years ago, people did not have the advantages of modern medical care, nor did they have great awareness of disease transmission. In small groups, discuss examples of what people at that time probably did to avoid infection. Look at the model below, and try to use the grammar from the chapter. Then, as a class, decide which approaches were probably helpful and which approaches were probably risky or ineffective, and explain why.

> *When people got sick in the past, they used natural treatments. I know that in ancient times people used honey to treat cuts and other skin problems.*

Listening

MyEnglishLab

Listen for it.

A BEFORE LISTENING You will listen to a lecture segment on lessons learned from three past pandemics. What facts do you think the lecturer, a professor of public health, will discuss? Brainstorm three specific ideas with a partner.

1. _____
   _____
   _____

2. _____
   _____
   _____

3. _____
   _____
   _____

B 🎧 LISTENING FOR MAIN IDEAS Listen to the lecture and answer the questions.

1. Which three pandemics did the lecturer discuss?

   _____   _____   _____

2. In what ways will the insights that were gained from past pandemics inform future prevention or lessen the impact of pandemics? List one way.

   _____

C 🎧 LISTENING FOR DETAILS Listen to the lecture again. What were the lessons the lecturer described? Did any of them match the predictions you made in Part A? Make brief notes. Then, discuss your answers with the class.

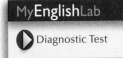
Writing

A Look at the sample flyer about pertussis. Then, work in small groups to design a health information flyer about the flu. Brainstorm and take notes on information that you think the public should know about the virus, its transmission, prevention measures, and treatment options. Include practical advice.

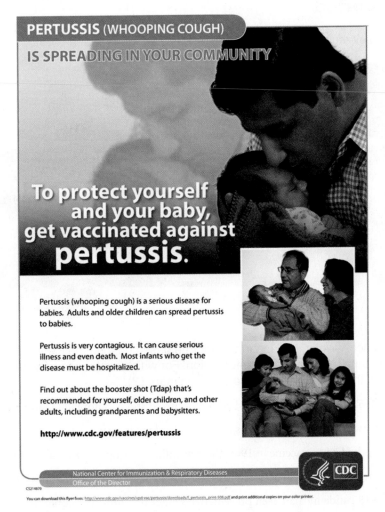

PERTUSSIS (WHOOPING COUGH)

IS SPREADING IN YOUR COMMUNITY

To protect yourself and your baby, get vaccinated against pertussis.

Pertussis (whooping cough) is a serious disease for babies. Adults and older children can spread pertussis to babies.

Pertussis is very contagious. It can cause serious illness and even death. Most infants who get the disease must be hospitalized.

Find out about the booster shot (Tdap) that's recommended for yourself, older children, and other adults, including grandparents and babysitters.

http://www.cdc.gov/features/pertussis

National Center for Immunization & Respiratory Diseases
Office of the Director

CDC

You can download this flyer from: http://www.cdc.gov/vaccines/vpd-vac/pertussis/downloads/f_pertussis_print-508.pdf and print additional copies on your color printer.

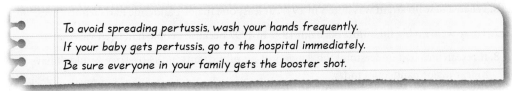

To avoid spreading pertussis, wash your hands frequently.

If your baby gets pertussis, go to the hospital immediately.

Be sure everyone in your family gets the booster shot.

B Working in the same groups, write the information for your flyer and decide what images, diagrams, or photos you could include. Use your notes from Part A. Try to use the grammar from the chapter.

C Share your flyers with your classmates. Vote on the flyer with the most helpful information and the most unique design.

CHAPTER 12

The Flu Pandemic of 1918

Getting Started

A What do you think the timeline illustrates? Discuss your ideas with a partner.

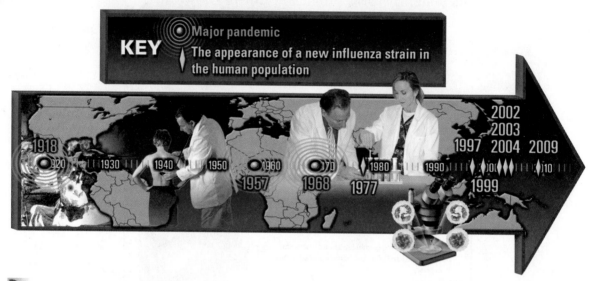

B Read the sentences. Which information is not true based on the timeline in Part A? Mark those sentences with an *X* and correct the information. For which sentences do you not have enough evidence? Mark those sentences with a question mark (*?*).

_____ **1.** Before 1957, a major flu outbreak had not occurred and had not killed numerous people.

_____ **2.** By 2009, two new influenza strains had been attacking humans.

_____ **3.** If doctors had had a vaccine in 1968, the new influenza strains would not have occurred.

_____ **4.** After a new flu strain had been recorded in 1977, a new strain didn't appear for 10 years.

_____ **5.** If the 1918 pandemic had been prevented, no other flu outbreaks would have happened.

_____ **6.** When a new flu strain was noted in 1977, at least one major pandemic had claimed lives.

_____ **7.** There were no big flu outbreaks from 1977 to 1997 because people had been vaccinated.

_____ **8.** If researchers had understood the dangers of new flu strains in the past, we wouldn't have to fear major pandemics today.

C Look back at Part B. Complete the tasks.

1. Circle those **past perfect verbs and time references** in sentences that show that **one event happened before another one.**
2. Underline the *if*-clause, and double-underline the **main clause**.
3. Following the model, make a chart with examples. Then, compare your chart with a partner's chart.

Past perfect with time reference	Conditionals (*if*-clauses + main clauses)

Reading

A WARM-UP What path do you think the flu pandemic of 1918 took as it affected and killed people around the world? On the map, continue the path of the outbreak from its origin in Kansas in the United States.

B UNDERSTANDING MAIN IDEAS Read about the flu pandemic of 1918. Then, compare the actual path of the pandemic with your prediction in Part A. Does anything surprise you?

THE GREAT PANDEMIC

During the early twentieth century, before antibiotics were discovered, communicable diseases were widespread. In 1918, the Public Health Service (PHS) in the United States had just begun to require state and local health departments to provide them with reports about specific diseases in their communities, but influenza was not on the list. In March 1918, officials in Kansas sent a worrisome report to the PHS after they became concerned that 18 cases of severe influenza had occurred. If the government had realized the severity of the cases, officials would have reacted more quickly and might have been able to prevent larger outbreaks. During May, reports of severe influenza were trickling in from Europe. Numerous young soldiers had become ill. Most of them recovered quickly, but some developed a deadly type of pneumonia. Within two months, after influenza had been spreading from the military to the civilian population in Europe, the disease was reported in Asia, Africa, South America, and back again in North America. If officials had made a connection between the Kansas cases and the soldier cases in Europe, a global pandemic could perhaps have been prevented.

By late August, influenza epidemics had struck port cities around the world. In Boston's harbor, dockworkers reported sick in massive numbers during late August. These workers had extremely high fevers and severe muscle and joint pains. For most of them, recovery quickly followed. But about 10 percent of them developed severe pneumonia that resulted in death. Many doctors later wished that they had been better informed about the connection between the different influenza occurrences. But without such knowledge, public health experts had little time to register their shock at the severity of this outbreak. Within days, people outside of Boston had contracted the disease. By mid-September, the epidemic had been making its way to California, North Dakota, Florida, and Texas. If the Boston PHS had had adequate knowledge about the nature of the disease, the rapid spread to the rest of the country might have been prevented.

Authorities quickly mobilized to fight the disease. On September 27, influenza became a reportable disease. However, influenza had become so widespread by that time that most states were unable to keep accurate records of their sick population. By then, public health officials had been working on ways to stop the rising panic through posters warning people of the dangers of influenza. Although the PHS was aware that the nation's immigrant population did not speak or read English, most posters had been printed in English. Among immigrants, the death toll might have been lower if they had been able to comprehend the warnings. Sadly, no measures proved effective in limiting the spread of the pandemic. By the time the pandemic finally subsided in the summer of 1919, nearly 675,000 Americans had died from influenza, and estimates are that worldwide 20 to 50 million people had passed away.

C UNDERSTANDING DETAILS Draw a timeline from March 1918 to Summer 1919 with the major events of the Great Pandemic and the months of occurrence. Then, discuss the questions in small groups.

What do you think officials should or could have done:
(1) after the reports from Kansas had come in?
(2) after the reports of ill soldiers in Europe had become known?
(3) after the Boston dockworkers had become sick?

Grammar Focus 1 Past perfect and past perfect progressive

Examples	Language notes
(1) In 1918, the PHS **had begun** to require states to provide reports about diseases. When the pandemic subsided, over 600,000 Americans **had died**. |————————————————————|———— March 1918 Summer 1919 People died Pandemic subsided	Use the **past perfect** for actions or events that were completed before another activity or time in the past. To form the past perfect, use **had + past participle**. The past perfect tends to be used in writing more than in speaking, particularly to clarify time sequence and to show that one event occurred before another.
(2) By late September, the disease **had become** widespread. By the time the pandemic finally subsided, nearly 675,000 Americans **had died** from influenza. Before antibiotics were discovered, communicable diseases **had been** widespread. Officials in Kansas sent a worrisome report to the PHS after they **became** concerned about cases of severe influenza.	We often use time references with the past perfect, such as **by the time, by [date], before,** and **after.** Both **by the time** and **by [date]** imply that the event mentioned in the main clause happened first, and the past perfect is used. The past perfect is optional in sentences with **before** or **after** because these time words themselves show the order of events.
(3) Because the PHS **had** not **recognized** the severity of the disease, the flu spread quickly without medical intervention.	We often use **because** with the past perfect.
(4) By then, public health officials **had been working** on ways to stop the rising panic. After influenza **had been spreading** from the military to the civilian population in Europe, the disease was reported in Asia.	The **past perfect progressive** expresses that an action was in progress before a specific past point in time. To form the past perfect progressive, use **had + been + present participle (verb + -ing)**. Like the past progressive, it also shows that an activity in the past was in progress when another event in the past interrupted it.

Time reference	Subject	Verb in past perfect		Complement
Within days,	people in Boston	**had**	**contracted**	the disease.
In 1918,	influenza	**had not been**	**placed**	on the list for reportable diseases.

Time reference	Subject	Verb in past perfect progressive		Complement
By then,	public officials	**had**	**been working**	on ways to stop the rising panic.
By mid-September,	the epidemic	**had**	**been making**	its way to California.

Grammar Practice

A Combine each pair of sentences, using the provided clues. One of the sentences in each pair should be in the past perfect or the past perfect progressive.

1. Trains were the primary form of transport for Americans in 1918. The number of passengers traveling by rail tripled.
   After *the number of passengers traveling by rail had tripled, trains were the primary form of transport for Americans in 1918.*

2. Telephone service in many countries became affordable. People relied on telegrams and letters to transmit information.
   Before _____.

3. In the early twentieth century, Americans flocked into movie theaters. Americans' love affair with Hollywood was already a significant part of the culture.
   When _____.

4. In 1917, young American men were required to register for the military. They were sent to camps across the United States.
   In 1917, after _____.

5. Europe's involvement in World War I enabled women to obtain jobs. In 1918, many women in war-torn European countries were employed in munition plants.
   Because _____.

6. In the early twentieth century, many developed countries built improved water and sewage systems in cities. The number of infections and deaths declined.
   After _____.

B Complete the paragraph with the past perfect, past perfect progressive, or past simple form of the verbs in parentheses.

During the late nineteenth century, doctors and scientists **1.** _____ (begin) to understand that diseases are caused by microorganisms. Earlier in that century, some doctors and public health experts **2.** _____ (believe) that diseases were caused by dirt. Others **3.** _____ (be) convinced that diseases were caused by bad weather or an abnormality in the body. Most early twentieth-century physicians **4.** _____ (be) familiar with influenza and its symptoms. But when the Great Pandemic hit in 1918, they still mistakenly **5.** _____ (believe) that influenza was caused by bacteria. They **6.** _____ (not, know) that influenza is in fact a viral infection. Moreover, they **7.** _____ (not, realize) that the flu is highly contagious, transmitted from person to person through coughing and sneezing. Even before 1918, influenza viruses **8.** _____ (mutate) and **9.** _____ (cause) global epidemics. In the early twentieth century, diagnosis **10.** _____ (be) often difficult as doctors frequently **11.** _____ (confuse) the disease with the common cold, cholera, or bubonic plague. In 1918, diagnosing influenza **12.** _____ (become) even more difficult because especially strong forms of the disease **13.** _____ (erupt): patients **14.** _____ (experience) symptoms not traditionally associated with influenza. Before vaccinations and antiviral remedies **15.** _____ (be, discover) in the 1940s, physicians **16.** _____ (rely) heavily on traditional therapies. During the pandemic, many doctors **17.** _____ (use) traditional treatments, such as sweating and quarantine, which at that time **18.** _____ (be) the most effective tool for controlling epidemics.

Grammar Focus 2 Past unreal conditionals

Examples	Language notes
(1) **If** the government **had realized** the severity of the cases, officials **would have reacted** more quickly. (= *The government did* <u>*not*</u> *realize the severity of the cases, and therefore, officials did* <u>*not*</u> *react quickly.*)	Past **unreal** (or **contrary-to-fact**) **conditionals** describe events or situations that are <u>untrue</u> or <u>impossible</u> because they happened in the past and cannot be changed. They are often used to express regret or unhappiness about events in the past. The dependent (subordinate) clause (**if-clause**) contains the condition, and the main clause contains the result of this condition.
(2) If officials **had made** a connection between the Kansas cases and the soldier cases in Europe, a global pandemic **could perhaps have been prevented**. The death toll **might have been lower** if immigrants **had been** able to comprehend the warnings. If we **had printed** posters in different languages, we **might have been** able to reach the immigrant population.	Use the **past perfect** in the *if*-clause and **would / could / might + have + past participle** in the main clause. The use of *could* and *might* suggests possible outcome options. When the subordinate clause comes first in the sentence, it is followed by a comma.
(3) Many doctors later **wished** (that) they **had been** better **informed** about the connection between the different influenza occurrences. We **wish** (that) we **had printed** posters in different languages.	The other type of conditional construction uses the verb *wish*. Sentences with *wish* express a regret, sadness about, or desire for a different outcome of past situations. Use *wish* followed by a **noun clause** (*that*-clause). Use the **past perfect** in the *that*-clause. *That* can be omitted in informal uses.
(4) If scientists **had recognized** (= *but they didn't*) mutations in the past seven flu strains *years ago*, they **might be** able to catch new viruses more easily *today*. If flu viruses **were** (= *but they aren't*) easy to recognize, scientists **would** probably **have found** a vaccine by now.	In some conditionals, the forms in the *if-clause* and the main clause are different because one of the clauses refers to the past while the other refers to the present. We call these constructions **mixed conditionals**: a. the past perfect in the *if-clause* and *would / could / might* + verb in the main clause b. the simple past in the *if-clause* and *would / could / might + have* + past participle in the main clause

If-clause: past perfect tense verb *had + past participle*	Main clause: *would / could / might + have + past participle*
If the Government **had realized** the severity of the cases,	officials **would have reacted** more quickly.
If we **had printed** posters in different languages,	we **might have been** able to reach immigrants.

Main clause: *would / could / might + have + past participle*	If-clause: past perfect tense verb *had + past participle*
The death toll **might have been** lower	if immigrants **had been** able to comprehend the warnings.
Officials **would have reacted** more quickly	if the Government **had realized** the severity of the cases.

Subject	Verb (*wish*)	Noun clause with past perfect tense verb form
We	**wish**	*that* we **had printed** posters in different languages.
Many doctors	**wished**	*that* they **had been** better **informed** about the flu.

Grammar Practice

A Combine the sentences as past unreal conditionals or *wish*-clauses. Remember to express the opposite of the facts conveyed in each sentence; decide which sentence should appear as the *if*-clause.

1. Underground trains were popular. They were a breeding ground for influenza. (if)
   If underground trains had not been popular, they would not have been a breeding ground for influenza.

2. The war required a lot of manpower. Communities experienced shortages in medical personnel. (if)
   _____

3. Epidemiologists were not able to predict the impact of the disease in different areas. Citizens failed to report severe cases to their local PHSs. (if)
   _____

4. Epidemiologists didn't have good records of cases of illness and death by October 1918. (wished)
   _____

5. Many people did not avoid public transportation, through which they probably contracted influenza. (wished)
   _____

6. Scientists did not develop a flu vaccine years ago. The influenza virus does have the ability to mutate very quickly. (if)
   _____

B Read the excerpts from comments of people during the 1918 flu pandemic. Use their ideas to make sentences that express contrary-to-fact ideas in conditionals and *wish*-clauses according to the prompts.

1. "There are six people sick in one house, and they are in two beds. None of the families in this community have enough bedding to keep warm nor the clothing needed in sickness. The Red Cross women have taken charge and are using one of the homes in the community as headquarters. This house is furnished with things needed for preparing nourishment and caring for the sick. Every precaution is taken to keep the disease from spreading. Masks are worn and disinfectants are used."
   From: *News and Courier* (Charleston), letter from a resident in Cheraw, South Carolina, October 10, 1918

   If the families *had had enough bedding, the sick would not have had to share beds.*
   The Red Cross Women wished that _____.
   If precautions _____.

2. "Indications are that influenza will become epidemic here soon. Active measures are not taken. Theaters must be closed. Other crowded places need to close. All amusement places are crowded. Reports show daily increase in cases and deaths."
   From: New Orleans telegram from a PHS Officer to Surgeon General Rupert Blue

   If active measures _____.
   If theaters and picture shows _____.
   If amusement parks _____.

3. "The epidemic has resurfaced in Oak Ridge. There have been seven deaths in that township. The doctors advocate staying away from public meetings. They repeat the classic preventive measures: always use separate cups, dishes, and towels; boil all utensils before using them. People are urged to hold a handkerchief over the mouth when sneezing or coughing."
   From: *Twin City Sentinel*, North Carolina, November 22, 1918

   Doctors wished that _____.
   If utensils _____.
   Many people wished that _____.

Speaking

A Work with a partner. Discuss what you have learned about the 1918 flu pandemic in this chapter. Answer the questions and take notes. Try to use the grammar from this chapter.

1. What circumstances might have affected the progress and spread of that pandemic or the recovery process of affected people differently?
2. What do you think doctors, officials, and people wished at that time?

B Think about a time when you or someone you know became sick or had an injury. Look at the model, and then answer the questions and take notes. Then, share your ideas with the whole class. Have you and your classmates had similar experiences and / or wishes?

1. Thinking about that condition today, what circumstances might have affected the progress of that disease or the recovery process differently?
2. What did you wish at the time? What do you wish could have been different today?

> When I was a child, my grandmother became very forgetful. She couldn't remember where she had put things, and within a short time, she couldn't remember where she lived. By the time my grandmother was . . .

Listening

A BEFORE LISTENING Discuss the questions with a partner.

1. Do you think flu pandemics can be prevented? If so, how? If not, why not?
2. Why might some people become much more severely ill from the flu than others—even if they contracted the virus from the same source?

B 🎧 LISTENING FOR MAIN IDEAS Listen to a report from a radio show. The report has two parts. Indicate what each part's main focus is. Throughout the report, you will also learn about several people: Ena, Bertha, Alexa and Gertrude Grant, Dina and Sigrid Friedman, and Klaus Kessler. Decide in which part of the report each person is the main character.

Part I discusses: _____   Part II discusses: _____

_____   _____

Relevant people: _____   Relevant people: _____

_____   _____

C 🎧 THINKING CRITICALLY Listen to the report again. Discuss the questions in small groups. Then, share your answers with the whole class.

1. How old was Ena when she became ill? What is the reason she provides for not becoming as ill as her two sisters who died? Why could this reason be a likely explanation for her survival?
2. Where did the two Friedman brothers very likely come in contact with flu-infected people? Why do you think they did not, however, get sick themselves?
3. The 1918 pandemic was not the first time that the flu had broken out, but why might the 1918 cases have been so severe?
4. The flu seems to attack people with a weak immune system. Why, then, were soldiers, whom we think of as healthy young men, so vulnerable to the 1918 flu?
5. What is Dr. Kessler's idea? Why does he think that people like Ena Grant can offer clues to helping humans protect themselves against the flu? But why is this such a complicated process?

Writing

A Imagine that you are a newspaper reporter in 1918. Your assignment is to write a brief news report about one of the disease outbreaks that have been reported in different places. Choose one report from the list and brainstorm ideas about the circumstances, the timeline, and potential outcomes of the outbreak. Take notes.

A news report about:
- the ill soldiers in Europe
- the dockworkers in Boston
- citizens on the outskirts of Boston
- citizens in California

> - very ill soldiers at a military base
> - 500 men sick
> - high fever
> - muscle and joint pain
> - some developed pneumonia
> - several dead
> - officials had never seen such severe cases
> - no appropriate medication
> - officials could have asked for help sooner
> - other outbreaks might have been prevented

B Use your notes from Part A to write your report. Explain the circumstances and the timeline of the outbreak, and then describe potential outcomes and wishes. Try to use the grammar from the chapter.

> ***Mysterious Disease Outbreak in Kansas.*** On Tuesday, officials in Kansas sent a report to the local Public Health Service (PHS) about cases of severely ill soldiers at a military base. Over 500 young men had become very sick within a few days. By the time doctors reacted, the men had developed extremely high fevers. Their muscles and joints had been aching since the onset of the disease, and they had been feeling unusually fatigued. Before doctors could provide appropriate help, some patients had developed pneumonia, and several patients had died. Officials said that they had never seen such severe cases of illness. They wished they had had appropriate medication to help the patients. If doctors had known that patients might be in danger of dying, they could have called for help from the PHS sooner, and an outbreak in other areas might have been prevented.

C Share your news reports with your classmates. Vote on the best report for each group of people (soldiers, dockworkers, citizens on the outskirts of Boston, citizens in California).

Grammar Summary

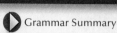

Coordinating conjunctions connect ideas in independent clauses; they connect ideas of equal importance.

Coordinating conjunctions, or FANBOYS, include: *for* [cause / reason] *and* [additional idea] *nor* [negative idea] *but* [contrast] *or* [alternative] *yet* [concession] *so* [result]	(1) Scientists were alarmed, for they had discovered a new flu virus. (2) Initial outbreaks occurred in Asia, and then they spread to Europe. (3) Scientists could not find the source, nor could they warn the public quickly. (4) People in Europe became sick, but South Americans remained healthy. (5) Citizens became sick, or they stayed healthy. (6) Citizens in North America remained healthy, yet many people panicked. (7) People's behavior is influenced by rumors, so governments may have to calm public opinion.

Adverbial time clauses and time phrases are dependent clauses that show time relationships.

Time clause subordinators are *after, before, when, while / as, since, until, as soon as / once, as / so long as,* and *whenever.* Time clauses can precede or follow main clause. Time clauses can be reduced if the subject in the main clause and the time clause is the same.	(1) Before a disease is called a pandemic, it must have spread from one continent to another. (2) Scientists work tirelessly until they find a cure. (3) As long as people travel, the spread of viruses can hardly be controlled. (4) While examining some test tubes, the scientist noticed a strange substance near the bottom. (5) When forced to visit sick patients in their homes, many doctors themselves became ill.

Past perfect and past perfect progressive describe actions or events that occurred before another action or event in the past.

The past perfect form is *had* + past participle; the past perfect progressive form is *had + been* + verb *-ing*. The progressive emphasizes duration. Past perfect sentences often occur with time references that clarify the sequence of events. The past perfect tends to be used in writing more than in speech.	(1) The virus had mutated before a vaccine could be found. (2) After the H1N1 virus had been spreading for months in 2009, it finally subsided in early 2010. (3) When people returned from overseas flights, they had often been exposed to H1N1 on airplanes. (4) By the time people realized that they were sick, they had often already developed pneumonia.

Past unreal conditionals (or contrary-to-fact conditionals) describe past untrue or impossible conditions and outcomes.

Past unreal conditionals are formed with past perfect in the *if-clause* (condition) and *would / could / might + have* + past participle (result) in the main clause. Their order can be reversed. The meaning is regret, unhappiness, or sadness. In contrary-to-fact wishes, *wish* is followed by a noun clause that contains the past perfect and expresses a wish for a different outcome of an event in the past.	(1) If travelers in 2009 had known about the dangers of getting the H1N1 virus during air travel, they might have canceled many of their flights. (2) Health officials would have warned travelers if they had known about the extent of the problem. (3) In 2009, many travelers wished (that) they had received better information and warnings about the dangers of H1N1. (4) Doctors wished that even patients with mild symptoms had come to see them.

Self-Assessment

A (6 points) Complete the paragraph with the coordinating conjunctions from the list below. Use each conjunction only once.

for   and   nor   but   or   yet   so

Small children with runny noses and dirty hands are said to be responsible for spreading sickness, **1.** _____ teens and young adults may be the main drivers of seasonal and pandemic flu. School-age children tend to have more close contact with a greater number of peers than very young children, **2.** _____ young adults are socially active. Very young kids may not be the main flu spreaders, **3.** _____ they are not as mobile, **4.** _____ do they congregate in as large a group as middle and high schoolers do. Many outbreaks start in schools, **5.** _____ the next place outbreaks are seen are in homes and families. To stop the spread of the virus, schoolchildren must be vaccinated early every fall, **6.** _____ the flu might not be slowed down.

B (4 points) Circle the correct time subordinators to complete the sentences.

1. Before / Since arriving on campus, many university students don't understand how serious an attack of the flu can be.

2. Until / Once students come down with the flu, they can be ill for up to two weeks.

3. While / After recovering, they may miss several classes and get behind in their work.

4. When / As seriously ill students are out for long periods of time, they also face the financial burden of missed classes that they paid for.

C (5 points) Complete the paragraph with the past perfect, past perfect progressive, or simple past form of the verbs in parentheses.

1. After we _____ (arrive) in England, my colleague _____ (begin) complaining about not feeling well, but despite her illness, we _____ (be) able to give a presentation at a conference. **2.** However, before we _____ (continue) the trip to Germany, I _____ (develop) severe joint pain. **3.** I _____ (feel) extremely fatigued, unable to enjoy the rest of the trip. **4.** After we _____ (return) home, I finally _____ (consult) my doctor because my symptoms _____ (get) so bad that I _____ (can, barely, stand). **5.** The doctor _____ (explain) that I _____ (develop) pneumonia, the last stage in swine flu, which _____ (sweep) countries across the globe in 2009.

D (5 points) Combine the sentences using past unreal conditionals and *wish*-clauses.

1. My colleague's symptoms were not recognized as swine flu symptoms. I didn't take my own joint pain and sleeplessness more seriously.

_____

2. Both my colleague and I wished something. We didn't have better information about swine flu.

_____

3. We didn't interpret my symptoms as swine flu. I didn't see a doctor and developed pneumonia.

_____

4. I wish something. I wasn't aware of the potential dangers of airplane travel at that time.

_____

5. We didn't realize that airplanes were a breeding ground for swine flu. We didn't cancel our trip.

_____

Unit Project: Public service advertisement

A **A** A public service advertisement (PSA) is a type of advertisement that appears on TV, radio, or in print. Its focus is on raising awareness and educating people about specific issues, such as health and safety. In this activity you will design a PSA on a current health issue. Follow the steps.

1. Work in teams of three students. Brainstorm on a health issue that you feel your classmates or community members should know more about (asthma, obesity, the flu, insomnia, etc.). Each team should select a different issue.

2. Decide on your PSA's main focus. This will guide the rest of your PSA. For example, if your selected health issue is asthma, you may want to focus only on the relationship between asthma and smoking or on asthma effects on children, but not both.

3. Create a "hook" (an interest device) to get your audience to pay attention. This could be a catchy phrase, a surprising fact, or statistic.

4. Decide what information you would like to share with your audience. You can define the problem or issue and length of time it has persisted by referring to statistics and dates and using causes and effects. You can also explain wishes and / or contrary-to-fact ideas from the point of view of those affected by the problem or issue.

5. Discuss what advice you will give your audience.

6. Decide what sound effects you will use in your PSA.

7. Write your PSA script. Make sure your PSA is no longer than 60 seconds.

8. Design a mini-poster for your PSA. Create an interesting visual (photo, drawing, etc.) accompanied by a catchy message line (this could be your message from step 5).

9. Present your PSA and poster to the class or record your PSA at home and play it for the class. For example:

By 2010, almost 300 million people worldwide had been diagnosed with asthma. In the United States alone, over 20 million people suffer from asthma, and almost 50 percent of them are smokers. (sound effect: person coughing) Until the number of smokers is reduced, the disease rate will continue to climb. Almost all asthma-suffering smokers wish they hadn't started smoking. If they had avoided the irritation of their lungs from cigarette smoke, they wouldn't have developed the breathing problems that they have now. When you choose a short-term solution, you avoid a long-term problem. Before picking up that cigarette, remember: stop smoking and start breathing!

B **B** Discuss the PSAs with your classmates. Follow the steps.

1. Discuss each PSA in terms of effectiveness of the oral portion and effectiveness of the poster. Would the message and poster have an impact on you? Why or why not? What could be improved?

2. Revise the scripts and poster and, if possible, present your PSAs in your school or community.

MyEnglishLab

▶ Unit Test

MyEnglishLab

▶ Search it!

Eradicating Poverty

OUTCOMES

After completing this unit, I will be able to use these grammar points.

CHAPTER 13

Grammar Focus 1
Connecting structures of cause / reason

Grammar Focus 2
Conjunctive adverbs of effect

CHAPTER 14

Grammar Focus 1
Articles

Grammar Focus 2
Parallel structures

My**English**Lab

 What do you know?

CHAPTER 13 Empowering Women

Getting Started

A Think about poverty around the world or in your country or region. Consider the impact of poverty on different segments of society. Discuss the questions in small groups.

1. How do poverty issues affect different age groups?
2. How does gender play a role in poverty?

B Read the statements about poverty. Some are based on fact, and others are misconceptions about the causes and effects of poverty. Write *T* next to the statements you believe are true and *F* next to those that may be popular beliefs but that are not based on research.

_____ 1. Men are the most affected by poverty since they are traditionally the main wage earners in families.

_____ 2. Poverty is a very complicated and widespread problem. Therefore, it is too big to address. Sufficient resources to eradicate poverty simply do not exist.

_____ 3. As we have poverty issues in our own country, we shouldn't be addressing global poverty.

_____ 4. Households in the developing world rely on the unpaid work of female members because girls and women provide the domestic labor needed for poor families to survive.

_____ 5. From local to national levels, corruption is widespread in poor counties; consequently, poverty eradication programs don't work as they are intended.

_____ 6. Due to traditional gender roles, most agricultural labor in developing nations is done by men, who also produce most of the food.

_____ 7. Poverty has become a global problem as a result of overpopulation. If people reduced the number of children they have, they could get out of poverty.

_____ 8. Gender inequality is a major fundamental cause of global poverty. Thus, aid and development programs must work to address basic rights, financial resources, health care, and education for women.

C Look back at Part B. Complete the tasks.

1. Underline **dependent (subordinate) clauses with connectors** that show cause or reason.
2. Circle **phrases with connectors** that show cause or reason.
3. Double-underline **independent clauses and their connectors (conjunctive adverbs)** that show result or effect.
4. Complete the chart with examples. Then, compare your chart with a partner's chart.

Subordinating conjunctions of cause / reason	Phrasal prepositions of cause / reason	Conjunctive adverbs of result / effect

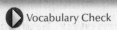
Reading

A WARM-UP With a partner, discuss how the words and phrases in the list are connected to the issue of global poverty and the role of gender. Then, share your ideas with the class.

control of assets	eradicate	hygiene	microfinance	nutrition
empower	food security	maternal health	mortality rates	vocational training

B SKIMMING Skim Part I of the article to identify three ways women are especially impacted by global poverty. Then, read the whole article.

Empowering Women to Eradicate Poverty

I. How are women impacted by poverty?

- Women bear a disproportionate burden of the world's poverty. In some estimates, women represent 70 percent of the world's poor. Statistics also show that women are more likely than men to be poor and at risk of hunger because of the regular discrimination they face in education, health care, employment, and control of assets.

- As a consequence of their status, many women are left without basic rights, such as access to clean water, sanitation, medical care, and decent employment.

- As a result of poverty and cultural norms, many women have little protection from domestic abuse or violence stemming from war, and they have no role in decision making.

- Women are usually paid less for their work. They also face discrimination when applying for credit for business, farming, or self-employment; consequently, they are forced to take unsafe and low-wage work.

- Women comprise the majority of small-scale farmers. As a result, they play a crucial role in food security and labor for post-harvest work.

- Because poor maternal health reduces women's capacity to work and generate income, communities that count on their contributions to household income and childcare experience the greatest setbacks in overcoming poverty.

- Global financial crises affect women particularly severely. Since many women in developing countries work in export-led factories or as migrant workers in service industries, they suffer greater job losses during economic downturns. However, in many countries the impact goes far beyond the loss of formal jobs, as women tend to do domestic work in cities.

II. How can empowering women help eradicate poverty?

- Women and girls in developing regions are often responsible for the time-consuming task of obtaining water. They are also in charge of caring for sick family members, raising children, and taking responsibility for household nutrition and hygiene. Various programs around the world provide access to clean water supplies. As a result, women increase the time they spend earning income, and girls are more likely to attend school. Additionally, family health and hygiene are improved.

- When women receive extra income, they tend to spend it on food and education first. Accordingly, programs that provide access to microfinance give women the chance to run their own businesses or farms. As a result, women have a direct role in overcoming poverty and discrimination.

- Basic education and vocational programs for women are especially effective since women often share their knowledge with others in the community.

- Women who are educated tend to have greater access to health care and are more likely to have fewer and healthier children. Therefore, programs that ensure women's access to health care and information can help reduce infant and maternal mortality rates.

C UNDERSTANDING DETAILS Read the article again. Identify at least three positive outcomes of aid programs for women. Share your ideas in small groups.

MyEnglishLab

▶ Reading Comprehension

Grammar Focus 1 Connecting structures of cause / reason

Examples	Language notes
(1) Women are the most affected by poverty **since** they are the primary caretakers in the family. **As a result of** their responsibilities, women benefit from aid programs differently than men.	Use connecting structures to express **cause of** or **reason for** something. The two types of cause / reason connectors are **subordinating conjunctions** and **phrasal prepositions**. (See Unit 3.)
(2) **Because** women in poor regions mainly work in manufacturing and service sectors, they suffer greater job losses in economic downturns. Basic education and vocational programs for women are effective **since** women often share their knowledge with others in the community.	**Subordinating conjunctions** connect dependent (subordinate) and independent (main) clauses. The dependent clause expresses the cause / reason while the independent clause shows the effect / result. If the dependent clause comes first in the sentence, it is followed by a comma. Subordinating conjunctions of cause / reason include *because, since,* and *as.* When *since* and *as* are used to express cause / reason, they do not show time relationships.
(3) Poor women have greater health issues **due to** a lack of access to health care. **As a consequence of** their status, many women are left without basic rights.	Some **phrasal prepositions** can also express cause / reason. They connect ideas to an independent clause and are followed by a noun or noun phrase. If phrasal prepositions begin a sentence, they are separated from the main clause by a comma. Examples include *as a result of, because of, due to,* and *as a consequence of*.
(4) *Incorrect:* **Due to** they contribute greatly to rural food production, women need more support for farming. **Due to** their great contribution to rural food production, women need more support for farming.	Phrasal prepositions cannot be followed by an independent clause.
	There are differing degrees of formality in these connecting structures. ***Because, since, as, because of, due to,*** and ***as a result of*** are used in both speaking and writing. ***As a consequence of*** is used mainly in writing. ***Because*** and ***since*** are most commonly used in informal conversation.

Independent clause	Subordinating conjunction	Dependent clause
Women are the most affected by poverty	**since** **because** **as**	they are the primary caretakers.

Subordinating conjunction	Dependent clause	Independent clause
Since **Because** **As**	women are often left out of leadership roles,	they are less able to affect change.

	Noun or noun phrase	Independent clause
As a result of **Due to** **As a consequence of**	clean water programs,	women can spend more time earning income.

Independent clause	Phrasal prepositions	Noun or noun phrase
Girls are more vulnerable to poverty	**as a result of** **due to** **as a consequence of**	early marriage.

Grammar Practice

A Circle the correct connecting structures.

Microfinance programs that target women in developing countries can be tools for fighting poverty. **1. As a result of / Because** women use income primarily to improve conditions for their families, microcredit programs for women with small businesses have been quite successful. Furthermore, by ensuring women participate at all levels of financial service programs, the benefits are even greater **2. because of / as** they earn the respect of the community. **3. As a consequence of / Thus,** their ability to plan more for the future, women participating in microfinance programs can help move their families beyond day-to-day survival. **4. Due to / Accordingly,** entire communities can gain from these credit programs.

B Read the pairs of sentences. Identify the pairs that clearly show a cause and an effect. Combine these sentences using a connector from the list. Depending on the type of connector you use, you may have to make changes to the dependent clause.

Subordinating conjunctions: as, because, since
Phrasal prepositions: as a consequence of, as a result of, because of, due to

1. Some nations in Sub-Saharan Africa have abolished school fees. / More children have access to primary education.

   _____

   _____

2. An increasing number of young girls and women are receiving an education in developing regions. / More communities are experiencing less poverty and improved living conditions.

   _____

   _____

3. Increasing the presence of women in national and local governments gives them a voice in decision making. / Their participation in government also facilitates their inclusion in the economic sphere.

   _____

   _____

4. Research shows that women are better able to improve their lives when they own land and other assets, such as livestock or small farm equipment. / They can use those assets to earn an income and access credit.

   _____

   _____

5. In some regions, rising land value, population growth, and confusion over land laws have increased conflicts. / Women are less likely to obtain access to farmland in those areas.

   _____

   _____

6. Women in developing countries comprise the vast majority of workers in the manufacturing sector. / Companies that initiate training and support programs not only improve the lives of their employees, but they also benefit from their increased skills.

   _____

   _____

Grammar Focus 2 Conjunctive adverbs of effect

Examples	Language notes
(1) Women who are educated tend to have greater access to health care and are more likely to have fewer and healthier children. **Therefore,** programs that ensure women's access to health care and information can help reduce infant and maternal mortality rates.	Use **conjunctive adverbs** (also known as transitions or sentence connectors) to connect ideas between sentences. Conjunctive adverbs can show an **effect** or **result** in a clause when you connect it with another clause that shows a **cause** or **reason**. (See Unit 3.) Conjunctive adverbs of effect include: *therefore, consequently, as a consequence, thus, as a result, hence,* and *accordingly.*
(2) Women comprise the majority of small-scale farmers. **As a result,** they play a crucial role in food security and labor. Women make up the majority of small-scale farmers. They, **therefore,** play a crucial role in food security and labor. *Incorrect:* They also face discrimination when applying for credit, **consequently,** they are forced to take unsafe, low-wage work. They also face discrimination when applying for credit; **consequently,** they are forced to take unsafe, low-wage work.	Conjunctive adverbs connect independent clauses, so they are preceded by a period or semicolon and followed by a comma. While it is less common, they can be placed after the subject of the sentence between commas. Conjunctive adverbs cannot be preceded by a comma. This is referred to as a **comma splice error.** There are differing degrees of formality in these connectors. *As a result* is used in both speaking and writing, but ***therefore, consequently, as a consequence, accordingly, thus,*** and ***hence*** are used mainly in writing. ***Thus*** and ***hence*** are the most formal and are used less commonly.

Independent clause	Conjunctive adverb	Independent clause
Women are key stakeholders in economic growth.	**Consequently,**	they merit greater consideration in development programs.
Funding for major budgets often excludes those with the greatest needs.	**As a result,**	programs that target small projects can be more effective.
Women make up the majority of small-scale farmers.	**Therefore,**	they play a crucial role in food security and labor for post-harvest activities.
Girls in poor families are typically needed to collect water and fuel for cooking;	**thus,**	they are forced to leave school at an early age.
Women often face discrimination when applying for credit;	**hence,**	they are often concentrated in insecure, unsafe, and low-wage work.
Women spend more of their income on family food and education;	**accordingly,**	more microfinance opportunities need to be open to them.
Girls and young women who drop out of school are less likely to find work.	**As a consequence,**	developing countries lose billions of dollars in unemployment costs.

Grammar Practice

A Read the passage about Dr. Yacoobi. Correct the five errors in the use of sentence connectors, including punctuation.

Dr. Sakena Yacoobi is founder and executive director of Afghan Institute of Learning (AIL). As an advocate for empowering poor women and children in her native country, her goal is to provide them access to education and health services designed and run by Afghan women. Dr. Yacoobi works in partnership with community leaders in villages in eight provinces and the refugee camps in Pakistan to share the effort needed to establish and maintain the health clinics and learning centers. As a consequence of her program has been successful.

Dr. Yacoobi was born in Herat, Afghanistan, and came to the United States at age 16. When she traveled to the Afghan refugee camps in Pakistan in 1992, she saw that the women were depressed and desperate, but she knew that they were strong. Because of they were uneducated and unhealthy, Dr. Yacoobi understood that they were not able to think of different ways to solve their problems.

In many villages, there aren't any public schools, therefore, AIL's centers operate as regular schools, teaching students through methods that promote critical thinking. Many adults struggle with illiteracy and a lack of job skills, thus the centers offer basic education, health education, and training in a variety of vocational skills. AIL has also developed programs on topics such as democracy, human rights, and leadership for both young Afghans and adults. Dr. Yacoobi has said that the programs and services offered by AIL work because of there is trust.

B Read the descriptions of two aid and development programs. Use the information to write sentences showing cause and effect relationships. You may select details directly from the description or draw your own conclusions. Use a conjunctive adverb of effect.

	Activities and programs	Results
(RED)	• works with brands like Apple, Nike, Starbucks, and The Gap, which donate up to 50% of each sale of selected products to (RED) • gives 100% of donations to The Global Fund, which gives direct aid to people with HIV/AIDS in Africa • has high-profile celebrity supporters	• since 2006, has brought over $170 million to The Global Fund and has helped over 7.5 million victims of HIV/AIDS • gives customers a chance to donate through their purchases and to become repeat customers of (RED) products
Women for Women (WFW)	• provides direct support to survivors of war and conflict in eight countries • uses a year-long program of direct aid • supports education, job training, and small business development	• has helped nearly 300,000 women become self-sufficient • over 250,000 men and women in 130 countries have worked with WFW

(RED):

1. _____

2. _____

WFW:

3. _____

4. _____

(RED) and WFW:

5. _____

Listening

A BEFORE LISTENING You will listen to an excerpt from a speech by the head of an international aid organization on the efforts of famous women to help eradicate poverty. Write any information you know about the philanthropic, or charitable, activities of these women below. Then, share your answers in small groups.

1. Angelina Jolie, actress _____

2. Rania Al Abdullah, Queen Consort of Jordan _____

3. Oprah Winfrey, media mogul and actress _____

4. Nicole Kidman, actress _____

B 🎧 UNDERSTANDING MAIN IDEAS Listen to the speech. In the middle column of the chart, note which organization or project each woman has been involved with.

Celebrity	Charitable organization and / or projects	Impacts of charitable activities
Angelina Jolie		
Rania Al Abdullah		
Oprah Winfrey		
Nicole Kidman		

C 🎧 UNDERSTANDING DETAILS Listen again. In the last column, note specific effects of the programs and activities each woman is involved with. Then, compare your notes to your predictions in Part A.

Speaking

A You and your partner will create a cause and effect visual aid for a presentation. Your topic is an approach to eradicating poverty that provides support to girls or young women. Follow the steps.

1. Topic: _____ Country or region: _____

2. Decide on an approach to eradicating poverty. (Examples: *education / retention in school, targeted health care, vocational training*)

3. Identify and describe the issues (causes) to be addressed.

4. Describe the methods of addressing the issues and describe the outcomes (effects).

5. Make your visual aid on paper or create a presentation slide(s) on a computer.

B Work with another pair of students and present your visual aid to each other. Look at the model. Try to use the grammar from the chapter in your presentation.

> *In our poster, you can see that we have focused on Sub-Saharan Africa. Because we think that providing education past primary school is essential, we think schools need help in creating programs that are sensitive to adolescent girls' needs. These programs also need to take their families' needs into account. Also, . . .*

Writing

MyEnglishLab

Linking Grammar to Writing

A Work with a partner. You will develop a pamphlet about a non-profit organization that focuses on eradicating poverty by helping a particular segment of the population in need in your own country or a country you select. This organization should be of your own creation. Brainstorm ideas on three different areas of need and programs the organization has undertaken. Use the chart as a guide.

Name of organization: _____

Areas of need: 1. _____ 2. _____ 3. _____

	Program 1	Program 2	Program 3
Program activities:			
Results / Outcomes:			

B Create a pamphlet about your non-profit organization. Use your notes from Part A. Try to use the grammar from the chapter.

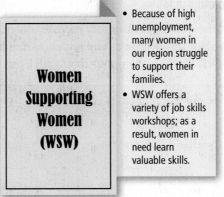

Women Supporting Women (WSW)

- Because of high unemployment, many women in our region struggle to support their families.
- WSW offers a variety of job skills workshops; as a result, women in need learn valuable skills.

C Post your pamphlets around the room. Which description has the most effective projects and outcomes? Why?

MyEnglishLab

Diagnostic Test

CHAPTER 14 Fair Trade

Getting Started

A Discuss the questions in small groups.

1. Do you drink coffee or tea? Do you eat chocolate, bananas, or pineapples? Do you care about where these products come from? Why or why not?
2. Do you care about product quality? How can you determine the quality of a product?

B Look at the two diagrams. The first one illustrates an Equal Exchange Coffee Chain, and the second one illustrates a Conventional Coffee Chain. Note the differences. Then, read the statements. Decide which coffee chain each statement describes. Write *EECC* or *CCC*.

_____ 1. The path from a small farmer to the consumer is both long and complex.

_____ 2. Farmers join groups of like-minded farmers and eliminate middlemen.

_____ 3. A partnership with small-scale farmers not only provides more money but also offers more agricultural support.

_____ 4. Consumers and producers in the coffee chain are neither connected nor do they know much about each other.

_____ 5. By the time the owners of coffee farms in countries like Ghana receive payment, the largest portion of the money has already been paid to intermediaries and middlemen.

_____ 6. The consumer is more aware of the product's origin when the supply chain is simple than when the supply chain is complex.

C Look back at Part B. Complete the tasks.

1. Circle all **articles** and the **nouns / noun phrases** they precede; also note **zero (Ø) articles**.
2. Underline all **groups of words, phrases, clauses, and sentences that have the same or parallel structure**.
3. Fill in the chart with examples. Then, compare your chart with a partner's chart.

	Articles and nouns / noun phrases	Parallel structures
a / an		
the		
Ø		

Reading

A WARM-UP Discuss the questions with a partner.

1. What is the difference between gourmet products and other products?

2. What is the process of cocoa bean harvesting? Who does the harvesting?

3. What do you know about fair trade and fair-trade products?

B SKIMMING Skim the article to find out what fair trade is and how it helps reduce poverty. Then, read the whole article.

FAIR-TRADE CHOCOLATE

The truth about how most cocoa beans are grown, harvested, and sold can make eating chocolates a guilty pleasure: 70 percent of the world's cocoa (the main ingredient in chocolate) comes from small farms in West Africa, most notably the Ivory Coast and Ghana. Family farms scrape by on about $100 per year. Children, working alongside their parents, neither attend school nor have any leisure. Many children are enslaved and work in dangerous and horrendous conditions, clearing fields with machetes and applying pesticides with their bare hands.

Today, thanks to a coalition of international nongovernmental organizations, the lives of cocoa farmers are improving. The improvements are financed through the sale of fair-trade chocolate, which has the potential of both easing the burden of the farmers and lifting them out of poverty. These chocolate products contain a higher percentage of cocoa than those of their traditional rivals. That's why the chocolate tastes richer and why it costs more than regular chocolate. Moreover, participating farmers keep a greater share of the profits than they would under non-fair-trade arrangements. The profits help improve labor conditions, build schools, and install sanitation systems. But most importantly, the chocolate is made from cocoa beans that come from farms where children are not enslaved or exposed to hazardous substances.

Behind the efforts are the groups that make up the growing fair-trade movement: humanitarian organizations, farmers' co-ops, and chocolate producers. Although the movement has existed for more than 40 years, and although fair-trade products have been available for decades, fair-trade chocolate products didn't exist until 2000, when Equal Exchange, a small company in Massachusetts, began to sell a fair-trade hot cocoa mix. The product was successful, and in 2004, the company introduced three chocolate bars. The basic idea of fair trade is for companies to buy not from a single farmer but from farming cooperatives (co-ops) so that the farmers, banding together, can charge a higher price for their product. Unless they organize and decide how to divide up the profits through democratic means, they have no bargaining power. But as a co-op, they are able to fund schools and clinics or hire specialists in sustainable agriculture.

As awareness of the plight of cocoa farmers and as the quality of fair-trade chocolate have grown, demand has increased. Responding to consumers' demands, bigger companies, such as Starbucks and Proctor & Gamble, are beginning to support fair-trade products. Now consumers can see from the label on the chocolate product that the cocoa came from a farm co-op that has been inspected to determine that the farmers have the freedom to form unions, that there's no slave labor, and that certain health and safety precautions are taken.

C UNDERSTANDING DETAILS On a separate piece of paper, complete the sentences with logical ideas (either explicit or inferred) from the text.

1. Because of the high level of poverty, parents _____ and _____.

2. Some international groups have found a way that _____ and _____.

3. Money earned from fair-trade sales can be used for _____, _____, and _____.

4. Three identifying factors of fair-trade products are _____, _____, and _____.

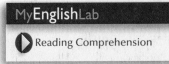

Grammar Focus 1 Articles

Examples	Language notes
(1) Thanks to **a** coalition of Ø international nongovernmental organizations, **the** lives of Ø cocoa farmers are improving.	We use **articles** before nouns or noun phrases to identify a specific or non-specific reference made by the noun.
(2) As **a** co-op, farmers are able to fund schools. Fair-trade chocolate has **a** rich flavor. The company began to sell **a** hot cocoa mix.	Use the indefinite article **a / an** with **non-specific countable, singular nouns**. We usually see it the first time a noun is mentioned, and neither the speaker nor the hearer has a specific noun in mind.
(3) Farmers keep **a share of the profits**. Fair-trade chocolate contains **a higher percentage of cocoa** than that of its rivals.	Use **a / an** when a part of a larger whole is first mentioned.
(4) **The** chocolate industry is beginning to be behind **the** fair-trade movement. Children are sold into slavery. **The** children work under horrendous conditions. **The** company began to sell **a** hot cocoa mix. **The** product was successful. **The** lives of cocoa farmers are improving. **The** improvements are financed through **the** sales of fair-trade chocolate. Awareness of **the plight of cocoa farmers** has grown. Fair-trade chocolate has a richer flavor than **the products (that are) sold by most competitors**.	Use the definite article **the** with **specific countable singular and plural nouns** and with **specific noncountable nouns.** We usually see it with nouns that are known to both speaker and hearer, usually the second time the noun is mentioned (either as the same noun or a synonym). A noun may also be identified by **a phrase or clause** that comes after the noun.
(5) Cocoa comes from **the** Ivory Coast. The Ivory Coast's southern border is along **the** Gulf of Guinea on **the** Atlantic Ocean. **The** best chocolate is fair-trade chocolate. **The** first fair-trade chocolate was sold in 2000. Cocoa is **the** main ingredient in chocolate.	The definite article **the** is also used with: • the names of certain countries • the names of certain geographical features • superlatives and ordinals • unique references.
(6) **The** consumer determines if fair-trade products become successful.	**The** can be used to refer to all members of a category in a generic, or general, sense.
(7) Ø Fair trade can help Ø farmers out of Ø poverty. Ø Children clear Ø fields with Ø machetes and apply Ø pesticides with their bare hands. Ø Cocoa comes from Ø farms in Ø West Africa, most notably Ø Ghana. Ø Starbucks and Ø Procter & Gamble are making an effort and are supporting Ø fair-trade products.	Do **not** use articles with noncount nouns and non-specific, general plural nouns. These "zero articles" (Ø) do not refer to a specific quantity or amount. Do **not** use articles with continents and most countries, as well as with some proper nouns, such as companies.
(8) Families get by on $100 **per year**. Children don't **attend school**. Fair-trade products have been available **for decades**. All the players are **in place**. The remaining companies will get **on board**. Fair-trade stores are open **in the morning** and **in the afternoon;** one is even open **at night**.	In certain phrases, article use is not predictable.

	a / an	*Ø*	*the*
Singular count noun	**a** cocoa bean **a** co-op **an** effort	———	**the** cocoa beans **the** co-op **the** effort
(Singular) Noncount noun	———	cocoa chocolate	**the** cocoa **the** chocolate
Plural noun	———	cocoa beans co-ops efforts	**the** cocoa beans **the** co-ops **the** efforts

Grammar Practice

A Circle the correct article or "zero article" to complete the paragraph.

Until about **1.** a / the / Ø 20th century, there were **2.** a / the / Ø small numbers of **3.** a / the / Ø cocoa plantations owned by **4.** a / the / Ø native farmers in **5.** a / the / Ø West African region. **6.** A / The / Ø farmers concentrated largely on growing **7.** a / the / Ø coffee. Most of **8.** a / the / Ø cocoa plantations belonged to and were run by **9.** a / the / Ø European settlers. But when **10.** a / the / Ø price for **11.** a / the / Ø cocoa beans went up, **12.** a / the / Ø West African farmers started to focus on growing **13.** a / the / Ø cocoa beans instead of **14.** a / the / Ø coffee, and within **15.** a / the / Ø short time, **16.** a / the / Ø farmers' main export became **17.** a / the / Ø cocoa. As **18.** a / the / Ø cocoa growing industry in **19.** a / the / Ø West Africa grew, **20.** a / the / Ø region attracted **21.** a / the / Ø more and more workers from **22.** an / the / Ø other regions. In fact, due to **23.** a / the / Ø availability of **24.** a / the / Ø jobs on **25.** a / the / Ø cocoa plantations, **26.** a / the / Ø families sent their children to work there. **27.** A / The / Ø children's work represented, and still represents, **28.** a / the / Ø large source of **29.** a / the / Ø income for **30.** a / the / Ø families who live in **31.** a / the / Ø poverty.

B Complete the paragraph with the correct articles. If an article is not necessary, write a "zero article" (Ø).

1. In _____ West African countries, it is common that _____ children work on _____ cocoa farms, or _____ coffee farm, or even in _____ mines, where they dig for _____ gold. **2.** Sometimes, _____ children's parents send them away to work on _____ farm or in _____ mine so that _____ children can help them with _____ little money that they earn. **3.** At other times, _____ children may be promised _____ material goods, such as _____ bicycle, for their labor. **4.** However, _____ children work under _____ dangerous and appalling conditions. **5.** They have to work _____ long hours; they have to carry _____ heavy bags of _____ cocoa or _____ coffee beans; they don't get _____ nutritious food; and they have to sleep in _____ wooden huts on _____ dirty floor. **6.** If _____ child does not work fast enough or doesn't carry enough _____ bags of _____ cocoa beans, he or she is often punished and beaten. **7.** In _____ gold mines, _____ child workers are preferred because they are small enough to crawl into _____ narrow shafts and pathways in _____ ground, and they aren't too tall for _____ caves in which they have to dig for _____ gold. **8.** However, _____ mines are not well constructed, and there is always _____ danger that _____ ceiling or _____ walls of _____ mines cave in and bury _____ children. **9.** It is difficult for _____ children to escape and return to their parents because someone watches _____ children all _____ time and locks _____ doors to _____ huts at _____ night. **10.** There are _____ organizations that are working to create _____ awareness of _____ child labor and _____ terrible conditions under which _____ children live and work. **11.** There are also _____ efforts among _____ humanitarian groups to stop _____ child labor, especially in _____ countries such as _____ Mali, _____ Ivory Coast, and _____ Ghana.

Grammar Focus 2 Parallel structures

Examples	Language notes
(1) Fair-trade products include **cocoa, coffee, and chocolate**. Fair-trade items include **not only** food products **but also** arts and crafts. Many people are aware of **neither** fair-trade food products **nor** fair-trade crafts items.	**Parallel structures** consist of **items in a series in the same grammatical form**. This structure shows that ideas or concepts in a series are of equal importance. Parallelism is typical of writing as it makes ideas balanced and coherent. Parallel structures are typically connected by **coordinating conjunctions** (*and, or*) or **correlative conjunctions** (*not only . . . but also, not . . . but, either . . . or, neither . . . nor*). We see parallel structures at the word, phrase, or clause / sentence level.
(2) Children work in **dangerous and horrendous** conditions. [2 adjectives] Companies buy **not from a single farmer but from farming co-ops**. [2 nouns]	At the **word level,** the same part of speech is repeated.
(3) The sales have the potential of **both easing the burden of the farmers and lifting them out of poverty**. [2 gerund phrases] Children **neither attend school nor have any leisure**. [2 verb phrases]	At the **phrase level,** the same grammatical group of words is repeated.
(4) Consumers can see **that farmers have the freedom to form unions, that there's no slave labor, and that certain health and safety precautions are taken.** [3 noun clauses] Fair-trade chocolate comes from farms **where children are not enslaved and where children are not exposed to hazardous substances**. [2 adjective clauses]	At the **clause level,** the same type of clause is repeated.
(5) Fair-trade chocolate **products** contain a <u>higher</u> percentage of cocoa <u>than</u> **those** of rival companies. *Incorrect:* Fair-trade chocolate **products** contain a <u>higher</u> percentage of cocoa <u>than</u> rival companies. (*illogical: Cocoa is in products, not in rival companies.*) That's why the **chocolate** tastes <u>richer</u> and why it costs <u>more than</u> **regular chocolate**. *Incorrect:* That's why the **chocolate** tastes <u>richer</u> and why it costs <u>more</u>. (*richer / more than what?*) Participating **farmers** keep a <u>greater</u> share of the profits <u>than</u> **they would** under non-fair-trade arrangements. *Incorrect:* Participating **farmers** keep a <u>greater</u> share of the profits <u>than</u> under non-fair-trade arrangements. (*they or others?*)	Parallelism is also used in **comparisons** (*-er / more / less . . . than, as . . . as*). Comparisons should be complete, clear, and between similar points. This means that all comparison words must be repeated so that the comparison is a logical comparison between related items. Additionally, the comparison must be explicit and not left up to the reader to guess.

Parallelism Level		Pattern 1	Pattern 2	Pattern 3
Word	Cocoa beans are	grown,	harvested,	**and** sold.
Phrase	Children	**neither** attend school	**nor** have any leisure.	
Clause	Consumers can see	that farmers are free to form co-ops,	that there's no slave labor,	**and** that certain health precautions are taken.

Grammar Practice

 A Complete the paragraph with appropriate words, phrases, or clauses from the list. Be sure the items are in parallel structure.

> **a.** although all its cocoa is of high quality
> **b.** encouraging young people to be the proactive consumers of the future
> **c.** 100 percent fair-trade chocolate companies can afford to do
> **d.** fiercely
> **e.** funding community projects through the fair-trade premium generated from fair trade
> **f.** if people show that they will buy it
> **g.** ~~to represent the interests of cocoa farmers~~
> **h.** that fair-trade markets are still relatively small
> **i.** their motto, "Pa Pa Pea," means "best of the best" in Twi
> **j.** what they have been able to sell so far

Kuapa Kokoo is a fair-trade co-op, an association of more than 45,000 cocoa farmers in Ghana. It was set up in 1998 to develop fairer trading practices and **1.** __g__. Kuapa Kokoo means "good cocoa farmer" in the Twi language of Ghana, and **2.** _____. Kuapa Kokoo is able to improve the lives of its members by ensuring reliable and prompt payment, providing training, a credit loan scheme, and access to market information, as well as **3.** _____. Although all its cocoa is certified fair trade, and **4.** _____, Kuapa Kokoo is able to sell only about ten percent of its cocoa to the fair-trade market. The reason is that Kuapa Kokoo is a large co-op, producing one percent of the world's cocoa output, and **5.** _____. The chocolate market is ferociously and **6.** _____ competitive. A few big chocolate companies are able to spend a lot more money on promoting their brands than **7.** _____. More shops will stock fair-trade chocolate not only if people say they like it but also **8.** _____. The Kuapa Kokoo resources are all about educating the next generation about fair trade and **9.** _____. By putting their understanding into action, they can create more demand for fair trade, so that Kuapa Kokoo and other small-scale producers can sell more of their produce on fair terms than **10.** _____.

 B Read the paragraph. On a separate sheet of paper, rewrite the paragraph revising the underlined parts to show parallel structures.

relatively recent and fairly new development

Use of fair-trade labels is a **1.** relatively recent development and a fairly new one. They didn't exist until 1989, when coffee became the first product to carry a fair-trade logo. Within 10 years, 17 different labeling organizations, each with its own **2.** logo and being symbolic, had sprung up and they gained recognition. In 1997, the organizations joined to form Fairtrade Labelling Organizations International (FLO), **3.** which works with 45 countries and overseeing product labeling efforts. The use of different labels can be **4.** confusing and it is puzzling, but this should become less so because the different organizations have settled on **5.** one European label and they also have one U.S. label.

Today, even **6.** the biggest and successful chocolate-producing companies in the world acknowledge that farmers in cocoa-growing countries need **7.** more financial help and more technological support. Formed in 2000 and responsible for **8.** both economic and social development and education in ecology in cocoa-growing communities, the World Cocoa Foundation (WCF) includes among its members such big companies as **9.** Nestlé, Hershey Foods, and there is also Mars, as well as **10.** Ghirardelli, Godiva company, and Starbucks coffee. Although the WCF is not part of the fair-trade movement, it, too, works **11.** to improve conditions and educates cocoa growers.

Speaking

A You will participate in a group discussion about the pros and cons of fair trade. Follow the steps.

1. Divide the class into seven groups. Each group assumes one of these roles:
   • Cocoa farmer, member of the Kuapa Kokoo co-op in Ghana
   • Cocoa farmer, individual grower in the Ivory Coast region
   • Teenager in the Ivory Coast, sent by parents to work on a cocoa farm
   • Member of the World Cocoa Foundation
   • Owner of chocolate company in developed country, not yet selling fair-trade chocolate
   • Representative of Equal Exchange, the company that first introduced fair-trade chocolate
   • Chocolate lover and consumer in a developed country

2. In your group, brainstorm arguments for or against cocoa farmer co-ops and fair trade that are consistent with your role. Use the explicit information that you have learned in this chapter, as well as inferences you can draw and other information that you may know to formulate your arguments. Take notes. Try to use the grammar from the chapter.

B Form new groups of seven with one representative for each role. Discuss the fair trade pros and cons for each role, using your notes from Part A. Try to come to a conclusion on whether fair trade is a good or a bad concept. List key pros and cons in the chart. Then, compare your group's conclusion with that of the other groups. Do all groups agree?

Role	Pros	Cons

Listening

A 🎧 UNDERSTANDING MAIN IDEAS Listen to a news report about fair trade. The reporter talks to three people, and refers to a fourth person, each from a different organization. As you listen, match each person with the organization he or she represents.

_____ 1. Sean Davenport   **a.** The Adam Smith Institute

_____ 2. Ellen Mayberry   **b.** Trade Aid Importers

_____ 3. Jeremy Pryor   **c.** The Fairtrade Foundation

_____ 4. Marcus Potter   **d.** WORLDwrite

B 🎧 UNDERSTANDING DETAILS Listen again. On a separate sheet of paper, identify each of the people in the report as being either for or against fair trade. Then, write each person's key arguments.

C DISCUSSION Compare and discuss your notes from Part B with a partner. Of the four people, who has the most reasonable and convincing argument for fair trade's positive or negative sides? Why? Then, discuss your conclusions with the whole class.

Writing

MyEnglishLab
▶ Linking Grammar to Writing

A Work in small groups. You will design announcements for a class symposium on approaches to eradicating poverty. Brainstorm ideas for each point in the outline shown below. Take notes on a separate sheet of paper.

> TITLE
> Brief background on poverty
> Facts and statistics from around the world
>
> Approaches to eradicating poverty
>   Approach and example
>   Approach and example
>   Approach and example
>
> (add a photo)
> Invitation to join symposium
>   When / where / what

B Write your announcement, using your notes from Part A. Try to use the grammar from the chapter.

2014 Eradicating Poverty Symposium

◼◼◼◼◼ Education and Poverty ◼◼◼◼◼

The vast majority of people living in poverty lack a basic level of education. Countless studies have shown the link between levels of education and levels of economic independence. Join us this year as we . . .

When taken as a whole, the statistics on education and poverty are staggering. In xx% of developing countries over xx% of children do not attend school of any kind. Of those that do attend school, only . . .

The 2014 Symposium will focus on three main approaches to providing education to those in poverty:
1.
2.
3.
(photo)
Join us on Saturday, March 22 in Kipling Hall on the University of Washington campus.
Registration opens at 8 A.M.; the symposium begins at 9 A.M. and runs until 4 P.M.

C Post your announcements around the room. Which announcement is the most likely to attract people to attend your symposium? Why?

MyEnglishLab
▶ Diagnostic Test

Grammar Summary

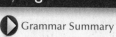
Connecting structures for cause / reason consist of three subordinating conjunctions and four phrasal prepositions. The type of structure affects the punctuation.

The subordinating conjunctions *because, since,* and *as* show cause or reason relationships and connect dependent and independent clauses. If the dependent clause comes first in the sentence, it is followed by a comma. Phrasal prepositions are followed by a noun or noun phrase and connect to an independent clause. The phrase usually comes first in the sentence and is followed by a comma. These phrasal prepositions show causes or reasons: *as a result of, because of, due to,* and *as a consequence of.*	(1) Many global aid programs target women because they are central to ending poverty. (2) Since boys and men play critical roles in gender equality campaigns, their needs must be addressed. (3) As a result of their heavy domestic workload, many girls in poor regions don't receive an education. (4) Women can be effective recipients of job skill training due to their willingness to share their knowledge with others.

Conjunctive adverbs of effect are used to connect sentences.

Conjunctive adverbs, or sentence connectors, can show an effect or result in a clause when joined with another clause that shows a cause or reason. They connect independent clauses and are preceded by a period or semicolon and followed by a comma.	(1) Access to land and equipment benefits female farmers. As a result, more agricultural programs devote funding to projects that aid women. (2) Women comprise the majority of small-scale farmers; therefore, their work is critical to global food security.

Articles identify nouns and noun phrases as specific or non-specific.

The indefinite article **a / an** identifies non-specific, countable nouns in the singular form. The definite article *the* refers to a specific countable noun, both singular and plural, and to a specific non-countable noun. It occurs the second time a noun or its synonym is mentioned. Non-count nouns and non-specific, general plural nouns do not use an article (Ø or "zero article"). **A / An** is also used to express a part of a larger whole. **The** is used when a noun is identified by the phrase that follows it. **Ø** is also used with first-mentioned non-count nouns.	(1) A cocoa seedling grows into a cocoa tree. (2) Cocoa pods grow on the cocoa trees, and the pods contain cocoa beans. The pods are harvested, and the beans are collected. (3) Ø Cocoa seedlings grow into Ø cocoa trees. (4) A cocoa plantation consists of a large group of cocoa trees. (5) The farmers of the Kuapa Kokoo Co-op harvest the cocoa pods that grow on the trees on their plantations. (6) Cocoa from co-ops is used for fair-trade chocolate.

Parallel structures consist of the same grammatical pattern to show that ideas or concepts are of equal importance.

Parallel structures are often joined through coordinating or correlative conjunctions at the word level, the phrase level, and the clause level. Parallelism is also used in comparisons to help make comparisons clear, complete, and non-ambiguous. Parallelism is typical of written discourse.	(1) Good quality chocolate is both shiny and smooth. (2) Good chocolate smells like a blend of aromas and tastes like a combination of flavors. (3) If the chocolate leaves a lasting taste in your mouth, and if you long for another piece, that's a sign of quality. (4) Fair-trade chocolate tastes better than regular chocolate. (5) The price of fair-trade chocolate is higher than that (the price) of regular chocolate.

Self-Assessment

A (4 points) Complete the paragraph with appropriate connectors from the list. More than one connector is possible in each blank.

as   as a consequence of   as a result of   because   because of   due to   since

   Boxgirls uses amateur boxing as a tool to help girls and young women develop the strength to become leaders in their communities. While they train them to know when to score and when to avoid risks in boxing, *Boxgirls* also helps them transfer these strategies to their own lives. **1.** _____ their training, they can identify chances for growth and take calculated risks to bring social change. They are able to apply discipline to their goals outside the ring **2.** _____ their boxing training teaches them that preparation and practice is key to winning. They are also able to expand their social and work skills **3.** _____ sports help them learn to work in a team and concentrate. **4.** _____ their training and experience, these young women learn leadership skills and gain self-confidence.

B (4 points) Rewrite the sentences using one of the conjunctive adverbs in the list. More than one connector is possible, but use a different one in each sentence.

as a consequence   as a result   consequently   hence   therefore   thus

1. Women benefit from disaster preparedness and response training since they are often the ones who care for the sick and injured after a disaster.

_____

2. Programs that teach rural women sustainable use of natural resources merit funding as these programs can bring positive environmental impacts.

_____

3. Because war brings further harm to vulnerable populations, efforts to find peaceful solutions to conflicts have wide-reaching benefits.

_____

4. Countries with developed economies must partner with developing nations in eradicating poverty because such collaboration is critical to fostering change.

_____

C (7 points) Complete the paragraph with *a, an,* or *the*. If an article is not necessary, write the null (ø) symbol. All articles within each sentence must be filled in correctly to receive a full score.

   1. _____ farmers grow _____ cocoa trees on _____ small farms in _____ hot, rainy environments near _____ equator. **2.** _____ farmers must look after _____ trees and protect them from ___ wind and _____ sun. **3.** _____ cocoa seedlings are often sheltered by _____ other trees, like _____ banana trees. **4.** When _____ trees are established, _____ farmers must fertilize _____ soil and watch _____ trees closely for _____ signs of _____ distress. **5.** _____ cocoa tree reaches _____ peak production in approximately ten years. **6.** It will continue to produce _____ pods at _____ high level for _____ years. **7.** Surprisingly, _____ cocoa beans from _____ old trees are just as good as those from _____ young trees.

D (5 points) Read the paragraph. Correct the mistakes in parallel structures in the underlined text. Rewrite the paragraph on a separate piece of paper.

   A chemical in cocoa beans can help <u>lower your blood pressure</u> and <u>preventing heart disease</u>. Some researchers suggest <u>that chocolate reduces pain</u> and <u>there's also a chance for it to reduce the</u> <u>risk of inflammation</u>. The <u>health benefits of dark chocolate are more pronounced than milk, or white, chocolate</u>. In order to reap the benefits of chocolate's beneficial influence, <u>you don't need to overindulge in chocolate bars or candy</u>, nor <u>you chew on tons of cocoa beans</u>. In fact, one piece of chocolate is <u>enough to promote the health benefits</u>, but it may not <u>stop your chocolate cravings</u>.

Unit Project: Symposium presentation

A Work in groups of three or four students. Prepare a presentation on eradicating poverty in three different countries. Follow the steps.

1. Choose one of the approaches to eradicating poverty from the list. Research how this approach has been used in three different countries. Your research should include poverty statistics for each country and the effectiveness of the approach. Divide the research among the members of your group. Take notes.

Approaches to eradicating poverty	Examples
Economic	microfinancing, project grants
Educational	literacy programs, vocational training programs
Health-focused	disease awareness and prevention campaigns, medical specialist volunteer programs
Social	free legal advice, awareness and prevention of domestic abuse and child abuse

2. Review your notes and prepare a slide presentation on the approach you have chosen. Follow the outline. Each point in the outline should be a separate slide.

1. Title slide
2. Overview
3. Definition of poverty
4. Definition of approach
5. Graph showing poverty statistics for country A
6. Examples of approach in country A
7. Evaluation of effectiveness / success
8. Graph showing poverty statistics for country B
9. Examples of approach in country B
10. Evaluation of effectiveness / success
11. Graph showing poverty statistics for country C
12. Examples of approach in country C
13. Evaluation of effectiveness / success
14. Recommendations
15. Conclusion
16. Questions and Answers

3. Practice your presentation. Make sure each member of your group has a chance to speak. As you prepare, anticipate audience questions and practice responses.

B Give your presentations within a formal setting. If possible, invite other teachers and classes to your symposium. Allow time for questions and answers after each presentation. Then, discuss the questions as a class.

1. Which team's presentation was the most informative? Why?
2. Which approaches to poverty reduction might be the most effective and realistic?
3. Which team's slides were the most well designed? Why?
4. Which team's presentation was the best? Why?

MyEnglishLab

▶ Unit Test

MyEnglishLab

▶ Search it!

Anthropology - Body Art

OUTCOMES

After completing this unit, I will be able to use these grammar points.

CHAPTER 15

Grammar Focus 1
Modals and phrasal expressions:
Degrees of necessity

Grammar Focus 2
Causatives

CHAPTER 16

Grammar Focus 1
Expressing purpose with infinitives:
Using *for* and *so that*

Grammar Focus 2
Conjunctive adverbs of exemplification, emphasis, and clarification

CHAPTER 15 Body Art in the Workplace

Getting Started

A Check (✓) the examples of body art you have worn. Then, describe the occasions and reasons for wearing it. Next, compare your responses with those of your classmates.

Body art	Worn	Occasion	Reason
Necklaces, bracelets, rings			
Earrings			
Make-up			
Nail polish			
Anklets and toe rings			

B Read some rules about appearance in the workplace. Do you think these rules apply in workplaces in your country or in other countries you are familiar with? Circle your answers. Discuss your answers with a classmate.

Rule	In my country			In other countries		
Employers should enforce dress codes.	Yes	No	Maybe	Yes	No	Maybe
Men must have their hair cut short.	Yes	No	Maybe	Yes	No	Maybe
Women can wear long pants.	Yes	No	Maybe	Yes	No	Maybe
Men and women must not wear flip-flops.	Yes	No	Maybe	Yes	No	Maybe
Employees are not allowed to have multiple earrings.	Yes	No	Maybe	Yes	No	Maybe
Companies make employees cover their tattoos.	Yes	No	Maybe	Yes	No	Maybe
Workers are not supposed to have body piercings.	Yes	No	Maybe	Yes	No	Maybe
Job applicants have to get tattoos / piercings removed.	Yes	No	Maybe	Yes	No	Maybe

C Look back at Part B. Complete the tasks.

1. Circle the **modals** and draw a rectangle around the **phrasal expressions** that show **permission** or **prohibition**.
2. Underline **verb phrases** that show that **one thing causes another**.
3. Following the model, make a chart with examples. Then, compare your chart with a partner's chart.

Expressions of permission / prohibition	Causatives
Modals:	Active causatives:
Phrasal expressions:	Passive causatives:

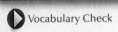
Reading

A WARM-UP With a partner, discuss what policies regarding body art you would expect in the companies listed in the chart. Check (✓) if you think earrings, piercings, and tattoos are permissible for employees in those organizations. Explain your answers.

	Accounting	Aircraft	Grocery	Theme park	Law firm	Day camp	Police
Earrings							
Piercings							
Tattoos							

B SCANNING Scan the article for policies regarding body art in various companies. Compare the actual policies with your predictions in Part A. Then, read the whole article. Do any of these policies surprise you? Why or why not?

Young Workers Have Something Up Their Sleeve

Nearly 50 percent of Americans between 21 and 32 have had at least one tattoo or body piercing done. Once associated with sailors, criminals, and bikers, tattoos have gone mainstream, putting employers in a bind: How to write rules that won't make customers feel alienated or get talented workers eliminated?

Policies are ambiguous. PricewaterhouseCoopers, an accountancy firm, says that employees must wear professional attire, not mentioning tattoos. Employees at aircraft maker Boeing can show off tattoos if the designs aren't "offensive." Employees at Vons grocery stores are advised to cover up. The dress code for Disney theme parks is explicit and conservative: employees are required to conceal tattoos and mustn't have more than one piercing per earlobe. Earrings have to be a simple matched pair, and hoops can't be bigger than a dime. Law firms also prefer conventional looks; associates should definitely not wear tongue studs.

For a day camp in Los Angeles, this divide has caused headaches. Although a few counselors have ladybugs or Asian characters for "luck" tattooed on themselves, some parents complain that inked, pierced counselors aren't appropriate role models. But the camp director says that if he didn't let tattooed counselors work for him, he would lose excellent employees. Ten years ago, the camp made its few tattooed staff members hide their body art, but today, the director has job candidates take the "is-it-offensive test": a butterfly tattoo may be exposed, but a skull and crossbones had better be covered up. Additionally, the director makes staffers remove belly rings or tongue studs when they are at work interacting with children.

Police departments tend to take a harder line than day camps. Officers can't display tattoos or piercings while in uniform; they are allowed to have only one stud per ear (hoops pose safety risks). In the past, police departments didn't need a policy on body art that told employees how they were or were not supposed to look on the job. But when tattooed war veterans applied for jobs, the police got them to look for jobs elsewhere because they had their entire forearms vividly decorated with tattoos. Some veterans had discrimination lawsuits filed against the police departments, but with little success because employers can legally make employees dress according to standards consistent with the images they want to convey.

Different standards have emerged for different industries. A pink rose discreetly inked on an ankle is perhaps acceptable at a hospital but not a day-care center; an eyebrow stud, viewed as charming at one store, should be removed at another. Ironically, in many cases, appearance policies that employees ought to follow are being set by Baby Boomers, a generation that was known for extremes and that had its employers shake their heads. In the past, Baby Boomers didn't get their hair cut and wore ripped clothes, but today they are passing judgment on nose rings and tattoos.

C UNDERSTANDING DETAILS Read the article again. Then, answer the questions in small groups.

1. What is the "divide" mentioned in the third paragraph? Why has it "caused headaches"?
2. What are the different standards, and why do different industries have different standards?
3. How is it ironic that many of today's appearance policies are being set by Baby Boomers?

Grammar Focus 1 Modals and phrasal expressions: Degrees of necessity

Examples	Language notes
Affirmative **Necessity** **Negative** 100% must, have (got) to, must not, be required to can't, be not allowed to had better, had better not, should, ought to, shouldn't, be advised to be not advised to be to, be supposed to, be not to, be not supposed to, be expected to, be not expected to, can, may, be allowed to not have to, be not required to 0%	The **modal auxiliaries** *must, had better, ought to, should, may,* and *can*—and their negative forms—express varying degrees of necessity (obligation, advice, expectation, and permission). Modals do not change forms to agree with the subject, and they are followed by the base form of the verb. Varying degrees of necessity can also be expressed through certain **phrasal expressions** that correspond in meaning to the modals: *be (not) advised to, be (not) allowed to, be (not) expect to, (not) have (got) to, be (not) required to,* and *be (not) supposed to.* Phrasal expressions tend to be used in formal policy statements and public announcements.
(1) Employees **must / have to / are required to wear** professional attire. Employees **mustn't / can't / may not / aren't allowed to have** more than one piercing per earlobe.	Use *must, have (got) to, be required to* to show **strong necessity** or **obligation**. They have a similar meaning, but *must* is more formal. Use *must not / mustn't, can't, may not,* and *be not allowed to* to express **prohibition**.
(2) Employees **had better** follow their company dress code. Associates **should** definitely not **wear** tongue studs. Employees **ought to / are advised to follow** appearance policies.	Use *had better* to express **strong advice** or **responsibility**. Use *should, ought to,* and *be advised to* to offer **advice**. (Refer back to Unit 1 for explanation of modals of advisability.)
(3) Policies tell employees how they **are** or **are not supposed to / expected to look** on the job. Employees **are to** conceal their tattoos at all times.	Use *be supposed to* and *be expected to* to show **expectation** or **requirement**. *Be to* can be used to show **strong** expectation. It is used formally.
(4) Employees at Boeing **can / may / are allowed to show off** inoffensive tattoos. The employees **don't have to / aren't required to** cover their tattoos if the tattoos aren't offensive.	Use *can, may, be allowed to, not have to,* and *be not required to* to express **permission** or **lack of necessity / obligation**.
(5) You **can / may** show off your tattoo. Officers **can't / may not display** tattoos or piercings. You **must / have to** cover your tattoo. You **must not** show off your tattoo. Employees **are not allowed to have** tattoos. You **don't have to** cover your tattoo. Employees **are not required** to dress formally.	The **negative form** changes the meaning for some of the modals and phrasal expressions: *Can / may / be allowed to* = permission *can not / may not* = prohibition *must / have to / be required to* = necessity / obligation *must not / be not allowed to* = prohibition *not have to / be not required to* = permission / lack of necessity

Grammar Practice

MyEnglishLab

▶ Grammar Plus 1
Activities 1 and 2

A Read the sentences. Decide what degree of necessity is expressed in each. Write *N* for *Necessity*, *PRO* for *Prohibition*, *A* for *Advice*, *E* for *Expectation*, and *PER* for *Permission*.

_____ 1. Accounting firms should convey a clean-cut image.

_____ 2. Aircraft technicians don't have to cover up tatoos.

_____ 3. Grocery store employees are expected to remove piercings.

_____ 4. Theme park workers can't have tattoos or piercings.

_____ 5. Lawyers ought to take out tongue studs or nose rings.

_____ 6. Camp counselors aren't allowed to display offensive body art.

_____ 7. Police officers are required to avoid dangling earrings.

_____ 8. Department store clerks may wear multiple earrings.

B Choose the correct modal or phrasal expression based on the clues in parentheses.

At a large organic food store chain in Boston, Juan Milano, a salesclerk, **1.** _____ (*strong necessity*) wear long sleeves to conceal the Buddha on his left forearm and the yellow-orange sun rays on his right arm. Also, he **2.** _____ (*obligation*) wear long pants to cover the image of Earth on one leg and wings on the other. Not surprisingly, he **3.** _____ (*prohibition*) reveal the sun spreading across his back. Of course, he **4.** _____ (*prohibition*) show the plugs in his earlobes and **5.** _____ (*advice*) cover them with bandages.

Han Liu works as a store manager for the same company in Los Angeles, overseeing health and beauty products departments at 25 stores. Han Liu **6.** _____ (*strong expectation*) wear the collared shirt and pleated khakis that all managers **7.** _____ (*advice*) wear when they are in the store, but he **8.** _____ (*permission*) follow looser appearance standards in Los Angeles than in Boston. He **9.** _____ (*lack of necessity*) cover the tattoo of a snake on his wrist, and he isn't told that he **10.** _____ (*strong advice*) remove his eyebrow ring. The only thing he **11.** _____ (*prohibition*) do is arriving late or not getting his job done.

Clearly, some companies with branches in different regions are setting standards for their employees, which reflect the non-universal acceptance of body art: what employees **12.** _____ (*advice*) do in one part of the country is often different from what they **13.** _____ (*lack of necessity*) or **14.** _____ (*prohibition*) do in another.

C Look at the photos of people from two different companies. What do you assume the policies on attire and body art are at these companies? Then, write three policy statements for each company, using modals and phrasal expressions.

Employees must dress professionally. They are not allowed to wear jeans.

Employees don't have to dress formally. They can wear casual shirts.

Grammar Focus 2 Causatives

Examples	Language notes
(1) The manager **has his employees cover** their tattoos. [active] Some people decide **to have their tattoos removed**. [passive]	**Causatives** are verb constructions that express the idea of someone or something causing something else to happen. There are two major causative constructions in English— **active** and **passive**.
(2) The day camp director **lets <u>tattooed counselors</u> work** for him. The camp **made <u>its tattooed staff members</u> hide** their body art. The director **has <u>job candidates</u> take** the "is-it-offensive" test. The police **got <u>them</u> to look** for jobs elsewhere.	To form an **active causative** construction, use: **let / make / have + direct object + base form** OR **get + direct object + to + base form**. The verb **let** conveys the idea of permission. The verb **make** conveys the idea of obligation. The verb **have** implies that instructions were given. The verb **get** conveys the idea of persuasion (someone convincing another person to do something).
(3) Many Americans **have had <u>at least one tattoo or piercing</u> done** (by a body art specialist). Baby Boomers didn't **get <u>their hair</u> cut** (by a hairstylist).	To form **passive causative** constructions, use: **have / get + direct object + past participle**. Both **have** and **get** convey the same idea, namely that a job was completed or that another entity completed the job. The **by-phrase** is usually omitted because the service provider's identity is either obvious or unimportant.

Subject	Causative—Active			Complement
	let / make / have / get	direct object	verb	
The director	**lets**	tattooed counselors	**work**	for him.
The camp	**made**	its staff members	**hide**	their body art.
The director	**has**	job candidates	**take**	the "is-it-offensive" test.
The police	**got**	them	**to look**	for jobs elsewhere.

Subject	Causative—Passive			(Optional *by*-phrase)
	have / get	direct object	past participle	
Many Americans	**have had**	one tattoo	**done**	(by a body art specialist).
Baby boomers	**didn't get**	their hair	**cut**	(by a hairstylist).

Grammar Practice

MyEnglishLab
Grammar Plus 2
Activities 1 and 2

A Read the sentences. Decide which of the following choices expresses the correct meaning for each sentence. Write *PER* for *Permission*, *O* for *Obligation*, *IG* for *Instructions Given*, *PRS* for *Persuasion*, and *JC* for *Job Completed*.

_____ **1.** PriceWaterhouseCoopers makes employees dress conservatively.

_____ **2.** Boeing had explicit policies regarding written body art.

_____ **3.** Vons gets its employees to conceal their body art.

_____ **4.** Disney lets staff wear one pair of earrings.

_____ **5.** Law offices have associates remove visible body art.

_____ **6.** Camp directors make counselors remove tongue studs.

B Complete the paragraph with appropriate causative verbs. Be sure to use the correct tense and other grammar forms.

In recent years, many companies **1.** _____*have had*_____ explicit appearance policies written in order to avoid **2.** _____ employees dress and "decorate" themselves in whichever way they want. These companies **3.** _____ their employees to reconsider unusual forms of body art, such as tattoos and facial piercings. In many cases, employers **4.** _____ employees remove earrings, tongue studs, and lip rings, and recently, employers **5.** _____ workers who deal with customers get rid of tattoos. In fact, workers have been asked to **6.** _____ their tattoos completely removed, and they can **7.** _____ this done correctly only at a professional tattoo removal service. To illustrate, a 20-year-old sales associate at a department store **8.** _____ numerous potential employers in retail sales tell him that the image he projected was "not the image they're trying to send." So he paid close to $700 to **9.** _____ the teardrop under his right eye erased, and he paid almost three times that much to **10.** _____ three small dots on his right hand removed. Another recent graduate in her early twenties decided to **11.** _____ a professional tattoo removal service take off the star on the inside of her left forearm. She worried that the star might **12.** _____ potential employers to think of her as unprofessional. It is estimated that twenty percent of clients at tattoo removal places undergo the painful laser removal treatments because they want to **13.** _____ job recruiters focus on their abilities and not on their appearance.

C Choose the appropriate verbs from the lists below to complete the paragraphs. Make the verbs active or passive.

add	associate	enter	put	~~show off~~	study

In the past two decades, there has been an increasing tolerance toward body art. More and more companies let their employees **1.** _____*show off*_____ their tattoos and piercings. When Texas Tech had some of its researchers **2.** _____ tattoos in the late 1980s, public attitudes toward tattoos got people **3.** _____ them with convicts and sailors but not with mainstream professionals. More recently popular culture has let tattoos **4.** _____ the mainstream. Studies have found that 25 percent of subjects have had some kind of tattoo **5.** _____ on themselves. Those numbers include not just bike messengers and rockers but also people in other professions who have had and are having tattoos or piercings **6.** _____.

apply	create	design	do	review	tattoo	wear

This development is making companies **7.** _____ their dress codes. Among the professionals who are getting visible tattoos **8.** _____, the numbers of those who are having more expansive arm, back, and leg work **9.** _____ are exploding. According to one tattoo artist, it is often the corporate executives who are getting the most extreme tattoos **10.** _____. He says that this makes sense because having someone **11.** _____ the tattoo work can be quite expensive, especially when someone gets a lot of tattoo work **12.** _____. Additionally, the corporate tattooed executives have the perfect cover because their bosses make them **13.** _____ suits all the time, so their tattoos are not visible during the daytime.

Speaking

A Read the three cases about people with body art. With a partner, discuss how you would feel if you were each person's colleague or someone who comes in contact with him or her (customer, student, patient, etc.). Look at the model. Then, take notes. Try to use the grammar from the chapter.

> *If I were in the hospital and my nurse had a huge tattoo that I could see, I wouldn't be worried. The nurse should wear what she wants. She needs to be able . . .*

> **Case 1:** A nurse working at a small town hospital was fired from her job for showing off the image of a snake which covered her arms from her left wrist all the way across her shoulders down to her right wrist. The tattoo showed the snake with its mouth open and fangs showing. The snake's tail and head showed prominently when she was wearing a short-sleeved uniform. Colleagues had made disapproving remarks, but it was not until the parent of a six-year-old patient complained to the hospital administration and said that the nurse's tattoo scared her son when she brought him in for treatment in the emergency room that the nurse was fired.

> **Case 2:** An employee at a car repair shop had rings inserted into his earlobes to stretch them and a ring pierced through the bottom of his nose. His supervisor questioned his good judgment, felt that the piercings were distracting, and concluded that anyone who has these types of piercings done must be associated with a suspect group of friends. When the employee refused to remove his body art, the supervisor fired him.

> **Case 3:** A female math teacher at a suburban high school was fired for refusing to cover up her ankle tattoo of Chinese characters. The school principal, upon discovery of the tattoo, had requested that the teacher wear long pants to hide the tattoo. He felt that exposing high school students to tattoos would constitute bad taste and a bad influence on teenage girls. In his opinion, teachers should be good role models for their students.

B In small groups, review the cases again. Discuss whether you feel each person's dismissal from his or her job was justified or not. Give reasons. Look at the model. Try to use the grammar from the chapter.

> *The car mechanic was fired because he had unusual ear and nose piercings done. His boss should not let him show his piercings because . . .*

Listening

A BEFORE LISTENING In small groups, discuss the situations or circumstances in which having body art might be an asset for someone and why. Make a list of such circumstances and reasons. Share your ideas with the rest of the class.

Body art can be an asset if / when . . .   *because . . .*

_____   _____

_____   _____

_____   _____

B 🎧 UNDERSTANDING DETAILS Listen to three people talk about their body art. Complete the chart with information you hear. Compare your responses with a classmate's answers.

	Person 1	Person 2	Person 3
Job?			
Body Art? Location?			
OK to display?			
Negative effects?			
Positive effects?			

C 🎧 MAKING INFERENCES What do you think the general policy regarding body art is at each person's place of work? Are you surprised by these apparent policies? Why or why not? Complete the chart. Listen again if necessary.

	Place of work	Policy regarding body art
Person 1		
Person 2		
Person 3		

Writing

MyEnglishLab

▶ Linking Grammar to Writing

A Brainstorm ideas on body art, clothing, and appearance policy for the school or program where you study English. What must faculty and students do? What can they not do? Take notes.

B Write a policy statement on body art, clothing, and appearance for the school or program where you study English. The policy should address faculty as well as students. Include at least 10 specific requirements. Use your notes from Part A. Try to use the grammar from the chapter.

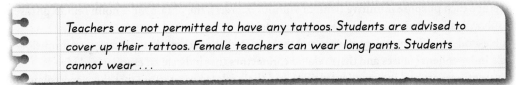

> Teachers are not permitted to have any tattoos. Students are advised to cover up their tattoos. Female teachers can wear long pants. Students cannot wear . . .

C Post your policy statements around the room. Which policy statement should the school or program adopt? Why?

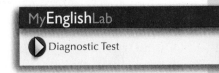

MyEnglishLab

▶ Diagnostic Test

CHAPTER 16 | Cultural Identity through Body Art

Getting Started

A Throughout history, cultures around the world have used various forms of body art or body modification. Read the descriptions of body art traditions around the world. Check (✓) those that you are familiar with. Then, discuss other forms of body art that you are familiar with that are not listed. Discuss reasons why people apply body art or undergo body modification.

_____ **1.** Some African tribes cut scars into their bodies in order to enhance their physical beauty. In fact, ashes and other dyes are often rubbed into the cuts so that the resulting scar is more prominent.

_____ **2.** To get a traditional *tatau*, or tattoo, Samoan men and women must undergo a painful process. Small, sharp combs are attached to a short stick, which the artist strikes repeatedly with a small mallet to make the designs. In other words, the tattoo is literally cut into the skin. Men's tattoos cover a large portion of the body and indicate their social standing; indeed, greater coverage brings higher status.

_____ **3.** In India, Hindu brides have their hands and feet painted with a paste made from the henna plant for good luck and a strong marriage. The process of the painting and the resulting stained patterns is called Mehndi.

_____ **4.** Head shaping was once practiced in the island nation of Vanuatu. Specifically, infants' heads were bound with soft strips of tree bark and then covered with a woven basket and fiber rope. The binding was done so that the head could be elongated, which signified intelligence, social status, and a connection to the spirit world.

B Look back at Part A. Complete the tasks.

1. Underline each **purpose infinitive** (with or without *in order*), the phrase *for* + **noun / noun phrase**, and the subordinating conjunction *so that* + **adverb clause**.
2. Double-underline **independent clauses and their related connectors** that indicate an **example**.
3. Circle **independent clauses and their related connectors** that indicate an **emphasized idea**.
4. Put parentheses around **independent clauses and their related connectors** that show an **explanation**.
5. Complete the chart with examples. Then, compare your chart with a partner's chart.

Expressions of purpose	Conjunctive adverbs: examples	Conjunctive adverbs: emphasis	Conjunctive adverbs: explanation

Reading

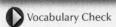

A WARM-UP With a partner, discuss the photos. As you describe the appearance of the people in the photos, discuss the meanings of the body modifications that you see. Use the words in the list to help you.

aethetics	to adorn	to depict	to file (filing)
motifs	to beautify	to embellish	to scar (scarify, scarification)

B SKIMMING Skim the text and underline the three main purposes of body art in various cultures. Then, read the whole text.

Cultural Expression through Body Art

For millennia, the human body has been a unique canvas decorated in many ways. Since the beginning of human history, people have embellished their bodies for many reasons. There is no known culture in which people do not paint, pierce, tattoo, reshape, or simply adorn their bodies in order to signal their place in society, mark a special moment, celebrate a life transition, or simply follow a fashion.

Body art can carry powerful messages about a person. That is, colors, designs, and the use of particular techniques are part of a visual language with specific cultural meanings. The techniques practiced for body decoration and alteration, both temporary and permanent; vary around the globe, as do the meanings behind the art.

A common motive for body art is aesthetics. For instance, in Ethiopia, women of the Karo and Hamer tribes scarify their chests and paint their faces with white chalk to beautify themselves. The cuts are made with a knife, and ash is rubbed in so that the resulting scar will stand out. These marks of beauty also represent a woman's ability to withstand the pain of childbearing. In the Indian state of Orissa, women of the Longia Soura tribe enhance their attractiveness by inserting increasingly larger discs of wood in their pierced ears to stretch their earlobes. They continue the stretching so that in time, their earlobes become elastic and eventually stretch nearly to their shoulders.

Representations of spiritual beliefs can also be seen in the body art of most cultures. For example, the Akha women of Thailand wear elaborate silver headdresses in order to appease the spirits. Although the headdresses often weigh as much as 10 pounds, the women wear them all the time; in fact, they wear them as they work in the fields and even to bed. Tooth filing is a religious practice of Hindus in the Indonesian island of Bali. Beginning at a young age, Balinese undergo the tooth filing ceremony, *matahtah*, so that they can expel the invisible forces of evil. They believe that the teeth, particularly the sharp canines, represent the uncivilized, animal aspect of human nature.

Across many cultures, body art also depicts important life transitions and events. Throughout Polynesia, tattoos are customary for both men and women. Specifically, body tattooing is used to signify young men's passage into adulthood. Using special handmade tools, the tattooist cuts the designs into the skin. Men who endure the painful tattooing process are respected for their courage. In many ethnic groups, paste made from the henna plant is used for body painting. In India and Pakistan, this practice is called Mehndi and is traditionally applied for special occasions, particularly weddings. A Mehndi artist draws the motifs on the bride's hands and feet and decorates the female wedding attendants. Mehndi motifs have various meanings, among them good fortune, blessings, and strength for the marriage.

C UNDERSTANDING DETAILS Read the text again and think about each purpose you underlined in Part B. Then, on a separate piece of paper, list at least one specific example of the way various cultures express beliefs and values through body art.

Grammar Focus 1 Expressing purpose with infinitives: Using *for* and *so that*

Examples	Language notes
(1) Some African tribes cut scars into their bodies **in order to enhance** their physical beauty. In many African cultures, women paint their faces with chalk **to beautify** themselves.	We use **infinitives** after the phrase **in order** to indicate a **specific purpose**. A purpose infinitive is used with a base verb and answers the question "Why?" *In order* is often omitted, particularly in speaking.
(2) The techniques used **for body decoration or alteration** vary around the globe.	For an **adverb phrase of purpose**, use *for* + a noun or noun phrase.
(3) In the past, bone, shell, and wood tools **were used for making tattoos**. In the past, bone, shell, and wood tools **were used to make tattoos**. These needles are **for cutting details** while those are **for making broader marks**. A tattoo artist uses a needle **to cut details with**.	To show a **general** or **common purpose** for something, use either *be used for* + a gerund or *be used* + an infinitive. To describe the **purpose of an object or action**, use *for* + a gerund. This construction answers the question "what is it used for?" When the subject of the sentence is **a person** (not the object described), *to* + infinitive is also common.
(4) **(In order) to get** a traditional tatau, Samoans must undergo a painful process.	You can use a purpose infinitive at the beginning of a sentence. This construction is less common.
(5) People use body art **to signal** their place in society, **mark** a special moment, or **celebrate** a life transition.	If multiple infinitives are used with the same verb, after the first infinitive, *to* is optional in the rest of the list.
(6) The binding was done **so that the head could be elongated**. Cuts are made with a knife and ash is rubbed in **so that the resulting scar will stand out**. The tattoo artist will work with an assistant **so that the process goes smoothly**.	Use the subordinating conjunction *so that* to express purpose. *So that* introduces an adverb clause, which typically includes modal verbs for ability: *can* in the present or future and *could* in the past. Other modals used in adverb clauses include *will* for future actions and *would* for the past. Use the simple present with a future meaning when the context makes it clear.
(7) The binding was done **in order that the head could be elongated**.	The more formal **in order that** has the same meaning as **so that** but is not commonly used.

Independent clause			Infinitive phrase of purpose
People	use	body art	**in order to** display their beliefs.
Many African women	paint	their faces and hair	**to** beautify themselves.

Infinitive phrase of purpose	Independent clause		
(In order) to get a traditional *tatau*,	Samoan men and women	must undergo	a painful process.

Subject	Verb	Prepositional phrase (*for* + noun / noun phrase)
Handmade tools	were used	**for** making tattoos.

Independent clause	Dependent clause (Adverb clause of purpose)		
Balinese undergo the tooth filing ceremony	**so that**	they	can expel	evil spirits.
Ash is rubbed into the cuts	**so that**	the scars	will stand out.

Grammar Practice

A Circle the correct expressions of purpose to complete the paragraph.

Around the world, people create body art **1. in order to mark / for to mark** important life events. In some cultures, it is used **2. for memories / to memorialize** loved ones who have passed away or **3. to symbolize / for a symbol** the transition of death. Women of the Dani tribe in West Papua paint their bodies with yellow clay **4. so that / in order to** others will know that they are mourning their deceased husband. In the past, Maori women in New Zealand would make cuts on their face and arms during mourning rituals. They also dyed the markings **5. to commemorate / for commemorating** the event. Hindu widows in India typically remove their nose studs **6. for showing / in order to show** respect for their deceased husband. In the Native American tribe of the Seminole, a warrior would paint himself with yellow pigments before battles **7. in order to / so that** his enemies would know that he was ready to fight to the death. In modern American culture, where tattooing in general is becoming more common, some people get "memorial tattoos" **8. in remembrance / to remember** of loved ones who have passed away.

B Identify and correct six errors in use of the purpose expressions.

Today, people seem to have varying motives for getting tattoos; sometimes they are intended in order that they mark a meaningful occasion or even simply to acquire a new, distinct accessory. While they might not be used for the same purposes as in the past, people still get them for expressing themselves. As in the past, popular culture influences tattoo choices today. Many use their bodies so they show their interests, choosing tattoo designs ranging from images of favorite athletes and university mascots to profiles of favorite singers and cartoon characters. Pop culture, religion, and loved ones all inspire tattoos. Of course, people also get tattoos for more serious and personal reasons. Many get tattoos for honoring ties to family members or friends. For instance, family members choose a meaningful symbol, image, or word for a "family" tattoo in order for each one can always feel connected to the others. Other customs are observed through tattooing as well. For decades, military recruits have gone to tattoo parlors during their basic training for tattoos so they mark the milestone of entering military service. However, whatever the motive is for the tattoos, most people would say that they are part of their identity.

Grammar Focus 2 Conjunctive adverbs of exemplification, emphasis, and clarification

Examples	Language notes
(1) People's reactions to body art are subjective. **In other words**, their perceptions are colored by their own cultural values and beliefs.	Use **conjunctive adverbs** (sentence connectors or transitions) to show relationships between independent clauses. (See Units 3 and 7.) Conjunctive adverbs can indicate an example, emphasized idea, or explanation.
(2) Body painting has had many roles throughout history. **For instance**, in India, Hindu brides have their hands and feet painted with henna for good luck and a strong marriage. (= *an example of a role of body art*)	Conjunctive adverbs that introduce **examples** include *for example, for instance, in particular,* and *specifically*.
(3) Although the headdresses often weigh as much as 10 pounds, the women wear them all the time; **in fact**, they wear them as they work in the fields and even to bed. (= *an emphasis of the idea "the women wear them all the time"*)	Conjunctive adverbs that **emphasize** a previous idea or make a stronger statement include *in fact, indeed,* and *as a matter of fact*.
(4) Body art carries powerful messages about the decorated person. **That is**, colors, designs, and the use of particular techniques are part of a visual language. (= *a clarification of "powerful messages about the decorated person"*)	Conjunctive adverbs that **clarify** or **explain** a previous idea include *in other words* and *that is*.
(5) In Ethiopia, **for instance**, women of the Karo and Hamer tribes scarify their chests and paint their faces with white chalk to beautify themselves. Men's tattoos cover a much larger portion of the body than women's; **indeed**, greater coverage brings higher status.	Conjunctive adverbs join independent clauses, so they are preceded by a period or semicolon and followed by a comma. While it is less common, they can be placed after the subject of the sentence between commas.
Incorrect: Men's tattoos cover a much larger portion of the body than women's, indeed, greater coverage brings higher status.	Conjunctive adverbs **cannot** be preceded by a comma. This is referred to as a **comma splice error**.

Independent clause	Conjunctive adverb	Independent clause
Spiritual beliefs are also conveyed in the body art of most cultures.	**For example,** **For instance,**	Akha women wear silver headdresses in order to appease the spirits.
Throughout Polynesia, tattoos are customary for both men and women.	**In particular,** **Specifically,**	body tattooing is used to signify young men's passage into adulthood.
Men's tattoos cover a large portion of the body and indicate their social standing;	**in fact,** **indeed,**	greater coverage brings higher status.
Tattooing, body piercing, and body painting are not new customs.	**As a matter of fact,**	these forms of body art have been around for thousands of years.
The artist strikes sharp combs repeatedly with a small mallet to make the designs;	**in other words,** **that is,**	the tattoo is literally cut into the skin.

Grammar Practice

A Read each pair of sentences and identify the relationship between them (exemplification, emphasis, or clarification). Then, connect the sentences using a logical conjunctive adverb from the list.

as a matter of fact	for instance	in fact	in particular	that is
for example	indeed	in other words	specifically	

1. The ancient Egyptians were innovative people whose inventions still impact modern society. They were one of the first cultures to develop cosmetics.

_____

2. Considering the time period, some of their creations did amazing things. Egyptians had cosmetics that would shrink wrinkles, get rid of scars, and make hair grow.

_____

3. Egyptians used cosmetic products for diverse needs. Many were used for all kinds of medicinal purposes.

_____

4. For ancient Egyptians, cosmetics were not gender-specific. Both men and women wore makeup.

_____

5. Cosmetics held a great deal of cultural significance for Egyptians. In their statues, even gods and goddesses were depicted wearing makeup.

_____

6. Physical appearance and adornment played key roles in social standing. To obtain greater status, it was necessary to wear more clothes and makeup.

_____

B Read each statement and identify the relationship between the clauses. Mark each *EX* (exemplification), *EM* (emphasis), or *CL* (clarification). Then, check if logical connectors are used and that the sentences are punctuated correctly. Correct any errors.

_____ **1.** As permanent body art, tattooing shouldn't be taken lightly, in other words, one should carefully consider the implications before deciding to get one.

_____ **2.** There are various aspects people need to consider before seeking the removal of a tattoo. That is, it is a time-consuming process that isn't always successful.

_____ **3.** Conventional tattoo removal is also quite costly. As a matter of fact, a tattoo that cost several hundred dollars to get could require several thousand dollars to be removed.

_____ **4.** New technologies are showing promise in the area of tattoo removal. One company, for instance, is marketing a new type of ink that breaks up after one treatment with a special laser.

_____ **5.** Other newer procedures are being used in place of traditional laser removal. In fact, one type involves the use of a special injected cream that bonds with and removes the ink as it comes out of the skin during the healing process.

Speaking

A With a partner, discuss what you have learned about the expression of cultural and personal beliefs through body decoration and body modification in various parts of the world. Answer the questions. Try to use the grammar from the chapter. Take notes.

1. What traditional expressions of cultural and personal body art have you learned about? Which of these expressions can you identify in modern society?
2. Are the types of body art the same or similar to those of the past? If yes, how? If not, how are they different?
3. What are the purposes of these types of body art?

B With your partner, form a group with another pair. Discuss the questions. Look at the model, and try to use the grammar from the chapter.

1. Share your ideas from Part A. Which of your ideas are similar? What are different?
2. Throughout world history, differences in cultural norms and attitudes toward the human body have resulted in conflict over and even prohibition of body art. These conflicting ideals have also contributed to the belief of some cultural groups that they are "superior" to others. Do you think that this conflict still occurs in today's society? If so, how, where, and with whom?

> When someone has body art that is visible to others, he may have problems. For example, if that person has multiple tattoos, people may think negatively about him. In fact, they might think . . .

Listening

A BEFORE LISTENING You will listen to a lecture by a professor of anthropology about four of the earliest forms of body art and their related traditions. With a partner, complete the chart with your predictions about the content of the lecture.

	Type	Places / People	Techniques / Materials	Purpose
1.				medical, cosmetic, spiritual, social
2.		Polynesia, Egypt, China, Japan		
3.			bone, wood, ivory, stone, metal	
4.	Body piercing			

B UNDERSTANDING MAIN IDEAS Listen to the lecture. As you listen, identify the four types of body art the professor discusses. Then, compare your notes to your predictions in Part A.

1. _____
2. _____
3. _____
4. _____

C 🎧 UNDERSTANDING DETAILS Listen to the lecture again. This time, listen for the specific signals that the speaker uses to indicate what type of detail he will provide (purpose expressions and conjunctive adverbs). Take notes on the information you hear in the appropriate category in the chart.

Purpose	Exemplification	Emphasis	Clarification

Writing

MyEnglishLab

▶ Linking Grammar to Writing

A You will write a short description of common types of body art or body modification in your culture, both in the past and the present. Brainstorm details for your description. Use the topics below and your own ideas.

Types	*Who*	*Purpose(s)*
make-up	men	beautification
special clothing or hairstyles	women	marital status
face or body painting	adolescents	social status
piercing	social status	personal or religious beliefs
tattooing	children or infants	significant events or memories
tooth alteration or decoration		

B Write your description. Use your notes from Part A. Your description should address the type(s), the recipients, and the purposes of the body art or body modification. Try to use the grammar from the chapter.

> Like other Pacific islanders, Hawaiians have used tattoos for centuries to indicate social position and personal identity. The tattoos are placed on various parts of the body, some of which are unusual. As a matter of fact, in the past, Hawaiian women actually had designs tattooed on their faces.

C Post your descriptions around the room. Which one had the most surprising or interesting information? Why?

MyEnglishLab

▶ Diagnostic Test

Grammar Summary

Modals and phrasal expressions can express varying degrees of necessity: obligation, prohibition, advice, expectation, and permission.

The modal auxiliaries are *can, may, should, ought to, had better, must*. Their phrasal equivalents are *be (not) allowed to, (not) have to, be (not) required to, be (not) advised to, be (not) supposed to, be (not) expected to, be (not) required to, be (not) allowed to*. With some modals and phrasal expressions, the negated form changes the meaning.	(1) In most schools, girls can wear pants. (2) In most schools, girls are allowed to wear pants. (3) Boys ought to wear belted pants. (4) Boys are expected to wear belted pants. (5) Students should wear appropriate clothes. (6) Students should not display offensive images on shirts. (7) Students must remove hats in school. (8) Girls must not wear low-cut shirts.

Causatives express the idea of someone or something causing something else to happen.

One type of causative construction is *let / make / have* + direct object + verb, and *get* + direct object + *to* + verb. *let* → permission; *make* → no choice; *have* → instructions given; *get* → persuasion. Another type of causative is *have / get* + direct object + past participle to indicate completion of a job or service, usually by someone else.	(1) Parents usually don't let their children get tattoos. (2) Schools make students follow their dress policies. (3) The principal had a student wear a school T-shirt over her tank top. (4) Teens sometimes get each other to get piercings. (5) The principal had several students' hair cut. (6) Teens sometimes get piercings done together.

Expressing purpose can be done with *in order* + infinitive, *for* + noun / noun phrase, or *so that* + adverb clause.

In order + infinitive (*in order* can be omitted) indicates a purpose for an action. An adverb phrase of purpose includes the preposition *for* + a noun / noun phrase, not an infinitive or gerund, except with the expression *be used for*. The subordinating conjunction *so that* introduces an adverb clause of purpose.	(1) Some people get tattoos (in order) to commemorate an event. (2) Others get tattoos to express their religious beliefs. (3) Samoans go to a master artist for their tattoos. (4) Special tools are used by Balinese priests for tooth filing. (5) In the past, Chinese mothers bound their daughters' feet so that they would become smaller.

Conjunctive adverbs can exemplify, emphasize, or clarify ideas in independent clauses.

Conjunctive adverbs that introduce examples include *for example, for instance, in particular*, and *specifically*. Conjunctive adverbs that emphasize ideas include *in fact, indeed*, and *as a matter of fact*. Conjunctive adverbs that clarify or explain previous ideas include *in other words* and *that is*.	(1) Body art takes many forms. For instance, nose piercing is customary in Indian cultures. (2) Piercing is not just limited to the face. In fact, in some cultures, people get multiple piercings on their bodies. (3) Individuals with extreme forms of body art can be ostracized; in other words, they are not accepted by people with different ideals about physical appearance.

Self-Assessment

A (5 points) Circle the modals or phrasal expressions that make the most sense.

Decorations, symbols, or words **1. must appear / may not appear** either on clothing or on the skin if they convey messages that are crude, violent, or reference items that are illegal. To ensure that undergarments do not show, sagging pants, spaghetti straps, and skirts shorter than fingertip length or a designated number of inches above the knee **2. are not allowed / are not required**. Head coverings, such as hats, caps, and hoods, **3. are not allowed to be / are required to be** removed; sunglasses **4. cannot be / may be** worn inside. Some piercings **5. can be / are expected to be** shown as long as they do not interfere with students' health and safety.

B (5 points) Complete the paragraph with appropriate, logical causative constructions from the list.

get / reduce   let / express   make / wear   had / uphold   let / find

School officials argue that a dress code, besides contributing to safety and discipline, **1.** _____ students _____ other ways to express their individuality. They say that uniforms **2.** _____ students _____ the visible differences between students of different socioeconomic classes and that parents **3.** _____ children _____ uniforms to remove pressure to dress in particular ways. Nevertheless, a U.S. Court of Appeals **4.** _____ a school district's uniform policy _____ with the opinion that the uniform policies limit only one form of student expression but **5.** _____ students _____ their individuality in many other ways.

C (5 points) Complete the sentences with *to, for,* or *so that*.

1. In many societies, hair is used _____ convey various ideals.

2. In certain rituals, a person's hair is cut or shaved _____ they can pass from one life stage to another.

3. Sikh men never cut their hair and cover their heads with turbans _____ show their religious commitment.

4. Some cultures reverse the customary treatment of hair _____ they can claim membership to a particular group.

5. Desiring to be different, some youth in the West adopt extreme hairstyles _____ attention.

D (5 points) Complete the paragraph with appropriate and logical conjunctive adverbs. Add proper punctuation.

In prisons, tattoos convey affiliation with a particular group **1.** _____ many inmates use tattoos to show that they are members of a gang. As tattooing in prison is illegal, it is quite difficult to practice **2.** _____ it has be done in secret without the usual resources. Prison tattooists do not have access to proper equipment and are forced to use unusual items **3.** _____ they have been known to use objects such as paper clips, staples, and even guitar strings. There are various symbols and numbers that represent multiple gangs or groups **4.** _____ images like spiderwebs and teardrops can represent the length of sentences. Prison tattooing is a clear example of a behavior practiced broadly in society that has been adopted and adapted by a social sub-group **5.** _____ inmates have made the art of tattooing a significant element of prison culture.

Unit Project: Poster presentation

A Work in groups of three or four students. Research a type of body art and prepare a poster presentation about it. Follow the steps.

1. Each member of your group should select one type of body art to research. Choose a type of body art from the box or one that you are familiar with. Fill in the chart with the appropriate information and find a picture of your art form.

African scarification	earlobe and lip stretching	makeup
Balinese tooth filing	ear piercing	neck rings of Padaung women
body piercing	henna tattooing (Mehndi)	other _____
Chinese foot binding	lip plates	

Type of body art	What is it? What does it involve?	Where is it used?	Who uses it?	What is its function or purpose?	What are related issues, restrictions, or prohibitions?

2. Share the details you collected with your group members. Choose one art form for your group presentation.
3. Prepare your group poster. Make sure you have a plain poster-size piece of paper and other necessary materials. Decide how you want to arrange any pictures or drawings you have collected or made.
4. Prepare your presentation. Divide the speaking parts equally so that each group member has a chance to speak.

B Present your poster to your classmates. Have a discussion after each presentation. Follow the steps.

1. Discuss each poster in terms of effectiveness of the oral portion and effectiveness of the poster. Were the different types of information presented clearly? Did the oral portion correspond to the poster?
2. Decide which poster or presentation was the most effective and which included the most surprising or unusual information about body art.

MyEnglishLab

▶ Unit Test

MyEnglishLab

▶ Search it!

UNIT 9

Community Service

Outcomes

After completing this unit, I will be able to use these grammar points.

Chapter 17

Grammar Focus 1
Gerunds as objects of prepositions

Grammar Focus 2
Reducing adverbial clauses of cause / reason

Chapter 18

Grammar Focus 1
Gerunds and infinitives as subjects and subject complements

Grammar Focus 2
Interaction of tenses: Time frame shifts

MyEnglishLab

 What do you know?

CHAPTER 17 | Professionals Making a Difference

Getting Started

A Discuss the questions with a partner.

1. What international volunteer organizations are you familiar with?
2. What types of activities are these organizations involved in?
3. What kinds of qualifications, if any, should people have if they want to volunteer?

B Read the statements. Check (✓) the statements that you agree with. Then, discuss your responses with a partner.

- ☐ 1. Community service volunteers need to be good at doing a wide range of activities.
- ☐ 2. Requiring serious time commitments, volunteer work is for people who have more free time, such as the young and the retired.
- ☐ 3. Companies who have an interest in expanding employees' skills should create opportunities for them to do volunteer work.
- ☐ 4. Volunteers who are dedicated to working on long-term projects have a greater impact than those who are only capable of working for short periods of time.
- ☐ 5. Having completed challenging projects in difficult conditions, volunteers should be satisfied with that experience. They shouldn't feel the need to do another project.
- ☐ 6. Communities that are accustomed to receiving very little outside support would probably be suspicious of volunteers at first.
- ☐ 7. Improving both physical and mental health, community service has benefits for volunteers, too.
- ☐ 8. People with valuable skills have the responsibility for sharing them with those in need.

C Look back at Part B. Complete the tasks.

1. Circle all **noun + preposition + gerund combinations** and put a rectangle around all **adjective + preposition + gerund combinations**. What prepositions seem to be the most common in these structures? Try grouping them in the chart.
2. Underline all **reduced adverbial clauses of cause and reason**. Consider what the complete clause would be.
3. Complete the chart with examples. Then, compare your chart with a partner's chart.

Noun + preposition + gerund	Adjective + preposition + gerund	Reduced adverbial clauses

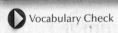
Reading

A WARM-UP Look at the engineering specializations in the list. What kind of work might these different types of engineers do in their jobs? Discuss your ideas with a partner.

chemical engineers   civil engineers   electrical engineers   mechanical engineers

B SCANNING Scan the article to identify three kinds of engineering projects volunteers have completed. Then, read the whole article.

Engineering without Borders

An engineering professor is using "people power" to build solutions for the developing world.

Bernard Amadei, a civil engineer and university professor, is a believer in using one's skills to help others. In 1997, requiring some landscaping work to be done at his home, he contacted a local company. The three men who came to complete the work were Mayan Indians from Belize. Amadei, an outgoing Frenchman who is good at connecting with others, listened as the men told him of the poverty in their home village of San Pablo. A few years later, he accepted an invitation to visit their families in Belize. There, he saw how difficult life was, especially for the young girls in the community. "Carrying water back and forth to the village all day, they couldn't go to school," Amadei says. "I knew that as an engineer, there had to be something I could do."

Amadei soon returned to San Pablo with a team of engineering students. They designed a pump that could supply water to the community without using electricity. That low-cost, simple solution transformed the lives of the villagers and that of Amadei. His reason for going to Belize was to use his engineering knowledge to help the people of San Pablo; however, the experience made him realize that he was no longer limited to teaching his students in the classroom. "The students were very interested in doing the project," he says. "I could also see the huge social impact that a small project can have."

His experience inspired Amadei to found Engineers Without Borders (EWB), a non-profit group that focuses on low-tech, high-impact projects in the developing world. Since 2002, more than 230 affiliated chapters have been formed in universities and professional groups around the United States, comprising over 8,000 members, with more overseas. EWB has built everything from solar panels in Rwanda to water filtration systems in Thailand, and the group has earned a reputation for attaining far-reaching results that go beyond projects. They strive to make a difference in communities that are weary of being told that there are no resources to help them. Furthermore, EWB is changing the way engineering is taught in schools and practiced in the field by addressing the long-neglected needs of the billions of people who live without clean water or decent sanitation.

The opportunity alone to pair learning with hands-on experience attracts many to EWB chapters, but an increasing number of young engineers believe their experience with EWB will shape their professional future. "Having participated in the critical work that EWB does, new generations of engineers will not be satisfied with going the usual route of client work and consulting," says one student. "We're looking to get out there and make a difference on the ground."

C UNDERSTANDING REASONS Read the article again. Then, answer the questions with information from the reading. Compare your responses with a partner.

1. Why was Amadei motivated to start Engineers Without Borders?
2. Why is the work that EWB volunteers do especially effective?
3. How can volunteering with EWB influence young engineers' professional goals?
4. Why does the organization use the term "Without Borders" in its name?

Grammar Focus 1 Gerunds as objects of prepositions

Examples	Language notes
(1) Amadei is **a believer in using** one's skills to help others. His team was **enthusiastic about helping** the residents of San Pablo.	Because **gerunds** function as nouns, they can appear in different positions within a sentence. A gerund can be the **object of a preposition** that is preceded a **noun** or **adjective**. (Refer to Unit 3 to review gerunds as objects of verbs.)
(2) EWB has **a reputation for attaining** far-reaching results.	The prepositions in **noun + preposition + gerund** combinations include *about, for, in, of* and *to*.
(3) Amadei is **good at connecting** with others. They will not be **satisfied with going** the usual route of client work and consulting.	The prepositions in **adjective + preposition + gerund** combinations include *about, at, for, in, of, to,* and *with*. We use both regular adjectives and past participial (*-ed*) adjectives in these combinations.
(4) The students were **interested in doing** the project. The EWB team was **excited about being invited** to the village.	We usually use **simple gerunds** in these combinations to make general statements. We can use **passive gerunds** to focus attention on the receiver of action. To form passive gerunds, use **being + past participle**.
(5) The program **was famous for having completed** many important projects in a short period of time.	These gerunds can also occur as **past gerunds** to emphasize a sequence of actions. The action in the past gerund happened before the action of the main verb. To form past gerunds, use **having + past participle**.

Subject	Verb	Noun	Preposition	Complement
EWB	has	a reputation	**for**	attaining far-reaching results.

Subject	Verb	Adjective	Preposition	Complement
The students	were	interested	**in**	doing the project.

See Appendix H on page A-10 for lists of common noun + preposition + gerund *and* adjective + preposition + gerund *combinations.*

Grammar Practice

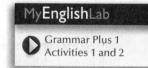
My**English**Lab

Grammar Plus 1
Activities 1 and 2

A Complete the paragraph with the correct prepositions from the list.

> about   for   in   to   with

Doctors Without Borders (Médecins Sans Frontières or MSF) is an international medical humanitarian organization. The doctors, nurses, and other medical specialists who work with MSF are dedicated **1.** _____ helping people in crisis situations regardless of their race, religion, or political affiliation. Since 1971, MSF teams have been responsible **2.** _____ providing quality medical care in nearly 60 countries. The teams have well-qualified specialists who are familiar **3.** _____ working in difficult, even dangerous, circumstances, and the majority of MSF's aid workers are from the communities where the crises are occurring. The work of MSF teams is not limited **4.** _____ offering direct medical care; they also share a commitment **5.** _____ serving as witnesses to the crises of the people they assist. However, as an organization, MSF is neutral. It has a reputation **6.** _____ not taking sides in armed conflicts and being concerned **7.** _____ providing care on the basis of need alone. This belief **8.** _____ operating independently of governments or other parties and obtaining independent funding is the key to MSF's ability to conduct its aid efforts.

B Read the sentences. Then, rewrite each sentence using the noun or adjective in parentheses with a preposition + gerund combination.

1. Amadei feels teaching engineering students in the field is important. (supporter)
   Amadei is a supporter of teaching engineering students in the field.

2. EWB volunteers complete projects by adapting centuries-old technology. (reputation)

3. The volunteers create inexpensive, low-tech solutions to serious problems. (proud)

4. Some volunteers were unsure about the completion of more complicated projects. (doubts)

5. At first, some professional volunteers do not know how to use low-tech tools. (unaccustomed)

6. Inexperienced volunteers realize that they can learn a great deal in the field. (capable)

7. EWB believes that it is important to partner with other agencies on projects. (advocate)

C Correct the errors in the noun or adjective + preposition + gerund constructions in the sentences. Write your correction above the line.

1. Professionals who can't join a volunteer agency find other methods for share their skills.

2. Many professionals, such as lawyers and accountants, are committed donating their services.

3. When volunteer agencies face difficult in raising funds for important services, these professionals can help by performing the work for free.

4. Some professionals are involved about helping volunteer agencies on a regular basis.

5. A professional's enthusiastic for contributing to volunteer projects can inspire his or her colleagues to help.

6. This approach to serve people in need works well for the professionals and the volunteer agencies who rely on their expertise.

Grammar Focus 2 Reducing adverbial clauses of cause / reason

Examples	Language notes
(1) **Because they lack access to clean water and proper sanitation,** many communities do not have healthy living conditions. **Lacking access to clean water and proper sanitation,** many communities do not have healthy living conditions.	**Adverbial clauses** are dependent (subordinate) clauses. They show relationships between ideas in terms of *time*, *cause* or *effect*, *contrast*, and *condition*. **Adverbial clauses of cause/reason** show why something happens. They begin with subordinators **because, since,** or **as** and can be reduced to **adverbial phrases** (present participle phrases). The adverbial phrase shows the cause or reason and the main clause shows the effect or result.
(2) *As volunteers complete* low-tech and low-cost projects, they can assist more communities in need. → **Completing low-tech and low-cost projects,** volunteers can assist more communities in need. *Because the girls were* carrying water back and forth to the village all day, they couldn't go to school. → **Carrying water back and forth to the village all day,** the girls couldn't go to school. *Since he needed* landscaping work to be done at his home, Amadei picked a company out of the phone book. → **Needing work to be done at his home,** Amadei picked a company out of the phone book.	To reduce an adverb clause of cause/reason, omit the subordinator, subject, and any auxiliary verbs. Then, change the main verb to its present participle form (-*ing* form). If the main verb is in the present progressive, it is already in the -*ing* form. You can create adverb clauses of cause/reason with the present and past verb forms.
(3) Since volunteers *have experienced* the satisfaction of using their skills to help others, many decide that they want more than a traditional job. → **Having experienced** the satisfaction of using their skills to help others, many volunteers decide that they want more than a traditional job.	An adverb clause with the verb in the present or past prefect form can be changed to an adverb clause with **having + past participle**. The resulting phrase emphasizes that the cause happened earlier than the effect.
(4) Because they **have never completed** hands-on work, some volunteers are able to expand their learning. → **Never having completed** hands-on work, some volunteers are able to expand their learning.	If the adverb clause is **negative**, put **not** or **never** in front of the -*ing* form when reducing it to a phrase.
(5) As a volunteer team **has recently received** funding for a water supply project in Central America, they will be able to give schools in the area access to clean water. → **Having recently received funding** for a water supply project in Central America, volunteers will be able to give schools in the area access to clean water.	The adverbs **recently** and **already** can also be used in the adverb phrase.
(6) As **volunteers** complete low-tech and low-cost projects, **their work** is highly effective. INCORRECT: Completing low-tech and low-cost projects, their work is highly effective.	An adverbial clause can be reduced to a phrase only when the subjects of the main clause and the adverbial clause are the same.

Adverbial (dependent) clause				Main (independent) clause
subordinator	subject	verb	complement	
Because	**they**	**lack**	access to clean water,	many communities do not have healthy living conditions.

Adverbial phrase	Main (independent) clause
Lacking access to clean water,	many communities do not have healthy living conditions.

Grammar Practice

A Read the sentences. Check (✓) the sentences that can be reduced to adverbial phrases. Then, write new sentences with the reduction.

☐ **1.** Since more companies are encouraging their employees to do volunteer work, attitudes about community service have changed.

_____

☐ **2.** Because employees have used skills like problem solving and networking in volunteer activities, they are able to transfer these skills to the workplace.

_____

☐ **3.** As work-supported volunteer programs motivate companies at all levels, they bring a strong sense of shared commitment.

_____

☐ **4.** Since it isn't possible for all companies to start their own programs, employees can seek opportunities to use their professional skills in volunteer organizations.

_____

☐ **5.** Since they have engaged in volunteer projects on their own, some professionals convince their employers of the benefits of sponsoring a program.

_____

☐ **6.** Because professionals in many fields have considerable expertise to offer, they have a major impact on struggling communities.

_____

B Identify the relationship between the two sentences. When possible, combine them by changing the first sentence into an adverbial phrase of cause or reason.

1. Volunteer biologists know how to fight the effects of water pollution. The biologists help countries like Thailand save their coral reefs.

_____

2. Psychologists volunteer in Southeast Asia for a variety of projects. Parents learn to help their children with learning difficulties.

_____

3. Volunteer economists advise businesses on local investment opportunities. They help improve local economies in Mongolia.

_____

4. Journalists are familiar with the newspaper publishing process. Local newspaper staff members are taught how to write and publish newspapers.

_____

5. Web developers have the ability to build and maintain websites. These developers assist nonprofit organizations in creating online fund-raising tools.

_____

6. Some teachers don't have sufficient training. They can learn a great deal from volunteers with extensive teaching experience.

_____

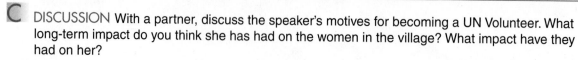
Speaking

 A Look at the list of professions that also have "Without Borders" volunteer organizations. Discuss your answers to the two questions in small groups. Use the words in the boxes for ideas. Try to use the grammar from the chapter. Look at the model.

Chemists Without Borders	Firefighters Without Borders	Teachers Without Borders
Farmers Without Borders	Lawyers Without Borders	Translators Without Borders

1. What kinds of activities do you think volunteers in each of the organizations carry out?

2. Where might they do their volunteer work?

Nouns			Adjectives			Prepositions	
(dis)advantage	enthusiasm	process	accustomed	famous	proud	about	in
advocate	experience	reaction	capable	good	reserved	at	of
belief	hope	reputation	committed	interested	responsible	for	to
chance	idea	responsibility	dedicated	involved	suitable		
commitment	interest	supporter	devoted	(well) known	used		
danger	knowledge	victim	engaged	limited			
dedication	method	way	excited	made			
devotion	problem		exposed	opposed			

> *I think that volunteers in Teachers Without Borders are engaged in teaching children in schools that don't have enough resources. They might also be involved in raising funds for . . .*

B Work with the same group. Draw conclusions about the reasons people join those organizations and discuss the potential benefits for them and the people they help. Look at the model.

> *Being dedicated to helping others learn, volunteer teachers use their skills to assist schools in poor communities. Volunteers can gain experience . . .*

Listening

 A 🎧 UNDERSTANDING MAIN IDEAS Listen to an interview with a United Nations Volunteer. Then, complete the information.

1. Country where the UN Volunteer works: _____

2. Volunteer's home country: _____

3. Volunteer's profession: _____

4. Volunteer's project: _____

B 🎧 UNDERSTANDING DETAILS Listen to the interview again. Use the model as you take notes on the information in the interview.

Motive(s) for volunteering	Challenges	Successes

C DISCUSSION With a partner, discuss the speaker's motives for becoming a UN Volunteer. What long-term impact do you think she has had on the women in the village? What impact have they had on her?

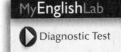
Writing

A In groups of three, brainstorm ideas for a volunteer organization, Students Without Borders. How could you and the students in your school help other students, in your country or in another, with basic, low-cost forms of assistance? Use the model to make notes on a piece of paper.

Where would you volunteer?	How do the students need support?	How would the projects be completed?

B As a group, write a funding proposal for a Students Without Borders organization at your school to be delivered to your school's administration or some other funding source. Try to use the grammar from the chapter. Follow the steps.

1. Choose a specific project idea from Part A.
2. Each group member writes about one of the three aspects discussed in Part A.
3. Combine the individual parts to create one proposal document (see the example below). Then, work together to write a brief opening to the proposal (the motivation for doing the project) and a short closing.

Date: November 5, 2013

Funding proposal for: Students Without Borders at Southeast University

Presented to: Southeast University Office of Student Organizations Funding Committee

Presented by: Adriana Gutierrez, Monica Popescu, and Gabriel Durand

As Southeast University students who are dedicated to helping others, we would like to formally request funding for a new campus organization, Students Without Borders. We believe that . . . .

Location of project

We are greatly interested in providing assistance to Greenville High School, which is near the Southeast campus. Having recently received severe funding cuts, Greenville has . . .

Identified needs

After consulting with the school's administration, we have identified two areas in which we think Students Without Borders could impact Greenville High. First, the free after-school tutoring program was eliminated, and many students are . . .

Project plan

The first part of our plan involves a low-cost method of providing tutoring services again. Students Without Borders would assume responsibility for . . .

In closing, we would like to thank you in advance for considering our proposal and we look forward to hearing your . . .

C Share your proposals with the rest of the class. As a class, discuss which proposal would most likely be accepted and why.

MyEnglishLab

Diagnostic Test

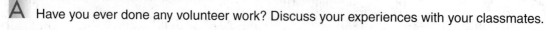

CHAPTER 18 | Youth Making a Difference

Getting Started

A Have you ever done any volunteer work? Discuss your experiences with your classmates.

B Work with a partner. First, read the examples of volunteer activities. Discuss whether these activities are good projects for young people to engage in. Then, read the reasons for doing community service. Discuss whether you agree or disagree. Give reasons for your answers.

Examples of volunteer activities

1. My team helped with earthquake relief efforts in Haiti. After a quake, a lot of rubble needs to be moved out of the way.
2. I went to Mexico to build schoolhouses. Kids can't have an education without a place to learn.
3. I organized a workshop on AIDS awareness in Rwanda. Awareness is key to AIDS reduction.
4. Our class has been involved in agricultural projects in India. People will benefit from the right techniques and equipment.

Reasons for doing community service

1. Helping underprivileged communities is a moral obligation.
2. It is important for one's resumé to be seen as a volunteer.
3. To have done disaster relief helps one see how fortunate one is.
4. Being thrown into community service is a way to spend one's vacation.

C Look back at Part B. Complete the tasks.

1. Circle all **gerunds** (**verb** + *-ing*) and draw a rectangle around all **infinitives** (*to* + **verb**).
2. Underline all **verbs**, and copy their **subject-verb-complement** structures into your chart under the appropriate tense.
3. Fill in the chart with examples. Then, compare your chart with a partner's chart.

Gerunds and infinitives	Tense shifts
Gerunds:	Past:
Infinitives:	Present:
	Future:

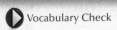
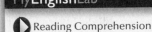

Reading

A WARM-UP Read the examples of specific community service activities. With a partner, discuss what the people's motives could be for engaging in these activities.

1. An American high school student travels to Russia to help build model farms.
2. A French university student travels to Honduras to teach children and adults computer skills.
3. A Canadian elementary school student collects trash in her neighborhood.

B SCANNING Read the title and then scan the magazine article to find answers to the questions. Discuss the answers with the class. Then, read the whole article.

1. What is SASVO and what are its mission and achievements?
2. What do you think the title of the article means?

Mixing Sweat with Earth

To dig trenches and haul construction material is probably not everyone's idea of a perfect vacation, but an increasing number of young people find fulfillment in community engagement. In 2001, South African student volunteers traveled to a deserted Mozambiquan village and were given the task of reconstructing the community's school building. Between 1993 and 2005, SASVO, which stands for the Southern African Student Volunteers Organization, was a pioneering body for community action across the region. To support poverty-stricken areas became the mantra of the organization, which sent out groups of students to spend part of their vacation on projects and fill gaps left by underresourced governments. But organizations like SASVO are not just about good deeds. Having participated in community projects was particularly meaningful for black students. Being offered service projects helps reaffirm young Africans' identity and sense of belonging. Mixing sweat with earth provides ownership of that land, and mixing sweat with the sweat of others provides joint ownership. SASVO had the potential to become a pan-continental volunteering body. By 2001, more than 6,000 student volunteers from 40 academic institutions in 10 African countries had participated in community development projects in South Africa and neighboring countries. The organization's key projects were renovating houses, building classrooms, and painting hospital wards. Student volunteers also did disaster relief work, ran human rights education workshops, and assisted with the general

elections in some countries. Future projects were expected to focus on HIV/AIDS awareness and agricultural projects. However, SASVO's promoting community engagement among young people in rural and disadvantaged communities remained the only volunteer effort by a local South African organization. For a number of reasons, SASVO's activities were suspended in 2005, but to be reactivated has been SASVO's goal.

In the opinion of its organizers, SASVO's greatest accomplishment was to instill in volunteers and community members alike ideals of self-reliance, volunteerism, and love of Africa through projects that help secure access to education and services for all. In many third-world countries, it is critical to bridge the divide between the political elite and destitute communities. The problem in those countries has always been that once people get to power, they lose contact with those whom they are meant to serve. But to have worked in a rural community will remain an important memory for volunteers. Being connected through strong links between volunteers and communities is essential. The communities' taking partial responsibility in their improvement gives them ownership of their projects, and volunteers' providing the sweat gets the work done. In the process, village people and volunteers—some of whom will probably become political and business leaders in the future—have time and opportunity to debate issues of pressing concern, such as human rights. People's and volunteers' sharing of ideas and resources creates links between people and the potential for lifelong community engagement.

C APPLYING IDEAS Read the article again. Make a list of the projects that SASVO was engaged in. They were all done in a third-world context. Then, discuss which projects could also be the focus of community engagement in developed countries. Explain your answers.

Grammar Focus 1 Gerunds and infinitives as subjects and subject complements

Examples	Language notes
(1) **Volunteering** is a meaningful experience for many young people. **To volunteer** is a meaningful experience for many young people. **Volunteering** *in underprivileged communities of rural Africa* is a meaningful experience for many young people. **To volunteer** *in underprivileged communities of rural Africa* is a meaningful experience for many young people.	A gerund is the **base form of the verb + -ing**. An infinitive is the word *to* + **the base form of the verb.** Gerunds and infinitives can functions as nouns and take the role of **sentence subject**. The gerund or infinitive construction can consist of a simple gerund or infinitive, or a more complex gerund or infinitive phrase, often a prepositional phrase that follows the gerund or infinitive.
(2) The organization's key projects *were* renovating **houses and building classrooms.** SASVO's greatest accomplishment *was* to instill in **volunteers and community members alike ideals of self-reliance.**	Gerunds and infinitives can also follow the linking verbs *be*, *become*, and *remain* as a **subject complement**.
(3) *It is critical* to bridge the divide. (Compare: **Bridging** the divide is critical.)	Infinitives as subjects are more formal than gerunds and occur more frequently in writing than in speaking. *It is* + **infinitive phrase** is a more common structure.
(4) <u>**Having participated**</u> in community projects was particularly meaningful for black students. <u>**To have worked**</u> in a rural community will remain an important memory for volunteers.	Gerunds and infinitives typically occur as simple gerunds and infinitives. We use simple gerunds and infinitives to make general statements. They can also occur as **past gerunds** and **past infinitives** to emphasize the time difference between actions. To form past gerunds and infinitives, use *having / to have* + **past participle.** Both past gerunds and past infinitives occur less frequently than simple gerunds and infinitives.
(5) <u>**Being connected**</u> through strong links between volunteers and communities is essential. <u>**To be reactivated**</u> has been SASVO's goal.	Gerunds and infinitives in the subject role can also occur in passive voice (*being / to be* + **past participle**).
(6) <u>**SASVO's promoting**</u> community engagement among young people remained the only indigenous organizational effort. <u>**Its promoting**</u> community engagement among young people remained the only indigenous organizational effort.	Gerunds as subjects can also occur with a possessive noun or pronoun to show **possessive relationship**. This structure is more typical of written discourse; in speech, the possessive tends to be replaced by the noun or its object pronoun.

	Subject	Verb	Complement
Simple gerund / infinitive	**Volunteering** in underprivileged communities of rural Africa	**is**	a meaningful experience for many young people.
	To support poverty-stricken areas	**became**	the mantra of the organization.
Past gerund / infinitive	**Having participated** in community projects	**was**	particularly meaningful for black students.
	To have worked in a rural community	**will remain**	an important memory for volunteers.
Passive voice	**Being connected** through strong links	**is**	essential.
	To be reactivated	**has been**	SASVO's goal.

Grammar Practice

A Match the subjects on the left with logical complements on the right to create sentences about volunteering in Africa.

A

_____ 1. Being able to access water and electricity

_____ 2. It is typical

_____ 3. Being annoyed by a slower pace of life

_____ 4. To compare the local situation with that of one's home environment

a. only leads to frustration.

b. tends to be a frequent reaction of volunteers.

c. is often not possible.

d. to be invited to stay with a local family.

B

_____ 1. Getting used to a different diet

_____ 2. Having informed oneself of local health issues before traveling

_____ 3. It's advisable

_____ 4. To be overwhelmed by project demands and cultural differences

a. is normal.

b. can take some time.

c. is helpful preparation.

d. to be flexible and not to expect organizations to run effectively.

B Rewrite the sentences, using gerunds, infinitives, or gerund / infinitive phrases as subjects or subject complements. Some sentences require changes in wording or omission of some words.

Example: The support of poverty-stricken areas became SASVO's mantra.

> *Supporting / To support poverty-stricken areas became SASVO's focus.*

1. SASVO's goals were the improvement of the quality of life in rural areas.

_____

2. Collaborative work with members of rural communities was the initial step.

_____

3. The 50/50 principle—the ideas that communities and volunteers "meet halfway"—meant that half the effort would come from SASVO and half from the communities.

_____

4. SASVO promoted self-reliance, regional cooperation, and unity, and that became one of its biggest achievements.

_____

5. The work as volunteers and the cooperation with disadvantaged communities enriched the students involved in the projects.

_____

6. One effect was that the young volunteers were encouraged to develop a commitment to uphold the spirit of volunteerism throughout their lives.

_____

7. SASVO was funded by a number of donors, such as banks and private foundations, and this might help in its reactivation.

_____

Examples	Language notes
(1) To dig trenches and haul construction material **is** probably not everyone's idea of a perfect vacation, but an increasing number of young people **find** fulfilment in community engagement. In 2001 South African student volunteers **traveled** to a deserted Mozambiquan village and **were given** the task of reconstructing the community's school building. Between 1993 and 2005, SASVO, which **stands** for the Southern African Student Volunteers Organization, **was** a pioneering body for community action across the region. To support poverty-stricken areas **became** the mantra of the organization, which **sent out** groups of students to spend part of their vacation on projects. But organizations like SASVO **are** not just about good deeds. Having participated in community projects **was** particularly meaningful for black students. Being offered service projects **helps** reaffirm young Africans' identity and sense of belonging. The problem in Africa **has** always **been** that once people **get** to power, they **lose** contact with those whom they **are meant** to serve. But to have worked in a rural community **will remain** an important memory for volunteers. SASVO's greatest accomplishment **was** to instill in volunteers and community members a love of Africa. In Africa, it **is** critical to bridge the divide between political elite and destitute communities.	The time frame is the perspective from which a writer explains ideas in a text. Tenses may change in order to express a shift in time frame, for example, from past to present, from present to present perfect, or from present to future. (You will learn about future tenses in more detail in Unit 10.) Explicit time references may sometimes signal the shift, but not always. Time shifts can occur for several reasons. 1. To illustrate a general topic sentence [present tense] through specific past experiences [past tense]. 2. To provide general background or factual information [present tense] as explanation for entities relevant in a past experience. 3. To offer generalizations [present tense] about past experiences or events [past tense]. 4. To emphasize a contrast, such as between a current or past situation [present perfect, present tense] and a future one [future tense]. 5. To express the writer's commentary [present tense] on a situation [past tense].

Grammar Practice

MyEnglishLab

Grammar Plus 2
Activities 1 and 2

A Complete each passage with the appropriate tense of the verbs in parentheses. Use time signals and / or context clues. Be ready to explain why you followed a time shift, or why you did not.

A. Over a decade ago, Operation Zenzele ("Do it yourself") **1.** _____ (pilot, *passive*) in South Africa. This project **2.** _____ (focus) on upgrading and repairing the infrastructure in disadvantaged communities. The project **3.** _____ (implement, *passive*) in conjunction with township youth. Advice on which communities to target within South Africa often **4.** _____ (come) from the government, whose ministries **5.** _____ (work) with the organization. Other organizations **6.** _____ (offer) long-term opportunities for college graduates to work in projects through which they **7.** _____ (gain) experience and practical skills. Volunteers also **8.** _____ (have) the option of working for non-governmental organizations and international agencies. To date, many long-term placements **9.** _____ (make, *passive*). With branches at seven universities in Africa, there **10.** _____ (be) no shortage of students.

B. Habitat for Humanity **1.** _____ (begin) in the 1960s in Americus, Georgia. Millard and Linda Fuller **2.** _____ (develop) a Fund for Humanity in 1968, and during the next five years, two houses **3.** _____ (complete, *passive*)—one in the United States and one in Africa. In 1976, Habitat for Humanity **4.** _____ (form, *passive*). Since then, Habitat **5.** _____ (build) over 500,000 houses around the world, providing more than 2 million people with homes. Habitat for Humanity **6.** _____ (have) partners in nearly 90 countries. The organization **7.** _____ (offer) programs for youth and college students, and there **8.** _____ (be) partnerships with churches and corporations. Disaster response **9.** _____ (become) an part of Habitat's work as well.

C. I 1. _____ (go) to Russia with Teens Uniting Globally (TUG).
TUG **2.** _____ (be) a subgroup of the Russian Farm Community Project and **3.** _____ (dedicate, *passive*) to improving the Russian economy by building "model farms" that farmers **4.** _____ (use) as templates. Since 1991, American youth **5.** _____ (team up) with Russian youth in towns, where they **6.** _____ (participate) in a project that **7.** _____ (require) manual labor but **8.** _____ (contribute) to a worthwhile cause.

B Complete the paragraphs with logical verbs and appropriate tenses from the lists below. Some verbs have to be in the passive form.

be	can / form	involve	realize	throw
can / fill	continue	oversee	return	use

A Georgetown student **1.** _____ next summer to earthquake-ravaged Haiti. He **2.** _____ work on the solar-powered structures he **3.** _____ _____ using recycled materials during spring break. The student's project at that time **4.** _____ the plastic bags that **5.** _____ by organizations to ship rations to disaster areas. While the bags **6.** _____ away after a single use, the student **7.** _____ that once the bags **8.** _____ empty, they **9.** _____ with rubble and **10.** _____ into bricks to create permanent structures.

be	be	enable	explain	go	look	support

With the help of a nonprofit organization that **11.** _____ environmentally friendly projects, the student **12.** _____ able to gain contacts in Haiti to begin the project. "We **13.** _____ to Haiti for spring break, which **14.** _____ incredible because it **15.** _____ us to get this project completed and have more experience when we **16.** _____ at larger projects for the summer," the student **17.** _____.

construct	learn	use

The building made from the rubble-filled bags **18.** _____ in an international compound, and both the local crew and aid workers from across the world **19.** _____ how to make the insulated and bulletproof structure. Micro solar technology **20.** _____, as well as an environmentally conscious septic system.

build	emphasize	make	recycle	use
compost	flush	purchase	set up	want

The volunteer group **21.** _____ to be responsive to community needs. The volunteers **22.** _____ a septic system that **23.** _____ gray water recycled from a shower that they **24.** _____. This septic system **25.** _____ toilets and then **26.** _____ the waste into a garden. The student **27.** _____ that all the materials (besides the plastic bags) for the building **28.** _____ in Haiti's capital, and the project **29.** _____ _____ use of local labor in addition to student volunteers "so we **30.** _____ _____ very much community integrated."

Listening

A BEFORE LISTENING Work with a partner. Make a list of what groups of people—other than high school or college students—might volunteer, and what volunteer activities they might choose.

B 🎧 UNDERSTANDING DETAILS First, complete the middle column with information you learned in the article on page 185. Then, listen to a speaker at a community service fair talk about his volunteer work. Complete the right-hand column of the chart. What are the similarities and differences between SASVO and the group described in the listening?

	SASVO	Tools for Self-Reliance
Type of volunteer work		
Age / profession		
When?		
Where?		
How often?		
Why?		
Who benefits?		

C 🎧 DISCUSSION Listen again. Then, discuss the questions with a partner.

1. Is the group of people who volunteer for Tools for Self-Reliance one of the groups of people you listed in Part A?
2. Is there anything that surprises you about this group of people? What is it?
3. Is the work that these members do the type of volunteer activity that you had predicted?
4. Is there anything that surprises you about their volunteer activity? What is it?

Speaking

A Divide the class into two groups. One group will discuss motives behind young people's (teens' and college students') volunteer work; the other group will discuss motives behind retired people's and senior citizens' volunteer work. Following the model, make a list of the motives your group discussed. Refer to specific examples or experiences. Try to use the grammar from the chapter.

Why do teens and college students volunteer?	Why do retired people and senior citizens volunteer?
Doing community service is a way to meet other people.	*To feel that they can contribute to their community is often a reason why retired people volunteer.*

B Share your group's notes with the whole class. What are the similarities and differences in young and older people's community service motives? Why? Complete the diagram.

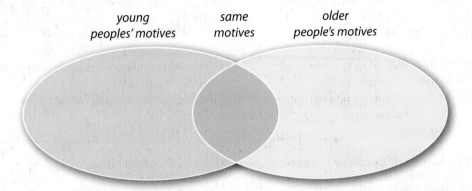

young peoples' motives   *same motives*   *older people's motives*

Writing

MyEnglishLab

▶ Linking Grammar to Writing

A Work in small groups. You will write a recruitment brochure for an actual volunteer organization to motivate people to join and dedicate their time. Research and brainstorm information for each element of the brochure.

Outside of brochure

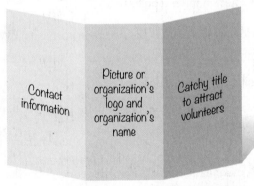

Contact information

Picture or organization's logo and organization's name

Catchy title to attract volunteers

Inside of brochure

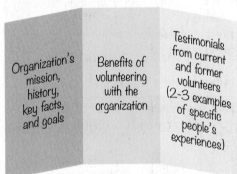

Organization's mission, history, key facts, and goals

Benefits of volunteering with the organization

Testimonials from current and former volunteers (2-3 examples of specific people's experiences)

B Create your brochure, using your notes from Part A. Be sure your brochure is visually interesting and contains relevant information so that people will be motivated to volunteer for your organization. Try to use the grammar from the chapter.

C Post your brochures around the room. Then, discuss the questions with the whole class.

1. Which group's brochure does the best job at attracting potential volunteers? Why?
2. Which organization might be the best to volunteer for? Why?

MyEnglishLab

▶ Diagnostic Test

Grammar Summary

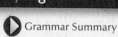
Gerunds as objects of prepositions can follow certain nouns and adjectives.

The prepositions that combine with nouns include *about, for, in, of,* and *to.* Those that combine with adjectives include *about, at, for, in, of, to,* and *with.* Past gerunds show that an action occurred before the action in the main verb. Passive gerunds put the focus on the receiver of actions. Past and passive gerunds occur less frequently than simple gerunds.	(1) Professionals have many reasons for sharing their skills. (2) They are responsible for organizing a variety of projects. (3) Volunteers are happy about having made a difference. (4) The engineers were excited about being invited to the village.

Adverbial phrases of cause or reason can be reduced to adverbial phrases.

Adverbial clauses of cause or reason begin with *because, since,* or *as.* This kind of clause can be reduced to an *-ing* phrase by omitting the subordinator, subject, and any auxiliary verbs. You can't reduce the adverbial clause if the subjects of the main and adverbial clauses are different. If the adverbial clause is negative, put *not* or *never* in front of the *-ing* form when reducing it to a phrase. The present perfect form of the verb is changed to *having* + past participle.	(1) Because professionals have many useful skills, they can contribute a great deal to volunteer projects. (2) Having many useful skills, professionals can contribute a great deal to volunteer projects. (3) Since communities need inexpensive sources of electricity, engineers can build low-tech solutions. (4) Not having extra time, the volunteers need to finish the project in three months. (5) Having successfully finished many projects, EWB is a respected organization.

Gerunds and infinitives can occur in the subject position of a sentence.

Gerunds / infinitives can occur as simple subjects and as gerund / infinitive phrases. They can also follow linking verbs as complements. Gerunds / infinitives can focus on the past. Gerunds / infinitives can be passive. *It is* + infinitives can be used to replace infinitives as subjects. Possessive gerunds are typical of writing.	(1) Volunteering / To volunteer helps people in the community. (2) Volunteering / To volunteer in a soup kitchen translates into food for homeless people. (3) A meaningful activity is volunteering / to volunteer with the handicapped. (4) Having prepared food / To have prepared food at a soup kitchen made me realize how unfortunate people can be. (5) Being trained / To be trained in early childhood education helps me in my volunteer work with children. (6) It is important to be trained in early childhood education. (7) A volunteer's helping with legal documents can be an important task in a women's shelter.

Interaction of tenses indicate a shift in time frame from the writer's or speaker's perspective.

Tense shifts occur for various reasons, such as to illustrate an idea through specific experiences, to give background or a generalization on past experiences, to emphasize contrast, or to express commentary on a situation.	(1) Several students from the university went to Central America and built homes for the poor as part of a Habitat for Humanity service project. Habitat for Humanity operates nationally and also works with organizations in other countries to build houses and school buildings. The young people who devote their time have to be commended.

Self-Assessment

A (5 points) Complete the paragraph with an appropriate noun or adjective + preposition combination from the list below. Use each combination only once.

credit for   engaged in   happy about   reputation for   way of

When their employees are **1.** _____ doing volunteer work, companies can benefit from their expanded skills. Another **2.** _____ benefiting from their volunteer work is to associate the company with the specific service project. That way, consumers are **3.** _____ doing business with a company who has a **4.** _____ using its resources to help others. Both parties can take **5.** _____ making a difference.

B (5 points) Read the sentences. If the sentence has an adverbial phrase, rewrite it with the adverbial clause. If it has an adverbial clause, reduce it to a phrase.

1. Requiring its volunteers to have professional qualifications, the British VSO aids developing countries.
_____
_____

2. Since the VSO recruits over 30 percent of its volunteers from developing countries, it helps professionals as they contribute to the programs in their own countries.
_____
_____

3. Having qualifications needed elsewhere, some of the volunteers from developing countries carry out their service in another country.
_____
_____

4. Because some volunteers are unable to do long-term service, they take shorter assignments.
_____
_____

5. As they share their skills with their local counterparts, VSO volunteers are especially effective.
_____
_____

C (5 points) Match the phrases on the left with logical complements on the right.

_____ **1.** Volunteering through community service applications

_____ **2.** To serve in one's community

_____ **3.** Having helped underprivileged people with challenging projects

_____ **4.** For many teens it is crucial

_____ **5.** Your engaging in community service as a professional

a. to volunteer because it might help with college.

b. signals that you have a well-balanced life.

c. can help people learn new skills.

d. is the best way to become part of the community.

e. often helps boost one's motivation and sense of achievement.

D (5 points) Complete the paragraph with appropriate tense forms of the verbs in parentheses.

After Hurricane Katrina, many university students **1.** _____ (become) involved in relief efforts to help rebuild communities that **2.** _____ (be) destroyed by the hurricane. Over the past decade, the student groups **3.** _____ (be) able to clean up debris and construct new homes. A large number of Gulf Coast citizens still **4.** _____ (live) in makeshift houses; therefore, student groups **5.** _____ (volunteer) their efforts for a while longer.

Unit Project: Research project

A **Studies** have shown that doing small things for others, including strangers, can have an impact on one's own happiness. These are often referred to as "random acts of kindness." In this project, you will carry out acts of kindness and report on the reactions you received as well as your own reaction to performing the acts. Follow the steps.

1. In small groups, brainstorm on acts of kindness that you could perform for people in your surroundings. Examples include holding the door open for someone, buying someone a cup of coffee, letting someone cut in line ahead of you, baking something for a new neighbor. In your group, choose different acts of kindness that each of you could perform. Each person should select three acts.

2. Carry out your acts of kindness at least once a day over the next three days. Write brief notes in a log for each day.

Act of kindness	Where?	To whom?	Receiver's reaction	My reaction	What I learned

3. Discuss the results of your acts of kindness in groups of three or four students.

> *Allowing a woman to cut in line in front of me brought a smile to her face. I was worried about being yelled at by other people in line. It was gratifying to make someone's day a little brighter.*

4. In your group, decide which acts of kindness resulted in the most positive reaction—by receivers and by you. What do you think was special about those particular acts of kindness?

B **Share** your group's discussion results with the rest of the class. As a class, work together to develop general observations about your research. Decide which random acts of kindness you will continue to do.

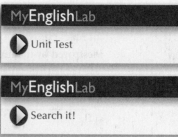

The Environment

OUTCOMES

After completing this unit, I will be able to use these grammar points.

CHAPTER 19

Grammar Focus 1
Infinitives as noun and adjective complements

Grammar Focus 2
Pronoun agreement and reference

CHAPTER 20

Grammar Focus 1
Future time

Grammar Focus 2
Modals of prediction and certainty

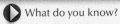

CHAPTER 19 | When Predators Disappear

Getting Started

A Work with a partner. Complete the activity.

1. Discuss how these organisms are related.

bird	caterpillar	flower

algae	fish	seal	shark

2. Put these organisms in "order." Explain how you decided on your "order" in each "chain of organisms."

frog	grasshopper	hawk	plant	snake

algae	dragonfly	fish	mosquito	raccoon

3. Using the chains you created in Step 2, predict what may happen if (a) the organism at the bottom of the chain disappears, (b) the organism at the top of the chain disappears, or (c) any organism in the chain disappears.

B Work in small groups. Read the definitions and explain them with specific examples.

1. A food chain is the sequence of who has a tendency to eat whom in a biological community (an ecosystem) to obtain nutrition. It starts with a primary energy source, like the sun, and moves to an organism that makes its own food from the primary energy source.
2. Herbivores are animals that eat plants. They are also called primary consumers.
3. Carnivores are animals that eat meat. This trait gives them a higher place in the food chain.
4. Predators are sure to have no natural enemies.
5. As carnivores in an ecosystem increase, they have opportunities to eat more of the herbivores, decreasing the herbivore population. Carnivores are then unlikely to find herbivores to eat, and the population of carnivores decreases. This keeps carnivores and herbivores in a relatively stable equilibrium, each limiting the other's population.

C Look back at Part B. Complete the tasks.

1. Circle all **nouns followed by infinitives**, and draw a rectangle around all **adjectives followed by infinitives**.
2. Underline all **pronouns** and **demonstrative pronouns**, and draw an arrow to the word or words to which they refer.
3. Fill in the chart with examples. Then, compare your chart with a partner's chart.

Nouns / Adjectives + Infinitives	Pronouns and Antecedents
Nouns + infinitives:	Sentences with pronouns:
Adjectives + infinitives:	Sentences with demonstrative pronouns:

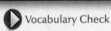

Reading

A **WARM-UP** Select the correct words to make the paragraph correct.

A change in the size of one population in a food chain is **1. apt / not apt** to affect other populations. This interdependence of the populations is certain to **2. maintain / disrupt** the balance of plant and animal within a community. For example, when there are too **3. many / few** giraffes, there will be **4. sufficient / insufficient** trees for them to eat. The giraffe population may **5. proliferate / starve**. **6. More / Fewer** giraffes also means **7. more / less** food is available for lions to eat, and **8. some / few** lions will starve. With **9. more / fewer** lions, the giraffe population can **10. increase / decrease**.

B **UNDERSTANDING MAIN IDEAS** Read the article. What happens to food chains all over the world? What is the difference between "bottom-up" and "top-down" research? Which type is discussed in the text?

NATURE OUT OF BALANCE

A team of scientists is reluctant to report that it believes humans have begun the world's latest mass extinction, and the consequences are being felt on land and in water systems as large predators vanish. The eagerness of hunters to slaughter lions and leopards in sub-Saharan Africa has caused a surge in disease-carrying baboons and they are inching closer to food crops and people. In East Africa, a reduction in big herbivores, such as buffalo and wildebeest, through disease and poachers determined to hunt has led to increases in woody vegetation that fuels wildfires in the dry season. Fishermen's readiness to decimate sharks along the U.S. Atlantic Coast has allowed their main prey, the cow-nosed ray, to proliferate: it now dines heavily on oysters. On the U.S. Pacific Coast, sea otters were hunted to near extinction for their fur. Sea otters feed on sea urchins, and sea urchins eat kelp. Without otters, the sea urchin population had an opportunity to explode, and the kelp forest began to disappear. The otters' absence started a chain of events that was almost certain to eliminate the habitat for marine life on the coast. On the Scottish island of Rum, where wolves have been absent for over 250 years, deer thrive, and the once forested island is now treeless. The decline of wolves in Yellowstone Park made the environment suitable for deer to flourish and feed on creekside trees. This threatened a crucial part of the forest on which creatures living in and near the water rely. Similarly, the lack of wolf populations throughout North America has led to an expansion of the deer population into suburban areas. Since deer carry ticks, humans have been almost certain to contract diseases spread by ticks, such as Lyme disease.

Much of the science in the study of food chains focused on the threat to life at the bottom of the food chain. Scientists theorized that small animals and plants are likely to be important because so many creatures rely on their survival. Although "bottom-up" research is fundamentally important, scientists say that "top-down" research deserves wider consideration. However, top-down research is difficult to conduct because decades may pass before the effects of the disappearance of large predators can be measured, often until after they have been lost and the ability to restore the species has also been lost. Their demise echoes further than previously anticipated. The declining number of predators creates an overabundance of prey, and it is sure to have contributed to the spread of disease, wildfires, and invasive species. Food chains are likely to be thrown out of balance. This outcome may be humankind's most pervasive influence on nature, and everyone must be aware of the consequences of his or her actions.

C **UNDERSTANDING DETAILS** Complete the food chains based on the information in the article. Which link in each chain has become weaker? Why? What have been the consequences for the other links in the chain? Indicate increases in the chain with *more* + noun, decreases with *fewer / less* + noun, and disappearance with *no* + noun. What could be done to rebalance these food chains?

Sub-Saharan Africa	*fewer lions, leopards*	→ _____	→ _____
East Africa	_____	→ *more vegetation*	→ _____
U.S. Atlantic Coast	_____	→ _____	→ *fewer oysters*
U.S. Pacific Coast	_____	→ _____	→ _____
Island of Rum	_____	→ _____	→ *no trees*
Yellowstone Park	_____	→ *more deer*	→ _____
North America	*fewer wolves*	→ _____	→ _____

Grammar Focus 1 Infinitives as noun and adjective complements

Examples	Language notes
	Infinitives can play the role of **noun complements** and **adjective complements** when they follow certain nouns and adjectives and complete their meaning.
(1) **The desire to hunt** made the environment suitable for deer to flourish.	We often use the infinitive to help define **abstract nouns.*** They can occur in various constructions. A simple infinitive follows an abstract noun. Together, the noun + infinitive function as the **subject** of the sentence.
(2) **The ability to restore** *the species* has been lost.	When the verb in the infinitive phrase is **transitive**, it can be followed by an object. Together, the noun + infinitive + object function as the **subject** of the sentence.
(3) The sea urchin population had **an opportunity to explode.**	A noun + infinitive can also occur in the **object** position of the sentence, following the main verb.
(4) Politicians set back **efforts to protect** <u>wolves</u>.	Similarly, the sentence object position can be made up of noun + infinitive + object when the verb in the infinitive phrase is **transitive**.
(5) **The desire to hunt** <u>for wolves</u> made the environment suitable for deer to flourish.	The noun + infinitive can also include a **prepositional phrase**.
(6) The scientists' **reluctance to report** <u>that humans are responsible for a mass extinction</u> was unusual.	The noun + infinitive can be followed by a **noun clause**.
(7) **The likelihood of the findings to be** <u>important</u> was never doubted.	The noun + infinitive can be followed by an **adjective**.
(8) **The possibility** <u>for deer</u> **to flourish** increases as wolf populations decline.	A noun + *for* + noun / pronoun + infinitive construction specifies **to whom or what the noun applies**.
(9) Top-down research is **difficult to conduct.** Food chains are **likely to be thrown** out of balance.	Infinitives can also follow certain **adjectives.**** A simple infinitive follows an adjective. The infinitive can also be in the passive form.
(10) Humans have been **almost certain to contract diseases** spread by ticks.	The adjective + infinitive can also be followed by a direct object if the verb in the infinitive phrase is transitive.
(11) The demise of predators is **sure to have contributed** <u>to the spread of disease</u>.	The adjective + infinitive can also include a **prepositional phrase**. The infinitive can also be in the **past form**.
(12) A team of scientists is **reluctant to report** <u>that humans have caused a mass extinction</u>.	The adjective + infinitive can be followed by a **noun clause**.
(13) Small animals and plants are **likely to be** <u>important</u>.	The adjective + *to be* can be followed by an **adjective**.
(14) The decline of wolves made the environment **suitable** <u>for deer</u> **to flourish**.	An adjective + *for* + noun / pronoun + infinitive construction specifies **to whom the adjective applies**.

*See Appendix I on page A-10 for a list of abstract nouns.
** See Appendix J on page A-10 for a list of adjectives commonly followed by infinitives.

Subject	Verb	Object / Complement
The desire to hunt	made	the environment apt for deer to flourish.
The sea urchin population	had	**an opportunity to explode.**

Subject	Linking verb	Complement
Top-down research	is	**difficult to be conducted.**
The Obama administration	was	**willing to sign a bill.**

Grammar Practice

A Complete the paragraph with the appropriate noun / verb combinations from the list in the correct infinitive structures.

eagerness / eliminate   likelihood / be deprived of   opportunity / shape
~~efforts / research~~   motivation / eradicate   tendency / hunt

The decline of large predators and other species at the top of the food chain has disrupted ecosystems all over the planet. The **1.** _____*efforts*_____ by Jeremy Jackson and Stuart Sandin of Scripps Institution of Oceanography in San Diego _____*to research*_____ a wide range of ecosystems resulted in their conclusion that the loss of these species is arguably humankind's most pervasive influence on the natural world. Large animals were once common across the globe, and they had the **2.** _____ the ecosystems. Humans' **3.** _____ the animals has resulted in the fragmentation of animal habitats and decline in animal populations. The **4.** _____ _____ of the ecosystems _____ big predators has been most pronounced among large species of carnivores. But there has also been **5.** _____ many large herbivores, such as elephants and bison. The **6.** _____ big predators from an ecosystem creates a chain of effects moving down through lower levels of the food chain.

B For each sentence, select the adjective + verb combination that makes sense and write it as an adjective complement with an infinitive. Use passive forms where necessary.

1. When the predators at the top of the food chain—lions, tigers, wolves, cougars—are removed, entire ecosystems are _____*likely to change*_____. (fortunate / likely; change / stabilize)

2. Humans have been _____ these top predators for ages due to fear, false information, hunting traditions, and other reasons. (motivated / careful; destroy / preserve)

3. In some regions, the loss of species at the top of the food chain has been happening because ecosystems had become fragmented and _____ these animals. (apt / unfit; support / eliminate)

4. Now people will be _____ that the loss of predators affects ecosystems worldwide in ways not apparent even a decade ago. (content / stunned; learn / select)

5. The disappearance of these large animals is _____ changes in the landscape and even increases in wildfires. (certain / ready; bring about / care for)

6. Researchers say that the absence of large predators creates an unpredictable cascade of effects, some of which are _____ for many years. (hesitant / unable; recognize / select)

7. For example, when whale populations vanished because of industrial whaling, many ocean areas became much less _____ the simple animals and plankton on which the entire ecosystem was based. (capable / prepared; eradicate / sustain)

Grammar Focus 2 Pronoun agreement and reference

Examples	Language notes
(1) **The cow-nosed ray** is proliferating, and **it** dines heavily on oysters.	We use **pronouns** in place of nouns and noun phrases to avoid repetition and to establish cohesion within spoken or written discourse. The nouns pronouns refer to are called **antecedents**. **Subject pronouns:** *I, you, he, she, it, we, you, they* **Object pronouns:** *me, you, him, her, it, us, you, them*
(2) Decades may pass before the effects of the disappearance of **large predators** can be measured, often until after **they** have been lost. **A scientist** reports that **he** has found evidence for humans' role in the latest mass extinction.	Just as there must be agreement between subjects and verbs, pronouns must agree with their antecedents in subject, possessive, or object form: The pronouns must also agree in gender with their antecedents if they refer to specific individuals whose gender is known.
(3) **Everyone** must be aware of the consequences of **his or her / their** actions. **The sea otter** was hunted to near-extinction for **its** fur. **A scientist** must ensure that **his or her** claims are supported with sufficient evidence. **A team** of scientists is reluctant to report that **it** believes humans have begun the world's latest mass extinction.	**Personal pronouns** can refer to indefinite pronouns, generic nouns, and collective nouns as their antecedents. Singular pronouns are used to refer to **indefinite pronouns** (*anybody, anyone, anything, everybody, everyone, everything, no one, nobody, nothing, somebody, someone, something*). If both genders are possible, use both masculine and feminine pronouns. In informal English, plural pronouns are often used to refer to indefinite pronouns even though they are grammatically inconsistent. A **generic noun** is a representative person or thing; it does not refer to a specific person or thing. Use both masculine and feminine pronouns to refer to a singular generic noun that describes a person. **Collective nouns** define a group (e.g., audience, class, committee, crowd, team) and take singular pronouns.
(4) **The dwindling number** <u>of predators</u> creates an overabundance of prey, and **it** is sure to contribute to the spread of disease.	In a complex noun phrase, the **head noun** determines whether the pronoun is singular or plural.
(5) *Incorrect:* **Small animals and plants** are likely to be important because so many creatures rely on **their** survival. (*ambiguous: two potential plural antecedents: animals, plants*)	Since pronouns replace nouns and noun phrases, their antecedent must be clear. If an antecedent is ambiguous, the meaning of the sentence may be confusing. Thus, a pronoun should not be used if it could have two or more possible antecedents—unless the meaning is logical.
(6) *Incorrect:* Although **"bottom-up" research** is fundamentally important, scientists say that **"top-down" research** deserves wider consideration. However, **it** is difficult to conduct. (*ambiguous: two potential singular antecedents*)	A pronoun should also not be used if the antecedent is **not** in the immediately preceding clause or sentence. In order to avoid an ambiguous sentence, the noun or noun phrase should be repeated. In this example, *top-down research* should be repeated in order to avoid ambiguity.
(7) *Incorrect:* The lack of wolf populations throughout North America has led to an expansion of the deer population into suburban areas, and **they** carry ticks.	A pronoun should be avoided if the antecedent is only implied but not explicitly mentioned. In this example, *deer* is the antecedent, but it is implied.
(8) *Incorrect:* In a scientific report, **they ~~say~~** that humans have begun the world's latest mass extinction. In a scientific report, **scientists claim** that humans have begun the world's latest mass extinction.	Do **not** use pronouns **they, it, you** if there is no explicit antecedent.
(9) <u>Food chains are thrown out of balance</u>. **This / This outcome** may be humankind's most pervasive influence on nature.	Do **not** use demonstrative pronouns **this / that** to refer to whole sentences.

Grammar Practice

A Complete the paragraph with correct pronouns.

The lynx and hare populations in Canada have a predator-prey relationship. **1.** _____ allows the ecosystem dynamic to work. Every ten years or so, the hares' reproduction rate increases. As more hares are born, **2.** _____ eat more of **3.** _____ food supply. **4.** _____ eat so much food that **5.** _____ are forced to supplement **6.** _____ diet with less desirable and nutritious food. As the hare population size grows, the lynx population size begins to increase in response. Because there are so many hares, other predators also hunt **7.** _____ along with the lynxes. The hares' less nutritious and varied diet begins to have an effect, and **8.** _____ causes the hares to die due to illness and disease. Fewer hares are born because **9.** _____ have less food to eat. The hare population declines, and because of **10.** _____ decline, the lynx population also begins to decline. Some lynxes starve and others die due to disease. Both the lynx and hare populations have fewer offspring, and **11.** _____ gives the vegetation a chance to recover. Once there is enough vegetation for the hares to begin to increase **12.** _____ population, the whole cycle begins again.

B Complete the sentences with appropriate pronouns or with nouns in those cases in which pronoun use would be ambiguous.

1. The destruction of lions in Africa resulted in an increase in baboons. *These primates / baboons* carry diseases that crossed over and began infecting nearby humans.

2. The reduction of lions and leopards in parts of Africa has led to population outbreaks and changes in behavior of olive baboons, increasing _____ contact with people and causing higher rates of intestinal parasites in both people and baboons than _____ presence would otherwise have caused.

3. The decimation of wolves in Yellowstone National Park led to elk overfeeding on aspen and willow trees, and _____ restoration has allowed the vegetation to recover.

4. When wolves were reintroduced to Yellowstone National Park, _____ brought down the elk and deer populations.

5. The decrease in elk and deer population allowed creekside willows to recover, and _____ led to a more fruitful environment for species living in and near the water.

6. Whales in the southern oceans dive deep to eat, and then _____ return to the surface to breathe. _____ waste deposits important nutrients from the ocean bottom into the upper water layers.

7. Rinderpest, a disease introduced by humans, almost wiped out the wildebeest population in parts of Africa. _____ in turn led to a buildup of woody vegetation. _____ resulted in devastating wildfires. When _____ was eradicated with a vaccine, the native grasslands returned and the number of fires decreased.

Speaking

A In small groups, review the food chains from the article on page 197. Researchers claim that humans are responsible for the decimation of predators through hunting and poaching practices. What other factors could have led to a decrease in the number of predators? Write down a possible non-human factor, and then explain its impact on each predator. Try to use the grammar from the chapter.

Sub-Saharan Africa	non-human factor: _____*lack of food*_____	→ fewer lions, leopards
East Africa	non-human factor: _____	→ fewer wildebeest
U.S. Atlantic Coast	non-human factor: _____	→ fewer sharks
U.S. Pacific Coast	non-human factor: _____	→ fewer sea otters
Island of Rum	non-human factor: _____	→ fewer wolves
Yellowstone Park	non-human factor: _____	→ fewer wolves
North America	non-human factor: _____	→ fewer wolves

B Work in small groups. Now that you have examined the impact that human and non-human factors may have on the increase or decrease of the number of predators, discuss the food chains in the Getting Started activity on page 196. What factors (human and non-human) might have an impact on the presence or absence of those organisms? Try to use the grammar from the chapter.

Listening

A BEFORE LISTENING You will listen to a lecture on the indirect effects of the absence of large predators. Discuss the questions with a partner.

1. What are the direct effects of the absence of large predators that you have learned about in this chapter so far?
2. What indirect effects do you think the lecturer will discuss?

B UNDERSTANDING MAIN IDEAS Listen to the lecture. Then, answer the questions.

1. What is the word that the lecturer uses for "large predators?" Why does she use this terminology?
2. What are the three indirect effects of predator disappearance that the lecturer discusses? List them in the top row of the table.

Effects on			
Examples of lakes			
Examples of oceans			
Examples of land			

C 🎧 UNDERSTANDING DETAILS Listen again. Focus on the specific examples that the lecturer provides to illustrate each indirect effect. Note them accordingly in the table in Part B. Compare your responses with those of a classmate, and together answer the questions below.

1. What do these indirect effects have in common? Why are scientists worried about them?
2. Is the presence or the absence of large predators better for our planet? Why or why not?

Writing

MyEnglishLab

▶ Linking Grammar to Writing

A Work with a partner. Select one predator and brainstorm on how this predator's disappearance or decline affects the food chain in which the predator resides. Take notes.

Predator: _____

Effects on the food chain:

_____ → _____ → _____ → _____

B Write your food chain analysis on a separate sheet of paper. Use your notes from Part A. Try to use the grammar from the chapter. Additionally, you can illustrate each step in the food chain through an appropriate visual image.

> In the Arctic region, the disappearance of the ice shelves due to global warming has reduced the habitat of polar bears. As a result of their shrinking habitat, many polar bears have lost their lives, and the polar bear population has decreased. With fewer polar bears around, seals in the Arctic waters have a greater chance at survival, and the number of seals has increased. As a result of their increased numbers, the fish . . .

C Share your food chain analyses in small groups. Examine each analysis for logic in the effects. Which food chain disruption through the disappearance of predators is the most serious? Why?

MyEnglishLab

▶ Diagnostic Test

Chapter 20 — Vanishing Islands

Getting Started

A With your partner, discuss which island nations you are familiar with. Then, identify unique challenges that small island nations might face compared to a country with greater land mass and natural resources. Rank the top five challenges according to how serious you think they are. Share and compare your rankings with the class.

B Read each statement about global climate change and rising sea levels. Decide if the meaning of each statement is based on: (A) a certainty, (B) a probability [a strong certainty], or (C) a possibility [a weak certainty].

_____ 1. Global climate change will become the greatest threat to the future of island and coastal communities in the next century.

_____ 2. Based on the current rate of increase, average global temperatures should rise by at least 5.8 degrees Fahrenheit (2 degrees Celsius) by the year 2100.

_____ 3. Once countries make a serious commitment to reducing their greenhouse gas emissions, they will understand the importance of using alternative energy sources.

_____ 4. Rising sea levels are going to continue causing eroded shorelines and poisoning fresh water sources and farmland.

_____ 5. Although some continue to believe that there must be other solutions, the governments of some island nations will need to consider permanent evacuations of their lands.

_____ 6. By midcentury, the severe impacts of global climate change will have forced nearly 150 million "climate refugees" to move to other countries.

_____ 7. The mining companies who stripped many island states of their vegetation and destroyed farming land should have known that they were risking the future survival of the islands.

_____ 8. A group of island nation leaders is holding a meeting next month to discuss potential strategies for dealing with rising sea levels and invading salt water.

C Look back at Part B. Complete the tasks.

1. Underline **verb phrases** that refer to **future states or events**.
2. Circle **present tense forms** that refer to **future states or events**.
3. Double-underline verb phrases that include a **modal verb** and show varying degrees of **predictability** and **certainty** in the past, present, or future.
4. Complete the chart with examples. Then, compare your chart with a partner's chart.

Future tense verbs	Present tense verbs with future meaning	Modal verbs of prediction and certainty

Reading

A WARM-UP With a partner, discuss the specific challenges the inhabitants of small islands face with issues such as food, fresh water, and energy. Decide which you think are the top three.

B UNDERSTANDING MAIN IDEAS Read the article and underline five major impacts of global climate change on small island countries.

The Uncertain Future of Island Nations

In the near future, many small island nations such as Kiribati, Nauru, the Maldives, the Bahamas, and Tuvalu may not survive the effects of global climate change. Because sea levels could rise three or more feet by the end of the century, global warming will likely threaten the very existence of islands such as these. For all small island states, climate change is soon going to present a challenge to their safety, security, and livelihoods. This threat should continue to grow with shifts in environmental conditions. The combination of climate change, security issues, and human rights factors make the future of small island states uncertain. The case for immediate action to reduce carbon emissions couldn't be more urgent.

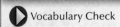

While rising sea levels may be the most obvious threat they face, small island states will also be exposed to an increasing number of extreme weather events. Higher temperatures will bring more heat waves, and higher sea levels will erode shorelines and increase flooding during storms and high tides. More frequent floods will bring salt water inland, poisoning limited water resources and destroying farmland. Higher temperatures will also change sea water chemistry, destroying reefs and fisheries. Altered weather patterns could also be changing the ranges of disease-carrying species, increasing islanders' exposure to new illnesses.

Although these nations only produce a small amount of greenhouse gasses, in the next few years, they will be experiencing the most severe impacts of climate change. In a recent interview, ecologist and island resident William Meares said, "The international community must be ignoring our crisis even though larger, more powerful countries have taken advantage of our natural resources for centuries. These nations must not realize how much damage they have caused our ecosystems because very few are taking serious steps to reduce their carbon output."

And the damage is considerable. Nauru's coast, the only habitable part of the island, is already steadily eroding. In 2008 and 2009, in what must have been frightening conditions, residents of Papua New Guinea and the Solomon Islands were forced to flee their homes to escape record tides. On Tuvalu, the groundwater is unsafe due to high salinity and pollution.

By the time the major carbon-emitting countries fully recognize the severe consequences of climate change, it will be too late to take the necessary steps to stop the continuing damage. Immediate and drastic reductions in emissions of greenhouse gasses are going to be necessary to buy time for these most vulnerable nations. According to some estimates, by 2050, between 250 million and one billion people will have moved to escape the effects of climate change. All the while, more islands and coastal regions will have been eroding away, adding a significant number of refugees to that figure.

C UNDERSTANDING DETAILS Read the article again. Identify statements that are based on probabilities, assumptions, or certainties. List them on a piece of paper and compare them with a partner's. Discuss any differences you have in your lists.

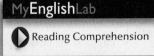

Grammar Focus 1 Future time

Examples	Language notes
(1) Higher temperatures **will bring** more heat waves. Higher temperatures **are going to bring** more heat waves.	We use both *will* (the simple future) and *be going to* when referring to **future events** or **states**, as they often have the same meaning. Either can be used when making **a general prediction** about something in the future and can refer to **general truths**, **facts**, or **habits**.
(2) When the government asked for volunteers for an environmental study, Meares said, "I'**ll help** conduct the study."	Use *will* to show **willingness** or **a quick decision** that was made at the moment of speaking. To form the simple future, combine the auxiliary *will* with the base form of the verb or use the contraction.
(3) Members of the Intergovernmental Panel on Climate Change **are going to meet** next month.	Use *be going to*, not *will*, when describing **a previously made plan** for the future, especially one that is going to take place in the <u>immediate future</u>. Use the appropriate form of *be* + *going to* + the base form of the main verb.
The members **are meeting** *on Tuesday* to finalize their annual report on climate change.	Similarly, we use the **present progressive tense** to describe **planned future activities**. In this case, we use **future time words** to show the future meaning or rely on the context to make the future meaning clear. Use the present progressive rather than *be going to* when the plan is **more definite**.
(4) The meeting tomorrow **starts** *at 10:00 A.M.* and **ends** *at 1:00 P.M.*	In some cases, we use the **simple present tense** with future time words to describe future events, such as activities that are **definite or on a schedule**.
By the time the major carbon-emitting countries fully **recognize** the severe consequences of climate change, it **will be** too late.	We also use the simple present tense in **dependent future clauses**. In these cases, the present tense is used in the dependent clause, and the future tense is used in the main, or independent, clause.
(5) These nations **will be experiencing** the most severe consequences of climate change *in the next few years*.	We use other future verb forms to make predictions about future activities, both in progress and completed.
These nations **will experience** the most severe consequences of climate change *in the next few years*.	Use the **future progressive** to show that an activity **will be in progress** at a time in the future. To form the future progressive, combine *will* + *be* + verb + *-ing*. Sometimes, the **simple future** and **future progressive** have a similar or same meaning.
(6) *By 2050*, between 250 million and one billion people worldwide **will have moved** to escape the effects of climate change.	To indicate that a future activity will be completed <u>before</u> another time or activity, use the **future perfect**. This tense is formed with *will* + *have* + **past participle**.
(7) *All the while*, more islands and coastal regions **will have been eroding** away, adding a significant number of refugees to that figure.	Use the **progressive** form of the **future perfect** to focus on the **duration** of an activity that will be in progress before another time or activity.

Grammar Practice

MyEnglishLab

Grammar Plus 1
Activities 1 and 2

A Using the base verb form and any negatives or adverbs in the parentheses, write an appropriate future verb phrase. Decide between the simple future, *be going to*, present progressive, or simple present forms. Note that more than one answer may be correct.

The UN's Intergovernmental Panel on Climate Change (IPCC) predicts that there **1.** _____

_____ (be) an increase in extreme weather events worldwide in the coming years. According to the climate

scientists on the IPCC, these weather events **2.** _____ (become) more severe in size and

strength. In its latest report, the panel notes that the serious weather events **3.** _____

(hit, not) every region in the same way. For example, Western Europe **4.** _____
(experience) major heat waves and North Africa **5.** _____ (sustain) more droughts.
The eastern and southern parts of the United States and the Caribbean **6.** _____
(have, probably) hurricanes with heavier rainfall and greater wind speeds. The IPCC report also cautions
that once rising sea levels **7.** _____ (reach) a certain level, small island states
8. _____ (face) destructive storm surges at earlier stages of severe weather events.
More critically, these small nations **9.** _____ (be) threatened by sea water
incursions, which **10.** _____ (poison) fresh water aquifers, **11.** _____
_____ (erode) shorelines, and **12.** _____ (ruin) farmland at greater rates. The
IPCC warns about the impact of such extreme weather on vulnerable areas of human settlement. In some
places, weather-related disasters **13.** _____ (wipe out) communities and
14. _____ (necessitate) evacuation or, as in the case of small island states,
permanent migration. Before policymakers **15.** _____ (receive) the report, it
16. _____ (review) by two IPCC working groups at a six-day meeting next month.

B Read the paragraph about environmental damage to coral reefs. Correct the seven verb
phrase errors.

   Scientists predict that the world's oceans will have been losing an additional 30 percent of coral reefs by
mid-century if damage caused by human activity is not reduced. As the destruction of reefs, or "bleaching,"
will continue, the effects are going to be felt in island ecosystems around the world. Reefs provide habitats
for over a million marine species and they protect coastlines from ocean wave action. Loss of that
protection is going to leave island communities more vulnerable to extreme weather events. Increased stress
on coral reefs will have threatened fresh water supplies and other natural resources on the islands. Because
reefs support fisheries and tourism, further loss of these ecosystems will be bringing economic impacts, too.
There will be fewer opportunities for sport fishing, scuba diving, and snorkeling, all of which are highly
popular tourist activities. Once these activities will decrease, the island tourism sector is seeing a significant
drop in employment. Another critical but lesser-known fact about coral reefs is that they contain chemical
compounds that are used to develop important medications for health issues such as ulcers, leukemia, skin
cancer, and cardiovascular diseases. Loss of these ecosystems will have meant the loss of potential cures for
life-threatening health conditions.

Grammar Focus 2 Modals of prediction and certainty

Examples	Language notes

Affirmative   **Certainty**   **Negative**
 will   100%   *will not / won't*
 must/have (got) to   ↑   *cannot / can't*
 should, ought to   │   *could not / couldn't*
 could   │   *must not
 might, may   ↓   *should not / shouldn't*
                        *might not, *may not
             0%
 	
 *These modals cannot be used in contractions.
	Use modal auxiliary verbs **must, should, ought to, could, might** and **may** to express varying degrees of certainty or prediction.
	 Earlier in this chapter, you used the auxiliary **will** to describe future actions or states; similarly, it works as a modal verb to describe a level of certainty about a future action or event.

(1) As sea levels **could rise** three or more feet by the end of the century, global warming will likely threaten the very existence of islands such as these. Altered weather patterns **could** also **be changing** the ranges of disease-carrying species. Many small island nations **may not survive** the effects of global climate change.	To show certainty of approximately 50% or less in **the present or future (possibility)**, use *may, might* or *could*. In the simple form, combine the modal with the base verb. In the progressive form, use the **modal + be + verb + -ing**. The **negative** forms of *may* and *might* show the same level of certainty.
(2) This threat **should continue** to increase with shifts in environmental conditions. In fact, islanders **should be experiencing** more negative effects as the conditions change. Based on current water temperatures, it **shouldn't be** long before more coral reefs are impacted.	To indicate an **assumption** about the present or future, use *should* or *ought to*, although *should* is more common. We use these modals with the base form of the verb to show our expectations based on our experience or knowledge. Also, use **modal + be + verb + -ing** for the progressive forms of these verbs. Typically, only *should* is used in the **negative** form, and it conveys the same level of certainty.
(3) Island residents **have to be** aware that significant changes to their ecosystems have occurred because the evidence is all around them. The international community **must be ignoring** our crisis. They **must not realize** how much damage they have caused. Global warming **will affect** many species of marine life because the changes in the water chemistry and temperatures **won't be stopping** anytime soon.	To show **strong certainty** (95%) about an action or state, use *must / have (got) to + base verb* or *+ be + verb + -ing*. These verbs express **high probability**. *Must* is more formal than *have (got) to*. *Have to* and *have got to* need to agree with the subject. Note that these modals are more commonly used to refer to the present, not the future, unless they are in progressive form. Only *must* is used in the **negative** form. To show **nearly 100% certainty** in the future, we tend to use *will + base verb* or *will + be + verb + -ing* instead. This is also true in the negative form.
(4) The case for immediate action to reduce carbon emissions **couldn't be** more urgent.	In the **negative** form, *could not / couldn't* = nearly 100% certain in the present. Use *could not / couldn't + have + past participle* for the past.
(5) Scientists believe that stricter carbon limits **might have slowed** the rise in sea levels. It's clear that countries **could have been doing** more to prevent the damage. The Panel **ought to have completed** the list of new restrictions. They started working on it last year. In what **must have been** frightening conditions, residents of Papua New Guinea and the Solomon Islands were forced to flee their homes to escape record tides. The residents **must have been wondering** if they would be able to return to their homes.	When expressing **weaker certainty** about past actions or states, use *may / might / could + have + past participle*. For the progressive form, use *may / might / could + have + been + verb + -ing*. Although not common, *should / ought to + have + past participle* (*should / ought to + have + been + verb + -ing* for the progressive form) can be used for **assumptions** about the past. To show **strong certainty** about past actions or states, use *must / had to + have + past participle*. For the progressive form, use *must + have + been + verb + -ing*. *Have to* is not commonly used in the past progressive form and *have got to* is not used in either past form.

Grammar Practice

A Complete the sentences with an appropriate modal based on the clues in the parentheses.

Tourism contributes greatly to the national economies of most small island states. For instance, nearly all of the national income of the Maldives comes from tourism, and most of the labor force in the Bahamas works in tourism. Unfortunately, negative data have shown that climate change **1.** _____ (*assumption*) be an issue that small island states will struggle with for years to come. Tourism-related activities **2.** _____ (*possibility*) be disrupted by the loss of coastal lands. Furthermore, coastal flooding and salt water intrusions **3.** _____ (*possibility*) hurt more than farms; they **4.** _____ (*possibility*) also disrupt tourism. Another change that the tourism sector **5.** _____ (*assumption*) be expecting is the decline of tourists from North America and northern Europe. This drop **6.** _____ (*certainty*) most likely be caused by potentially warmer winters. Island states **7.** _____ (*probability*) also be worrying about stricter regulations on aircraft emissions. Clearly, small island states **8.** _____ (*certainty, negative*) be expecting their tourism industries to stay the same.

B Read each statement. Then, write a sentence about it that indicates a possibility, assumption, probability, or certainty. Use one of the modals from the box in simple or progressive form. Try to use a variety of tenses in your sentences.

could not / couldn't   may / might / could (not)   must (not)   should (not) / ought to   will (not)

1. Small island states rely heavily on imported goods and services. This reliance often leads to very high costs for energy, transportation, and communication.
They could develop cheaper energy such as solar or wind power. _____

2. Until recently, native island cultures have remained relatively isolated and unchanged by the outside world. The introduction of television, air travel, and other modern advances has negatively impacted these native cultures.
_____
_____

3. Due to their small and isolated ecosystems, islands are ideal for conducting environmental research, particularly on the effects of habitat destruction and uncontrolled development.
_____
_____

4. Because of their isolation, most island states have a disproportionately greater number of species that are unique to their ecosystems and endangered.
_____
_____

5. Over the years, non-native domestic farm animals that were introduced to island systems have caused serious damage to native plant and animal species.
_____
_____

Speaking

A In groups of three or four, discuss the following scenarios. Make general and specific predictions about the future of the two places described in the scenarios. Indicate what you think will happen in the near future and what will happen at a later time. Discuss any assumptions that can be made about the scenarios. Look at the model, and try to use the grammar from the chapter.

> **Scenario 1:** A highly populated coastal community in Southeast Asia has been experiencing greater periods of inland flooding due to rising sea levels. The repeated flooding has begun contaminating the freshwater sources and eroding the shoreline. The community depends on the local farms for its main food supplies, and the local economy is heavily dependent on fishing.

> **Scenario 2:** A tiny island nation in the Pacific is slowly losing its land to rising sea levels. Despite its size, it has been a highly popular tourist destination for many years, and the country has prospered economically. However, recent decreases in the number of tourists coming to the island have caused concern. The country also depends on the nearby countries of Australia and New Zealand for the majority of its food and energy sources.

> *Residents of the coastal community must be . . . The community is going to need . . . As the situation . . . the community also needs to consider . . .*

B Share your conclusions and predictions with another group.

Listening

A BEFORE LISTENING You will listen to a news segment about the island nation of the Maldives. The country is facing the loss of its territory due to rising sea levels and other effects of climate change. With a partner, predict what actions the country may take to ensure its future.

B 🎧 UNDERSTANDING MAIN IDEAS Listen to the news segment. Take notes on the environmental conditions the country is facing and the present or future actions the government is taking to address the problems. Then, compare your notes with your predictions in Part A.

C 🎧 LISTENING FOR DETAILS Listen again and identify statements in which the speaker indicates possibilities, assumptions, probabilities, and certainties in different tenses. Following the model, make a chart with examples.

Weaker certainties / possibilities	Assumptions	Stronger certainties / probabilities	Certainties

Writing

A You and a partner will write a brief report on potential future impacts of climate change on your local community or a selected region of your country. With your partner, select the area you will write about. Follow the instructions and use the chart to brainstorm information for your report.

Situation: An international nonprofit organization has funds available to help communities improve their environmental conditions and prevent future damage from climate change. Imagine that you are using your report to apply for this funding.

Location	Current conditions / issues	Future impacts on the environment	Future impacts on population	Necessary changes or adaptations

B Write your report on a separate sheet of paper. Use your notes from Part A. Try to use the grammar from the chapter.

> The Chesapeake Bay on the Atlantic coast of the United States is the largest estuary, a body of water where fresh and salt water mix, in the country. Six states and Washington, D.C. are part of the greater Chesapeake Bay watershed, the main source of fresh water in the region, and the bay is also home to thousands of species of plants and animals, including fish and shellfish. Because of its low elevation and extensive coastline, it is quite vulnerable to . . .

C Share your report with the class. Decide which report makes the strongest case for funding.

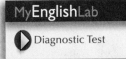

Grammar Summary

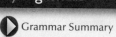

Infinitives as noun and adjective complements help complete the meaning of the respective noun or adjective.

Infinitives can follow various abstract nouns and adjectives, and they can occur in subject or object position with nouns.	(1) The motivation to obtain animal parts for food or dress has been a main reason for poaching.
With adjectives, infinitive complements typically follow linking verbs, like *be*.	(2) Many poachers have disobeyed orders to stop hunting animals. (3) Sharks are bound to be killed by poachers for their fins.
Infinitives as noun / adjective complements can occur with various constructions, such as prepositional phrases, and they can also occur as passives or as past infinitives.	(4) Some administrations' wish to have poachers punished for their crimes has come too late. (5) Many poachers have not been pleased to have been singled out as troublemakers.

Pronoun agreement and reference help avoid repetition and establish cohesion within spoken or written discourse.

Pronouns must agree with the entity to which they refer in subject, possessive, or object form.	(1) An alligator has few enemies. It preys on smaller animals.
Singular antecedents (indefinite pronouns, generic and collective nouns, head nouns in complex noun phrases) take singular pronouns; plural antecedents take plural pronouns.	(2) Each small animal has its enemy. (3) A group of baboons fled from its lion enemy. (4) An organism that produces its own food is an autotrophy; it is usually a plant organism. (5) Herbivores are called primary consumers because they feed on plants.
Antecedents must be clear; pronouns should refer to one single antecedent, which must be close to the pronoun in the preceding clause. In case of ambiguity, the noun should be used.	(6) Lions eat giraffes. Lions are top-predators. *Incorrect:* Lions eat giraffes. They are predators.

Future time is used to describe or predict events and states in the immediate future or a later point in time. Some present tense forms are used for future time. Perfect forms show that one future action is completed before another action or time (or the duration of those future actions).

Will and *be going to* both describe general predictions, but only *be going to* is used for previously made plans that will happen in the immediate future.	(1) Many island nations will lose land to rising sea levels.
Will can also indicate "willingness" or a quick decision.	(2) Water temperatures are going to increase each year. (3) The researcher said, "I'll help with the analysis of the results."
The present progressive is used with planned and definite future activities.	(4) The waste water recycling program is starting next week.
The present simple is used with scheduled activities and in time clauses.	(5) The panel meets the first Monday of each month.
The future progressive describes an action in progress in the future while the future perfect indicates that one action will be completed before another action or time in the future.	(6) At this time next year, the panel will be completing its next report. (7) By that time, the field research teams will have identified new issues and they will have been collecting data on all the major island ecosystems for a full year.
The future perfect progressive describes the duration of the action in progress before the other action or time.	

Modals of prediction and certainty can describe varying degrees of possibility, probability, and certainty.

To show possibility (50% or less certainty) in the present or future, use *may / might / could* + base verb or future verb + *-ing*.	(1) Ocean levels could rise higher than anticipated.
	(2) Many countries may not be planning for these levels.
For assumptions about the present or future based on expectations or experience, use *should* or *ought to* + base verb or *be* + verb + *-ing*. Only *should* is used in the negative.	(3) Currently, island states and coastal communities should be experiencing the effects of increasing severe weather. They shouldn't be seeing dropping sea levels.
	(4) With changes to the world's oceans, most marine ecosystems have to be damaged to some degree.
To show strong certainty (95% probability) about the present, use *must / have (got) to* + base verb or + *be* + verb + *-ing*.	(5) There must not be any simple solutions to the problem.
Only *must* is used in the negative form.	(6) They couldn't evacuate such a large area so quickly.
Could not / couldn't show nearly 100% certainty in the present and *could not / couldn't* + *have* + past participle show the same meaning in the past.	(7) Farmers couldn't have known that they were causing so much water pollution.
	(8) Island nations may have been able to make emergency plans if they had known that sea levels would rise.
To show past possibility (weaker certainty), use *may / might / could* + *have* + past participle; for the progressive use *may / might / could* + *have* + *been* + verb + *-ing*.	(9) Private corporations should have known that they were damaging the islands; the damage was clear.
	(10) We should have been seeing better results from the energy-saving measures we took.
Although less common, *should / ought to* + *have* + past participle or *should / ought to* + *have* + been + verb + *-ing* can describe assumptions about the past.	(11) Mining companies must have only been thinking about their profits when they stripped islands of their resources.
To show strong certainty about past actions or states, use *must / had to* + *have* + past participle or *must* + *have* + *been* + verb + *-ing*. *Must* is the most common modal used here.	

Self-Assessment

A (5 points) Change the sentences into sentences with infinitives as noun / adjective complements, using the nouns / adjectives in parentheses. Note that some infinitives need to be passive.

1. Administration officials did not follow _____ the hunting ban on wolves in the Rockies. (the advice, maintain)

2. Animal conservation groups are _____ that the lifting of the ban will again decimate the number of wolves and disproportionately increase the number of deer. (afraid, learn)

3. With _____ (the opportunity for wolves, hunt and kill), the growing deer population is _____ the plant life in the area. (likely, destroy)

4. However, this is also _____ that the presence of deer actually has a positive effect on soil in forested areas. (a reminder, understand)

B (5 points) Find the five unclear pronoun uses and replace the pronouns with logical nouns.

The animal ecologist Charles Elton introduced the concept of the food web. He originally called it a food cycle. He described it as follows: "The herbivores are usually preyed upon by carnivores, and they get the energy of the sunlight at third-hand. They again may be preyed upon by other carnivores, and so on, until we reach an animal which has no enemies, and it forms a terminus on it. There are, in fact, chains of them linked together by food, and they are all dependent in the long run upon plants. We refer to such relationships among them as 'food-chains.'"

C (5 points) Circle the correct verb phrase to complete the paragraph.

Since island states and coastal communities **1. experience / will be experiencing** greater threats to their homes, resources, and livelihoods from climate change, it **2. will become / will have become** necessary for them to find more efficient methods to grow their crops and maintain their fisheries. Residents **3. will have been needing / are going to need** to implement practical, low-cost techniques, such as the use of floating fields. It is clear that people **4. will have seen / will be seeing** opportunities to create new businesses from the changing needs, and by the end of the century, entrepreneurs **5. will have found / are going to find** successful approaches to adapting to life after climate change.

D (5 points) Correct the bolded modal verb phrase error in each sentence. Check the form and tense of the verbs and make sure the sentence makes sense.

1. Climate change **ought to cause** health problems in tropical regions.

2. In the past, native islanders **must not have known** about the connection between weather and health connections because they were greatly in tune with their natural environment.

3. Global warming **should be leading** to increased outbreaks of diseases that are associated with warmer temperatures, like malaria.

4. Outbreaks of waterborne illnesses in island states **couldn't be** on the rise as more extreme weather events disrupt fresh water and sewage systems.

5. More consistent weather patterns in the past **may prevent** the expansion of certain tropical diseases.

Unit Project: Personal action plan

 A   Many people feel that an individual alone cannot reduce human impact on the environment. However, developing a personal plan to lessen one's own impact on the environment can make a major difference. In this project, you will make and follow through with a personal action plan to make changes that will result in less damage to the environment.

1. In small groups, brainstorm on activities that you do every day and that consume energy (e.g., using lights), use resources (e.g., printing documents on paper), or in some way pollute the environment (e.g., using plastic bags from stores).

Activities that consume energy	Activities that use resources	Activities that pollute

2. Choose one activity from each column and decide how you can reduce or change what you normally do to make it less harmful to the environment. Use the following format:

Activity	Current habit	Planned change to habit	Desired outcome

3. Follow your plan for one week and record your activities in the chart. Use the following format:

Activity	New habit	Outcome

B   In small groups, share your action plan and outcomes from Part A. Discuss whether or not your plan was successful and how you plan to continue your efforts. Look at the model, and then try to use the grammar from the unit.

> *My motivation to reduce my use of plastic came from hearing about how bad plastic bags are for the environment. In the beginning, I wasn't able to remember to take my reusable cloth bags to the store. But eventually, I used every opportunity to bring them. I'm going to use these bags from now on, and I think that it could have a great impact in the long term.*

As a class, decide which new habits are the most effective and the most likely to help the environment. What makes these new habits particularly useful?

My**English**Lab

▶ Unit Test

My**English**Lab

▶ Search it!

Appendices

A Irregular verbs

Base Form	Simple Past	Past Participle
A		
arise	arose	arisen
awake	awakened / awoke	awakened / awoken
B		
be	was, were	been
bear	bore	born / borne
beat	beat	beaten / beat
become	became	become
begin	began	begun
bend	bent	bent
bet	bet	bet
bid (farewell)	bid / bade	bidden
bid (offer amount)	bid	bid
bind	bound	bound
bite	bit	bitten
bleed	bled	bled
blow	blew	blown
break	broke	broken
breed	bred	bred
bring	brought	brought
broadcast	broadcast / broadcasted	broadcast / broadcasted
build	built	built
burn	burned / burnt	burned / burnt
burst	burst	burst
buy	bought	bought
C		
catch	caught	caught
choose	chose	chosen
cling	clung	clung
come	came	come
cost	cost	cost
creep	crept	crept
cut	cut	cut
D		
deal	dealt	dealt
dig	dug	dug
disprove	disproved	disproved / disproven
dive (jump head-first)	dove / dived	dived
dive (scuba diving)	dived / dove	dived
do	did	done
draw	drew	drawn

dream	dreamed / dreamt	dreamed / dreamt
drink	drank	drunk
drive	drove	driven
dwell	dwelt / dwelled	dwelt / dwelled
E		
eat	ate	eaten
F		
fall	fell	fallen
feed	fed	fed
feel	felt	felt
fight	fought	fought
find	found	found
fit (tailor, change size)	fitted / fit	fitted / fit
fit (be right size)	fit / fitted	fit / fitted
flee	fled	fled
fling	flung	flung
fly	flew	flown
forbid	forbade	forbidden
forecast	forecast	forecast
forego / forgo	forewent	foregone
foresee	foresaw	foreseen
foretell	foretold	foretold
forget	forgot	forgotten
forgive	forgave	forgiven
forsake	forsook	forsaken
freeze	froze	frozen
G		
get	got	gotten / got
give	gave	given
go	went	gone
grind	ground	ground
grow	grew	grown
H		
hang (an object)	hung	hung
hang (executed by hanging)	hanged	hanged
have	had	had
hear	heard	heard
hide	hid	hidden
hit	hit	hit
hold	held	held
hurt	hurt	hurt
I		
input	input	input
interweave	interwove / interweaved	interwoven / interweaved

K		
keep	kept	kept
kneel	knelt / kneeled	knelt / kneeled
knit	knitted / knit	knitted / knit
know	knew	known

L		
lay	laid	laid
lead	led	led
leap	leaped / leapt	leaped / leapt
learn	learned / learnt	learned / learnt
leave	left	left
lend	lent	lent
let	let	let
lie (be positioned)	lay	lain
light	lit / lighted	lit / lighted
lose	lost	lost

M		
make	made	made
mean	meant	meant
meet	met	met
mislead	misled	misled
mistake	mistook	mistaken
misunderstand	misunderstood	misunderstood
mow	mowed	mowed / mown

O		
offset	offset	offset
outbid	outbid	outbid
outdo	outdid	outdone
outgrow	outgrew	outgrown
outsell	outsold	outsold
overcome	overcame	overcome
oversee	oversaw	overseen
oversleep	overslept	overslept

P		
pay	paid	paid
prepay	prepaid	prepaid
prove	proved	proven / proved
put	put	put

Q		
quit	quit	quit

R		
read	read (sounds like "red")	read (sounds like "red")
repay	repaid	repaid

rewrite	rewrote	rewritten
rid	rid	rid
ride	rode	ridden
ring	rang	rung
rise	rose	risen
run	ran	run
S		
say	said	said
see	saw	seen
seek	sought	sought
sell	sold	sold
send	sent	sent
set	set	set
sew	sewed	sewn / sewed
shake	shook	shaken
shave	shaved	shaved / shaven
shed	shed	shed
shine	shined / shone	shined / shone
shoot	shot	shot
show	showed	shown
shrink	shrank	shrunk
shut	shut	shut
sing	sang	sung
sink	sank / sunk	sunk
sit	sat	sat
sleep	slept	slept
slide	slid	slid
sling	slung	slung
slit	slit	slit
sow	sowed	sown / sowed
speak	spoke	spoken
speed	sped / speeded	sped / speeded
spend	spent	spent
spill	spilled / spilt	spilled / spilt
spin	spun	spun
spit	spit / spat	spit / spat
split	split	split
spread	spread	spread
spring	sprang / sprung	sprung
stand	stood	stood
steal	stole	stolen
stick	stuck	stuck
sting	stung	stung
stink	stunk / stank	stunk

strew	strewed	strewn / strewed
stride	strode	stridden
strike (to delete)	struck	stricken
strike (to hit)	struck	struck / stricken
string	strung	strung
strive	strove / strived	striven / strived
swear	swore	sworn
sweep	swept	swept
swell	swelled	swollen / swelled
swim	swam	swum
swing	swung	swung
T		
take	took	taken
teach	taught	taught
tear	tore	torn
tell	told	told
think	thought	thought
throw	threw	thrown
thrust	thrust	thrust
tread	trod	trodden / trod
U		
unbend	unbent	unbent
unbind	unbound	unbound
undergo	underwent	undergone
underlie	underlay	underlain
understand	understood	understood
undertake	undertook	undertaken
undo	undid	undone
uphold	upheld	upheld
upset	upset	upset
W		
wake	woke / waked	woken / waked
wear	wore	worn
weave	wove / weaved	woven / weaved
wed	wed / wedded	wed / wedded
weep	wept	wept
win	won	won
wind	wound	wound
withdraw	withdrew	withdrawn
withhold	withheld	withheld
withstand	withstood	withstood
wring	wrung	wrung
write	wrote	written

B Verbs and adjectives followed by the subjunctive

Verbs followed by the subjunctive			
advise	demand	order	resolve
ask	desire	petition	suggest
beg	dictate	propose	urge
command	insist	recommend	vote
decide	intend	request	
decree	move	require	

Adjectives followed by the subjunctive			
advisable	desirable	imperative	necessary
critical	essential	important	urgent
crucial	fitting	indispensable	vital

C Verbs followed by gerunds and infinitives

Verbs followed by a gerund						
admit	can't stand	enjoy	get through	miss	recollect	risk
advise	complete	escape	imagine	permit	recommend	spend (time)
anticipate	consider	excuse	involve	postpone	report	suggest
appreciate	delay	fear	keep	practice	resent	teach
avoid	deny	finish	mention	quit	resist	tolerate
can't help	dislike	forbid	mind	recall	resume	waste (time)

Verbs followed by a preposition and a gerund					
admit to	believe in	depend on	forget about	participate in	take part in
aim at	care about	disapprove of	give up	plan on	think about/of
apologize for	complain about	discourage from	insist on	refrain from	win by
approve of	concentrate on	dream about	look forward to	succeed in	worry about
argue about	confess to	feel like	object to	talk about	

Verbs followed by an object, a preposition, and a gerund						
accuse of	blame for	charge with	fine for	keep from	prevent from	stop from	thank for

Verbs followed by an infinitive								
afford	attempt	condescend	expect	hope	long	plan	refuse	volunteer
agree	be able	consent	fail	hurry	manage	prepare	say	wait
aim	beg	dare	forget	intend	mean	pretend	shoot	want
appear	care	decide	get	leap	need	proceed	strive	wish
arrange	choose	demand	happen	learn	neglect	promise	swear	
ask	claim	deserve	hesitate	leave	offer	propose	threaten	

Verbs followed by an object and an infinitive								
advise	bring	challenge	dare	forbid	invite	love	persuade	tell
allow	build	choose	direct	force	lead	need	remind	urge
ask	buy	command	encourage	hire	leave	order	require	want
beg	cause	convince	expect	instruct	like	permit	teach	warn

Verbs followed by either a gerund or an infinitive with no change in meaning										
begin	continue	can't stand	can't bear	detest	hate	like	love	prefer	start

Verbs followed by either a gerund or an infinitive, but with change in meaning				
forget	stop	regret	remember	try

D Common noncount nouns

Common noncount nouns								
advice	courage	fish	happiness	jealousy	management	paper	salt	toothpaste
air	detergent	fog	hate	jelly	manufacturing	peace	satisfaction	traffic
anger	disinfectant	food	health	jewelry	meat	perfume	sauce	truth
beauty	dirt	fuel	heat	juice	mustard	plastic	scenery	violence
bread	dust	fun	homework	justice	medicine	pollution	soap	water
butter	education	fur	honesty	ketchup	metal	poverty	silver	wealth
chalk	energy	furniture	independence	land	milk	precision	soil	weather
cheese	engineering	gasoline	information	leisure	money	progress	soup	wine
cloth	equipment	garbage	ink	lotion	moonlight	rain	snow	wood
clothing	evidence	glue	intelligence	love	nature	research	sugar	work
coffee	fabric	gold	ice	luggage	news	ribbon	sunshine	yarn
confidence	fair trade	grass	ice cream	machinery	oil	rice	support	
copper	finance	gravy	jam	make-up	paint	salad	tea	

E Tense and place/time shifts

	Tense Shifts
Employee: "I **discuss** work issues online."	The employee said that he **discusses** work issues online.
Employee: "I **discussed** work issues online."	The employee said that he **had discussed** work issues online.
Employee: "I **have discussed** work issues online."	
Employee: "I **had discussed** work issues online."	
Employee: "I **will discuss** work issues online."	The employee said that he **would discuss** work issues online.
Employee: "I **can discuss** work issues online."	The employee said that he **could discuss** work issues online.
Employee: "I **may discuss** work issues online."	The employee said that he **might discuss** work issues online.
Employee: "I **would discuss** work issues online." **(could, might, should, ought to)**	The employee said that he **would discuss** work issues online. **(could, might, should, ought to)**
Progressive forms	
Employee: "I**'m discussing** work issues online."	The employee said that he **was discussing** work issues online.
Employee: "I **was discussing** work issues online."	The employee said that he **had been discussing** work issues online.
Employee: "I **have been discussing** work issues online."	
Employee: "I **had been discussing** work issues online."	
Employee: "I **will be discussing** work issues online."	The employee said that he **would be discussing** work issues online.
Employee: "I **will have been discussing** work issues online."	The employee said that he **would have been discussing** work issues online.
Questions	
Employee: "**Is** the boss **discussing** work issues online?"	The employee asked **if/weather** the boss **was discussing** work issues online.
Employee: "Why **is** the boss **discussing** work issues online?"	The employee asked/wondered **why** the boss **was discussing** work issues online.
Requests	
Employee: "**Stop** discussing work issues online!"	The employee told his colleague **to stop** discussing work issues online.
Employee: "**Don't discuss** work issues online!"	The employee asked his colleague **not to discuss** work issues online.
Employee: "**Let's not discuss** work issues online!"	The employee told his colleague **that they should not discuss** work issues online.
Place/Time Shifts	
this (morning)	that (morning)
today/this day	that day
these (days)	those (days)
now	then
(a week) ago	(a week) before/earlier
last weekend	the weekend before / the previous weekend
tomorrow	the next/following day
next (week)	the following (week)
last century	in the 20th century
here	there

F Common stative passive + preposition combinations

Common stative passive + preposition combinations				
about	**against**	**as**	**by**	**for**
be concerned be excited be worried	be discriminated	be known be organized be qualified be realized be recognized be understood	be annoyed be bored be covered be frightened be scared be surrounded be terrified	be designated be (well) known be made be prepared be qualified be remembered be reserved be used
from	**in**	**of**	**to**	**with**
be divorced be distinguished be exhausted be gone be protected be tired	be disappointed be dressed be enclosed (also with *within*) be found be interested be involved be located be measured be organized be reflected be rooted	be composed be frightened be made be made up be scared be terrified be tired	be accustomed be addicted be committed be connected be dedicated be devoted be engaged be exposed be intended be limited be married be opposed be referred be related be tied	be acquainted be aligned be annoyed be associated be bored be cluttered be coordinated be covered be crowded be decorated be disappointed be done be equipped be filled be finished be graced be impressed be pleased be provided be satisfied
No preposition	**into**	**on**		
be born be broken be called be crowded be listed be locked be used	be divided	be based be located be positioned be situated		

G Common intransitive verbs

Common intransitive verbs									
agree	believe	contain	disappear	happen	live	resemble	stand	vanish	
appear	belong	cost	emerge	have	look	rise	stay	wait	
arrive	collapse	cry	exist	know	last	sit	suppose	weigh	
awake	collide	depend	fall	laugh	occur	seem	swim		
become	consist	die	go	lie	remain	sleep	think		

H Common noun + preposition + gerund and adjective + preposition + gerund combinations

Noun + preposition + gerund						
about	*for*	*in*	*of*			*to*
anxiety doubt enthusiasm	credit fondness method preference reason reputation responsibility talent tolerance	belief believer delay difficulty experience interest mistake research success	(dis)advantage advocate benefit chance criticism critic danger fear	fondness habit hope idea knowledge love memory	method practice problem process supporter victim way	addiction alternative approach commitment dedication devotion introduction opposition reaction

Adjective + preposition + gerund						
about	*at*	*for*	*in*	*of*	*to*	*with*
angry *crazy disappointed enthusiastic excited glad (un)happy nervous sad sorry upset worried	*bad *good	famous good (well) known made perfect reserved responsible sorry suitable used useful	engaged interested involved successful	afraid ashamed (in)capable critical fond frightened guilty proud scared *sick terrified *tired tolerant weary	(un)accustomed addicted committed dedicated devoted exposed limited (un)opposed used	bored concerned content familiar *fed up satisfied

*(*Note: These phrases are used in informal language.)*

I Abstract nouns

Abstract nouns commonly followed by infinitives									
advice appeal anxiety certainty	command decision delight desire	eagerness effort fact hesitation	instruction liability likelihood luck	motivation need opportunity order	permission plan possibility preparation	pride proposal recommendation readiness	refusal reluctance reminder request	requirement suggestion tendency wish

J Adjectives commonly followed by infinitives

Adjectives commonly followed by infinitives						
anxious apt ashamed bound	careful certain content delighted	determined disappointed eager eligible	fortunate glad happy hesitant	liable likely lucky pleased	proud ready reluctant sad	shocked sorry surprised upset

Index

A / an, 144,146, 152
A lot of, 104
A number of, 104
About, 178, 192
Abstract nouns, 104, 198, 212
Accordingly, 140
Active causatives, 156, 160
Adjective clauses
    function of, 24, 28, 40
    method to shorten, 40
    non-restrictive, 28, 34, 40, 94,
        97, 112
    with object relative
        pronouns, 32, 34, 40
    with quantifiers, 90, 97, 112
    reduced to adjective phrases,
        36, 40
    restrictive, 28, 34, 40, 94, 112
    with subject relative
        pronouns, 28, 36, 40
    with *where, when*, and *why*,
        90, 94, 95, 112
Adjective complements
    infinitives as, 196, 198, 212
    noun clauses as, 46
Adjective phrases, 36
Adjectives
    adverbs that modify, 24, 26,
        40
    attributive, 26
    as comparative, 68, 72, 86
    degree complements
        following, 68, 74, 86
    explanation of, 24, 26, 40
    to form equatives, 68, 70, 86
    infinitives following, 196,
        198, 212
    noun plus infinitive followed
        by, 198, 212
    participial, 26, 40
    placement of, 26, 40
    predicative, 26
Adverb clauses
    of cause / reason, 176, 180,
        192
    explanation of, 116, 120
    modals in, 166
    negative, 180, 192
    of purpose, 164, 166, 172

    reducing, 180, 192
    of time, 120, 132
Adverb phrases
    of cause / reason, 180, 192
    of purpose, 166, 172
    of time, 116, 120, 132
Adverbs
    of certainty, 26
    as comparatives, 72, 86
    conjunctive, 59, 60, 140, 152,
        164, 168, 172
    degree complements
        following, 68, 74, 86
    explanation of, 24, 26, 40
    to form equatives, 68, 70, 86
    of frequency, 26
    of manner, 26
    that modify adverbs, 24, 26
    that modify adjectives, 24, 26
    that modify verbs, 24, 26
    placement of, 26, 40
Advice, 2, 6, 15, 20, 158, 172
After, 120, 126, 132
Agent, 107
And, 104, 118, 132
Antecedents, 200, 212
Articles, use of, 144, 146, 152
As, 138, 152, 180, 192
As a consequence, 140, 152
As a consequence of, 138, 152
As a matter of fact, 168, 172
As a result, 140, 152
As a result of, 138, 152
As . . . as, 148
As long as, 120, 132
As soon as, 120, 132
At, 178
Assumption, 208, 213
Attributive adjectives, 26
Auxiliary verbs, 6

Be
    adjectives following, 24, 26,
        40, 198, 212
    in conditional constructions,
        80
    with past participle, 90, 92,
        107, 108, 112
    in time clauses, 120

Be advised to, 158, 172
Be allowed to, 158, 172
Be expected to, 158, 172
Be going to, 108, 206, 212
Be required to, 158, 172
Be supposed to, 158, 172
Because, 126, 138, 152, 180,
    192
Before, 120, 126, 132
Being + past participle, 178
But, 118, 132
By (date), 126
By- phrase, 92, 102, 107, 108,
    112, 160
By the time, 120, 126

Can, 6, 158, 172
Can't, 158, 172, 208, 213
Causatives, 156, 160, 172
Cause / reason, 136, 138, 152,
    176, 180, 192
Certainty, 204, 208, 213
Collective nouns
    explanation of, 104, 200, 212
    subject-verb agreement with,
        104, 112
Commas
    with adjective clauses, 28, 34,
        36, 40
    with adverbial clauses, 120
    with conjunctive adverbs, 59,
        64, 136, 140, 152, 168
    with coordinating
        conjunctions, 59, 64,
        118, 132
    with non-restrictive clauses,
        28, 34, 36, 40, 94, 95, 112
    with past unreal
        conditionals, 128
    with phrasal prepositions, 59,
        64, 136, 138, 152
    with restrictive clauses, 28,
        34, 40, 94, 95, 112
    with subordinating
        conjunctions, 59, 64,
        136, 138, 152
Commas splice errors, 140, 168
Comparative clauses, 72, 86
Comparatives, 72, 86

Comparison
  connecting structures for, 54,
    59, 60, 64
  equatives for, 70, 72, 86
  parallel structures for, 148,
    152
Complement clauses, 74
Complements, 46, 47, 64
Compound sentences, 118
Concession, 118, 132
Conditionals
  future unreal, 78, 80, 86
  past unreal, 128, 132
  unreal, 78, 80, 86
Conjunctions
  coordinating, 59, 60, 64, 118,
    132, 148, 152
  correlative, 148, 152
  subordinating, 59, 60, 64,
    136, 138, 152
Conjunctive adverbs
  of exemplification, emphasis,
    and clarification, 164,
    168, 172
  explanation of, 59, 64
  to show effect, 136, 140, 152
  to show similarity or
    difference, 59, 60, 64
Connecting structures
  for cause / reason, 136, 138, 152
  for comparison and contrast,
    59, 60, 64
Consequently, 140
Coordinating conjunctions
  explanation of, 59, 64, 118,
    132
  to join independent clauses,
    118, 132
  to join parallel structures,
    144, 148, 152
  to show similarity or
    difference, 59, 60, 64
Correlative conjunctions, 148,
  152
Could, 6, 20, 128, 132, 208, 213
Could not / couldn't, 208, 213
Count nouns
  definite articles with, 146, 152
  quantifiers with, 54, 56, 64

Dangling modifiers, 120
Degree complements, 74, 86
Dependent clauses
  adjective clauses as, 28
  adverb clauses as, 120, 132
  future, 206
  noun clauses as, 15, 46, 64
  past progressive in, 4
  subordinating conjunctions
    connecting, 138, 152
  with unreal conditionals, 78,
    80, 86
Due to, 138, 152
Dynamic passives, 107, 108,
  112

Each, 104
Each of, 104
-ed, 26
Effect, 136, 140, 152
Either . . . or, 148
Embedded questions, 46
Enough . . . to, 74
Equatives, 68, 70, 86
-er . . . than, 148
Every, 104
Every one of, 104
Example, 164, 168, 172

For
  combined with nouns or
    adjectives, 178, 192
  expressing purpose with
    infinitives, 166, 172
  with present perfect, 12, 20
  to show cause or reason, 118,
    132
For example, 168, 172
For instance, 168, 172
Formal language
  in adjective clauses with
    quantifiers, 97
  in adjective clauses with
    where, *when*, and *why*,
    34
  in coordinating
    conjunctions, 118
  to express cause or reason,
    138

  with *in order that*, 166
  with infinitives as subjects,
    186
  with modals of certainty, 208
  with modals of necessity, 158
  in object adjective clauses, 34
  passives in, 107
  to show effect, 140
Frequency, 26
Future perfect
  explanation of, 206, 212
  passives in, 108
Future perfect progressive, 204,
  206, 212
Future progressive, 204, 206,
  212
Future time, 204, 206, 212
Future unreal conditionals, 78,
  80, 86

Generic nouns, 200, 212
Gerunds
  explanation of, 49, 64, 184, 186
  as objects, 49, 64
  as objects of prepositions,
    176, 178, 192
  passive, 178, 186, 192
  past, 178, 186, 192
  to show possessive
    relationship, 186, 192
  simple, 178, 184
  as subjects, 104, 184, 192
  as subject complements, 184,
    186, 192
  verbs followed by, 49, 50, 64
Get, 160, 172
Go + gerund, 49

Had, 126, 132
Had better, 6, 20, 158, 172
Have, 160, 172
Have got to, 158, 172, 208, 213
Have to, 158, 172, 208, 213
Having + past participle, 178,
  180, 186
Head nouns, 104, 105, 112,
  200, 212
Help, 49
Hence, 140

If, 46
If-clauses, 80, 86, 124, 128, 132
If / whether, 82
Imperatives, 82
In, 178, 192
In fact, 168, 172
In order (that), 166, 172
In other words, 168, 172
In particular, 168, 172
Indeed, 168, 172
Indefinite pronouns, 200, 212
Independent clauses
    conjunctive adverbs to
        connect, 140, 152, 168,
        172
    coordinating conjunctions to
        connect, 118, 132
    with past progressive, 4
    subordinating conjunctions
        to connect, 136, 138, 152
    with unreal conditionals, 80
Indirect speech. *See* Reported
    speech
Infinitives
    explanation of, 49, 64, 186,
        192
    as noun and adjective
        complements, 192, 198,
        212
    as objects, 49, 64, 198, 212
    past, 186, 192
    purpose, 164, 166, 172
    to report imperatives, 82
    as subjects, 104, 184, 186,
        192, 198, 212
    verbs followed by, 49, 50, 64
-ing, 26, 180, 192
Intransitive. *See* Verbs.

Less . . . than, 72, 148
Let, 49, 160, 172
Likely, 72
-ly, 26

Main clauses. *See* Independent
    clauses.
Make, 160, 172
Many, 104
Mass nouns, 104

May, 6, 20, 158, 172, 208, 213
Might, 6, 20, 128, 132, 208, 213
Modals
    in adverb clauses, 166
    of advisability and
        suggestion, 2, 6, 20
    explanation of, 2, 6, 20
    passives with, 107, 108
    of prediction and certainty,
        208, 213
    to show degrees of necessity,
        158, 172
More . . . than, 72, 148
Must, 6, 20, 158, 172, 208, 213

Necessity, 158, 172
Negative statements, 49, 107
Neither . . . nor, 148
Noncount nouns
    definite articles with, 146, 152
    quantifiers with, 54, 56, 64
    subject-verb agreement with,
        102, 104, 112
Non-restrictive adjective clauses
    with quantifiers as, 97, 112
    explanation of, 28, 34, 40
    with object relative
        pronouns, 34, 40
    reduced to adjective phrases,
        36, 40
    with subject relative
        pronouns, 28, 40
    with *where* and *when*, 94, 95,
        112
Nor, 118, 132
Not . . . but, 148
Not only . . . but also, 148
Noun clauses
    noun plus infinitive with,
        196, 198, 212
    in reported speech, 82, 86
    as subjects, objects, or
        complements, 44, 46, 47,
        64, 104
    with the subjunctive, 15, 20
    as subordinate clauses, 15, 46
    with unreal conditionals, 80,
        86, 128, 132
Noun complements, 198, 212

Nouns
    abstract, 21, 104, 198
    collective, 104, 200
    as comparatives, 68, 72, 86
    count, 54, 56, 64, 112, 146, 152
    degree complements
        following, 74, 86
    to form equatives, 70, 86
    generic, 200
    head, 104, 200
    mass, 104
    noncount, 56, 146

Object adjective clauses, 34, 36,
    40
Object of prepositions
    gerunds as, 176, 178, 192
    relative pronouns as, 34
Object pronouns, 200
Object relative pronouns, 34
Objects
    gerunds as, 44, 49, 64
    nouns and infinitives as, 196,
        198, 212
    noun clauses as, 46, 47, 64
    in passive sentences, 107, 112
Of, 56, 104, 178, 192
Of + the, 56
Once, 120, 132
One of, 104
Or, 118, 132
Ought to, 6, 20, 158, 172, 208,
    213

Parallel structures, 144, 148, 152
Participial adjectives, 26
Passive causatives, 156, 160
Passive gerunds, 178, 186, 192
Passives
    dynamic, 107, 108, 112
    stative, 90, 92, 112
Past gerunds, 178, 186, 192
Past infinitives, 186, 192
Past modals, 108
Past participles
    being with, 178, 186
    be with, 90, 92, 107, 108, 112
    to form stative passive, 90,
        92, 107, 108, 112

Past perfect
    method to form, 126
    passives in, 108
    use of, 124, 126, 128, 132
Past perfect progressive, 126,
    132
Past progressive
    passives in, 108
    time expressions with, 4
    use of, 2, 4, 20
Past unreal conditionals, 128,
    132
Phrasal expressions, 158, 172
Phrasal prepositions
    explanation of, 59, 60, 64
    to show cause or reason, 136,
        138, 152
Plural verbs, 104
Possessive nouns, 186
Possessive pronouns, 200, 212
Prediction, 206, 213
Predictive adjectives, 26
Prepositional phrases, 40, 198,
    212
Prepositions
    to express similarity or
        difference, 59, 60, 64
    following stative passives, 92,
        112
    objects of, 34
    phrasal, 59, 60, 64, 136, 138,
        152
Present. *See* Simple present
Present participle, 36, 40
Present perfect
    passives in, 108
    time expressions in, 10, 12, 20
    use of, 10, 12, 20
Present progressive
    in future time, 204, 206, 212
    passives in, 108
Present simple
    in future time, 204, 206, 212
    passives in, 108
Progressive. *See* Future perfect
    progressive; Future
    progressive; Past
    progressive; Present
    progressive

Prohibition, 156, 158, 172
Pronoun-antecedent
    agreement, 196, 200,
    212
Pronouns
    agreement between
        antecedents and, 200,
        212
    demonstrative, 196, 200
    indefinite, 200, 212
    object, 200, 212
    personal, 200
    possessive, 200, 212
    relative, 28, 32, 34, 36, 38, 40
    subject, 200, 212
Purpose infinitives, 164, 166,
    172

Quantifiers
    adjective clauses with, 90, 97,
        112
    explanation of, 54, 56
    subject-verb agreement with,
        104
    use of, 54, 56, 97, 112
Questions
    embedded, 46
    wh-, 46, 64
    yes / no, 82

Reason. *See* Cause / reason
Recommendations, 2, 15
Relative pronouns
    as objects of adjective
        clauses, 34, 40
    as objects of prepositions, 32,
        34, 40
    as subjects of adjective
        clauses, 28, 36
    in adjective phrases, 32, 36,
        40
    use of, 28, 32, 36, 40
Reported speech, 78, 82, 86
Reporting verb, 82
Restrictive adjective clauses
    explanation of, 28, 34, 40
    with adjective phrases, 36, 40
    with object adjective clauses,
        34, 40

with subject adjective
        clauses, 28, 40
    with *where*, *why*, and *when*,
        94, 95, 112
Results, 136, 140, 152

Semicolons, 140
Sentence connectors. *See*
    Conjunctive adverbs
Series, items in, 148
Should, 6, 20, 158, 172, 208,
    213
Simple future, 108, 204, 206
Simple gerunds, 44, 49, 50, 64,
    176, 178, 184, 186, 192
Simple modals, 108
Simple past
    passives in, 108
    reporting verbs in, 78, 82, 86
    time expressions in, 2, 4, 10,
        12, 20
    use of, 2, 4, 10, 12, 20
Simple present
    passives in, 108
    in future time, 206, 212
Since
    in adverb clauses or phrases,
        120, 132, 180, 192
    to express cause or reason,
        138, 152
    with present perfect, 12, 20
Singular verbs, 104, 112
So, 118, 132
So that, 166, 172
So . . . that, 74
Specifically, 168, 172
Statements. *See* Negative
    statements
Stative passives, 90, 92, 112
Subject adjective clauses, 28,
    36, 40
Subject complements
    gerunds and infinitives as,
        184, 186, 192
    noun clauses as, 42, 46, 47, 64
Subject pronouns, 200, 212
Subjects
    gerunds and infinitives as,
        104, 186, 192, 198, 212

noun clauses as, 42, 46, 47, 64, 104
in passives, 92, 107, 112
Subject-verb agreement, 102, 104, 112
Subjunctive form, 10, 15, 20
Subjunctive verbs, 10, 15, 20
Subordinate clauses. *See* Dependent clauses
Subordinating conjunctions
explanation of, 59, 60, 64
to show cause or reason, 136, 138, 152
to show similarity or difference, 59, 60, 64
Subordinators, 120, 132, 180, 192
Suggestions, 2, 6, 20

That
in adjective clauses, 28, 34, 36, 40
to introduce noun clauses, 46, 47, 64
to introduce a reported statement, 82
to introduce subjunctives, 10, 15, 20
That-clause, 80, 86
That is, 168, 172
The, 144, 146, 152
The fact that, 46
Therefore, 140
Thus, 140

Time expressions
adverb, 116, 120, 132
with future perfect, 206, 212
with future progressive, 206, 212
interaction of tenses with, 188, 192
with past perfect, 124, 126
with past perfect progressive, 126
with past progressive, 4, 20
with present perfect, 12, 20
with present progressive, 206, 212
with simple past, 4, 12, 20
with simple present, 206, 212
To, 178, 192
Too . . . to, 74
Transitions. *See* Conjunctive adverbs.
Transitive. *See* Verbs.

Unreal conditionals
future, 78, 80, 86
past, 128, 132
Until, 120, 132

Verbs
agreement between subjects and, 102, 104, 112
auxiliary, 6
followed by gerunds, 44, 49, 50, 64
followed by infinitives, 44, 49, 50, 64
intransitive, 107, 198
plural, 104, 112
reporting, 78, 82, 86
singular, 104, 112
subjunctive, 10, 15, 20
transitive, 107, 198

When
adjective clauses with, 90, 94, 95, 112
with past progressive, 4
with simple past, 4
in time clauses or time phrases, 120, 132
Where, 90, 94, 95, 112
Whether (or not), 46
Which, 28, 34, 36, 40, 97, 112
While, 4, 120, 132
Who, 28, 34, 36, 40
Whom, 34, 40, 97, 112
Whose, 28, 40, 97, 112
Wh- questions, 46. *See also* Questions
Why, 90, 94, 95, 112
Will, 6, 20, 206, 208, 212, 213
Wish, 80, 86, 128
With, 178, 192
Would, 6, 20, 128, 132

Yes / no questions, 82
Yet, 118, 132

Credits